From the Welsh Border
to the World

From the Welsh Border to the World: Travels in Minority Languages

by
Simon Gwyn Roberts

University of Chester Press

First published 2020
by University of Chester Press
University of Chester
Parkgate Road
Chester CH1 4BJ

Printed and bound in the UK by
T J International
Padstow PL28 8RW

Cover designed by the
LIS Graphics Team
University of Chester

A catalogue record for this book is available
from the British Library

ISBN 978-1-908258-37-3

CONTENTS

ACKNOWLEDGEMENTS

Part of this work was made possible by the award of a research grant by the University of Chester in 2018.

With thanks to Ato Erzan-Essien, Martin Evans, Rhian Waller, Steve Toogood, Ian Rasmussen and my family.

Figure 1: Bilingual English–Welsh signs

INTRODUCTION
MINORITY LANGUAGES IN THE
AGE OF SOCIAL MEDIA

It was the last day of a long weekend in the mountains of the south-west of Ireland, tracing the outer fringes of Europe along the Atlantic coast. I had not visited County Kerry for a couple of decades, and entered the Gaeltacht via the winding roads beyond Tralee on the Dingle Peninsula. I was looking for the tiny village of Cloghane at the foot of Brandon Mountain, but until I worked out its Irish equivalent – An Clochán – I was unable to find it. The Dublin government's policy had changed since I was last here: in 2005, a decision was taken to remove all English place names, in addition to all English commands, from road signs in the Gaeltacht.

The Gaeltacht (theoretically, areas in which more than 25% of the population speak Irish, or did so in 1926, when it was established) inevitably has the effect of producing a dual nation, something of a 'two-speed' solution to the issue of language preservation. There is a certain allure to this, a tourist-friendly frisson derived from the concept of crossing an internal frontier into an exotic land where a culture is being actively preserved from the predations of global English.

But it is different to the Welsh approach – where nothing is allowed to compromise the indigenous language's ubiquity, at least in terms of public signage and the outward symbolism of its official status. In Wales, whether you are in the exclusively English-speaking Chester suburb of Saltney, or the wildest corner of Welsh-speaking Ceredigion, everything is strictly bilingual regardless of the cultural reality. The intention and effect is to reflect Welsh's relevance, its continuing vibrancy, the fact that it still exists in an unforced way as a majority language in parts of the country. In Ireland, the Gaeltacht removes English entirely in an effort to protect it from further erosion, a rearguard action to

1

preserve a rural culture in aspic. And although almost 40% of the Irish population claim some facility with the language, the reality is that less than 2% of those speak it on a daily basis.[1] There is no real equivalent of a town like Caernarfon, where tracksuited youths hurl salty abuse in their own distinctive form of Welsh, not as a political act, not because the area is protected from modernity, but because it is the language they have naturally grown up speaking.

The contexts are very different (and I am guilty of over-simplifying both) but the underlying issue is the same and gives rise to an obvious question: which approach to the preservation of minority languages is best – uneasy co-existence with the majority tongue, or some level of separation from it?

This book does not seek to provide a definitive answer to that question, nor is it a comprehensive treatment of the subject: a volume on minority languages never could be (there are more than 6,000 extant global languages[2]). Neither is it about linguistics, the mechanics of language. Instead, the anecdotal chapters that follow attempt to make a case for a comparative approach, arguing that a global examination of what is perhaps best described as the cultural geography of minority languages reveals wider truths about their status and future. There is an inherent conundrum common to all the case studies: how do you preserve a fragile culture in a globalised world without resorting to narrow exclusivity or destructive protectionism?

That central question requires a corollary if it is to remain relevant in the post-web world: how can minority languages negotiate a global media culture facilitated by social media and dominated by ubiquitous languages like English and Spanish?

***

Language extinction on an enormous scale has been occurring for decades and has sped up dramatically over the last century. But there are also grounds for optimism. If we consider the classic cycle through which languages are lost: where a period of dominance (by an incoming 'colonial' language which becomes a powerful force in a region) is followed by bilingualism (where people become proficient in both 'native' and 'colonial' languages) through to monolingualism (where younger generations are proficient only in the 'colonial' form),[3] then European exemplars like Welsh and Basque provide a kind of model to escape that cycle, where the crucial second bilingual stage is negotiated in such a way that the indigenous tongue survives and is celebrated. The slide towards the monolingual final stage, in which the indigenous minority tongue is a source of shame for younger generations, is halted.

This often requires funding and intervention, of course, and that is not always feasible in developing countries. But the power of language lies in its ability to frame a specific culture and landscape, to provide a distinctive and irreplaceable framework for the understanding of a particular environment.

Language defines the human relationship to place and it is this additional factor that potentially holds the key to salvation for minority tongues. Harrison argues that the death of any language means the loss of 'long cultivated knowledge that has guided human-environment interaction for millennia (and the) accumulated wisdom and observations of generations of people about the natural world, plants, animals, weather, soil. The loss is incalculable, the knowledge mostly unrecoverable.'[4] It is, however, the *awareness* of loss that provides additional grounds for optimism: exposure to the outside world, whether through personal experience or the media, reveals the fragility and value of one's own linguistic heritage in the sense that it is analogous to biodiversity, the preservation of a threatened species. Indeed, a counter-intuitive feature of a truly globalised online media is that it tends to shed new light on the value of diversity. We are made *aware* of what we stand to lose.

In some cases, we are made aware of what we have already lost. Consider the revival of Cornish, for example. Although organisations like Gorsedh Kernow were established in the early twentieth century, it is only in recent years that there has been any official recognition of Cornish culture by external authorities. In 2002 the UK government recognised the language (in line with the Council of Europe's Charter for Minority Languages) and in 2014 the Cornish were granted National Minority status within the UK.[5] The last native speaker, popularly supposed to have been Dolly Pentreath, died in 1777. Now, media technology facilitates its revival and expansion – with podcasts, web-streamed news and social media all playing a role.[i]

My travels revolved around particularly linguistically diverse regions of the world, where I found that almost everybody was delighted to talk about language – it is central to life, culture and identity in West Africa in much the same way as it is in the South Pacific, the Balkans, Central America, Gwynedd or the Gaeltacht. People are not reluctant to discuss their linguistic heritage, they do not need to have their thoughts on its meaning teased out of them: they are proud of it, and they absolutely understand its significance in a globalised world and the way in which the negotiation with lingua francas like English, Hindi, Russian or French is conducted.

This comparative approach sees me examine – in a necessarily superficial way – case studies drawn from every continent, all with very different contexts, and assessed in relation to established European exemplars like Welsh, Basque and Breton. In most of Western Europe views of minority languages have shifted over time, from being seen as a threat to the

---

i In early 2019, I witnessed a crowd of at least 1,500 in Manchester's famous Ritz music venue singing along to Gwenno's 'Eus Keus?' (Is There Cheese?), the standout track on her Cornish language album *Le Kov*. Gwenno Saunders is perhaps the ultimate Brythonic Celt, brought up in Cardiff by a Cornish-speaking father and Welsh-speaking mother.

4

'centre', to being embraced and sometimes even celebrated as an indication of cultural vibrancy, intangible heritage and diversity.

None of this means that the futures of European minority languages are assured. Indeed, research on Skye and Tiree suggests that Scottish Gaelic is at the point of 'societal collapse', because policies to celebrate and promote it have focused too heavily on encouraging new speakers – and not enough on its preservation in its heartlands, like the Hebrides. Critics have suggested that the increasing number of Gaelic schools in urban areas of the Central Belt often benefit middle-class children whose parents see the educational advantages of dual-language learning.[6] Identical concerns, albeit from a much higher baseline, have long been expressed in relation to Welsh – with pressure group 'Cymuned' ('Community') gaining prominence in the early 2000s with its calls for the protection of fragile Welsh-speaking communities. It is often argued that the healthy statistics suggesting that the language is thriving (875,000 speakers in 2018) are somewhat misleading, and mask a serious decline in 'Y Fro Gymraeg', those culturally distinct areas where first-language speakers predominate.[7]

***

Some have observed that there is a liberal tendency to celebrate 'good' localism (thriving communities, locally sourced food, vernacular architecture, and – by extension – indigenous languages) while simultaneously deriding 'bad' localism (hostility to immigration, nativism, bombastic nationalism).[8] The suggestion is that there is a fundamental hypocrisy in so doing, that the two are inherently connected. David Goodhart articulated a different but related observation in his much-reported take on Brexit, where he suggested that the UK and much of the developed world has split into two opposing tribes: 'somewheres' (those rooted in place and community) versus 'anywheres' (mobile, open to change, tolerant). This, he says, is the contemporary fault-line that made Brexit inevitable;[9] and Theresa May then transplanted the observation into populist politics with her 'citizens of nowhere' speech.

I am not so sure: you *can* come from a specific place, value that place's distinctiveness, and simultaneously embrace the rest of the world. Indeed, the two are frequently mutually reinforcing, not mutually exclusive – in the sense that travelling reveals the distinctiveness of one's own culture by forcing you to see it afresh and discern an infinitely nuanced blend of differences and similarities which provoke empathy, not antipathy. It is something of a cliché, but the more we travel, the more likely we are to make connections and see similarities. The less we travel, the more likely we are to see differences. In the words of Alexander von Humboldt: 'There is no worldview so dangerous as the worldview of those who have not viewed the world.' And, as Andrew Solomon observes: 'Too often, policy is determined by just such people.' Writing of George W. Bush, Solomon adds: 'His lack of curiosity was stunning, and his failure to consider travel a prerequisite to negotiating his country's place in a larger world smacked of arrogance and incompetence'.[10] In this context, a reference to the subsequent reign of Donald Trump seems redundant.

I am from a Welsh-speaking background (father and paternal family from Penmachno in the heart of Welsh-speaking Wales), but am not fluent in Welsh (mother from Stoke-on-Trent, raised in the north-east Wales borderland). I have therefore lost part of my cultural and linguistic heritage, but have always been imbued with the politics of the language and an awareness of its fragility and significance.

This is an unusual combination, which informs the work and, I hope, lends an interesting perspective on Welsh and the case studies that follow in the sense that I am simultaneously removed from, and immersed in, that cultural heritage. To that end, this book is inevitably underpinned by Welsh, with reflections on its place in the modern world and the status and significance of minority languages in general. This is partly as an exemplar of the previously cited 'evolution' from threat to celebration, but also a case study of how a language can thrive in relation to the global dominance of English.

This approach raises an obvious question about the celebration and preservation of diversity which critics frequently cite as a further charge of hypocrisy: why are some forms of identity worth celebrating and others treated with suspicion, or even considered toxic? Spectator columnist Rory Sutherland, for example, claimed in a radio interview to be 'three eighths English and three eighths Welsh', arguing that it was fine for him to celebrate his Welshness, but not fine for him to celebrate his Englishness.[11] It is a very familiar refrain, with a very obvious answer: it is all about numbers, scale, size, influence and power. Small nation identity is inherently defensive, protecting a fragile and vulnerable culture from a dominant globalised culture. This is by no means always positive or pleasant, but it does have a logic attached.

By contrast, as an expression of a very different form of identity, Brexit was also frequently framed in terms of language, which remains central to the debate albeit not always overtly articulated as such. Freedland reminds us that the Brexiteers 'were itching to shake off the shackles of Brussels and run into the embrace of the "Anglosphere" where our chief trading partners would no longer be those countries on our doorstep but the English speakers of Australia, New Zealand, Canada, and above all the US'.[12]

So an appreciation of diversity, not least the linguistic version that exists within the four (or more) nations of the UK, might have helped to normalise the English, to detoxify the brand, to see themselves as just another Germanic tribe – an unusually successful group who migrated to Britain and called the people they found there 'foreigners' ('Welsch' remains the modern German word for a Southern European, implying a non-German with origins in the Roman Empire).

Referencing ancient history in this way is, generally speaking, a terrible idea. Serbian nationalists and hardline Ulster Loyalists are good examples of where this leads – it is a destructive dead-end to engage in a continual rehashing of a redundant past, and certainly not a sustainable basis for civic society and inclusivity. And, equally obviously, the multiple waves of migration in the intervening centuries render the very notion of 'indigenous' peoples problematic at best, absurd at worst.[ii] However, it might at some level have acted as a valuable corrective to decades or even centuries of avoiding the obvious reality: the English as just another distinctive piece in the wonderful mosaic of European peoples.

It is too late now – and indeed this version of historical revisionism seems unlikely to resonate in a world where the notion of 'identity politics', so central to the survival of fragile minority cultures and languages, has suddenly morphed into something that can be mobilised by dominant groups who – for the first time perhaps – feel that their own cultures are under threat. That tendency, the driving force behind Brexit, Trump, Alternative für Deutschland and other manifestations of Western populism grew exponentially while this book was being researched, adding an additional dimension to its underpinning rationale. In a worldview that emphasises the lost power of a

---

ii Indeed, in the eighteenth century Daniel Defoe and many of his successors contrasted England, as a nation of immigrants, with the apparent ethnic and cultural homogeneity of the Welsh and the Scots '… all other nations would eventually have to catch up with the English, since cosmopolitanism was the shape of the future' (P. Parrinder (2006). Character, Identity and Nationality in the English Novel. In R. Burden and S. Kohl (Eds.), *Landscape and Englishness* (p. 94). Amsterdam, Netherlands: Rodopi).

once dominant group, concepts of cooperation and pooled resources have little traction.

Meek cites a further common concern framing contemporary politics – that distinctiveness of place is being erased by a creeping uniformity whose paradoxical hallmark is a shallow diversity, arguing that the blame for this is distributed differently in another illustration of the culture wars afflicting politics in the West: one side interprets it as a result of immigration and the EU, the other blames austerity and globalisation.[13] In reality the erosion of place is largely down to global corporate power, mainly derived from the US, which has (since its inception) been embraced particularly enthusiastically in the UK and writ large in our town centres.

If this book has any kind of message, it is to call for a renewed emphasis on *regionalism* in multiple global contexts, with minority languages acting as a political corrective – a 'reality check' – to exclusive and bombastic nationalism when these forces are dangerously ascendant. Devolution and regional power are the real key to 'taking back control' – a fact rarely acknowledged in the context of the UK, where sovereignty and notions of democracy are almost always framed in national terms, and (in the case of the Brexit debate) only loosely connected with political reality. Contrast this with Germany (for example) where the Lander (federal states) have real political power over core issues including education, law enforcement and media regulation.

***

Just six years ago, authors like Castells and Mason took an optimistic view about the web-based power of the network to take on elites in authoritarian environments (Arab Spring, Iran, former Soviet Union).[14] Now, reflections on the value of linguistic diversity in the post-web world must be viewed in a very different global context: with many countries characterised by growing populism, a tendency towards isolation and nationalism, and the associated mobilisation of identity politics by the majority (with social media central to these processes).

There are, however, ways in which fragile cultures and languages can be protected without resorting to exclusivity, hostility, or the 'othering' of those seen as threatening to that culture. Travels in the most diverse regions of the world almost always suggest that protecting a culture need not be combined with introspection or notions of purity: quite the opposite, in fact. Wales is a model, not perfect but not bad, for the way in which an overwhelmingly dominant culture can be accommodated whilst preserving and celebrating a fragile minority revolving around the centrality of language. And if, further to that, the experience of living with that dominant culture actually helps these processes, because it reveals something about the value of diversity, the value of preserving that which is distinctive, then there are signs that this model, or a version of it, is being adopted elsewhere.

Technology can help, not hinder this. Some have suggested that minority language social media might have special relevance for indigenous language communities in West Africa (for example) – particularly those which transcend state borders – because the technology relates to issues of identity and social mobility and might create new communities online.

In Senegal, (covered in Chapter 1) colonial French was traditionally the language of writing, whilst Wolof (and many others) were the languages of speech. But social media is arguably changing this by mirroring the oral traditions of spoken Wolof more effectively than traditional media and text. Social media have also liberated mediated communication from the centre and given more agency to networks and individuals in terms of participatory governance and civic action.

In Struga, near the Macedonian–Albanian border, I met a man who uses Twitter and Facebook to celebrate the distinctive local version of Macedonian. He told me that he tries to frame comments in such a way that they revolve around the features of his dialect that are unique – but which might in other circumstances be in danger of being lost. There is nothing exclusive about this – he also tweeted in standard Macedonian and English – but the vibrancy of the local form is something he felt was worth celebrating and social media is the perfect vehicle for doing this as it reflects the oral nature of these kinds of regional dialects while simultaneously extending their reach and 'proving' their contemporary relevance. The story is far more encouraging than lazy pronouncements about the global dominance of English on increasingly ubiquitous social media platforms often suggests.

A META-NET study of 2017 conceded that in the digital era, Europe's rich linguistic heritage, its mosaic of minority tongues, 'faced challenges' but went on to suggest that the new communicative world offered 'many possibilities and opportunities'. It found that language technology support varied dramatically from 'weak or non-existent' for some small languages to 'fragmentary' for languages like Basque, where a clear political dimension adds an extra dimension to the notion of preservation.

But while minority languages might be starved of the investment required to invest in big-scale language technology, at grassroots level people do understand the role and importance of social media in maintaining and diversifying the use of minority languages. As META-NET itself conceded: 'linguistic borders often do not coincide with political borders'.[15] Herein lies the true value of social media, as the recent experience of the Welsh in Argentinian Patagonia proves. The pre-web reality saw fragmented communities struggling to articulate a coherent political position as a result of geographical separation. Social media has supplanted the local newspaper-reading tradition of Welsh Patagonia and now forms a meaningful public sphere, which transcends geography and looks set to maintain and perhaps develop Welsh speakers' sense of community and political representation.

'Fragmented' in this context means language communities separated by distance or political divisions: it strikes me that these environments offer an interesting opportunity to study meaningfully the advantages of social media communication strategies – connecting places and people without the need for physical proximity.

The criteria for the selection of the regions discussed also invite a comparison with biodiversity, which lends an additional theme to the work. Mountains act as isolating agents (in the natural world), ensuring the development of refugia where unique species have evolved and thrived. The regions covered in this book are all characterised by varying degrees of topographical isolation, and all are therefore marked by rich linguistic and cultural diversity.

The concept of bioregionalism is a further useful prism in this context: a celebration of the unique and indescribable features of a place. It is widely understood to stress the primacy of environmental 'regions' over political ones (in the sense that the natural environmental conditions in any given place affect human interaction more positively and naturally than political boundaries). But it is not as naïve as it might sound: it also stresses the totality of the human experience, the cultural elements that make us who we are. Bioregions are not the same as environmental regions: they are fundamentally human – informed by the environment, giving rise to political regionalism, or localism, underpinned by an awareness of the ecological surroundings.

For Jeremy Rifkin, the stakes are high: if we lose the sense of place, the sense of being, we lose something irreplaceable and vital to us all as a species. His prognosis is that geography counts, and culture matters: 'If you lose the rich cultural diversity of thousands of years, it's as final and devastating as losing biodiversity.'[16]

Each chapter that follows is an account of travels in one particularly diverse region in each continent (bookended by what UNESCO defines as the two most linguistically diverse regions on Earth: West Africa and the South Pacific).[17] It is not intended to be definitive or comprehensive – merely a snapshot of countries at various stages of what I suggest is a natural evolution from conflict to compromise. There are some contextual similarities between the languages examined, in the sense that all are minority tongues within their nation state – but the underlying geographical, technological, economic and political circumstances are very different (ranging from Tamil, a major global language and yet a minority tongue within Sri Lanka with an associated highly charged political significance, to the languages of Vanuatu, spoken in some cases by a few hundred people). The message is, in general, a positive one: a comparative approach suggests that, although there are pressing threats to minority languages from a wide range of global and domestic forces, there are also realistic grounds for optimism.

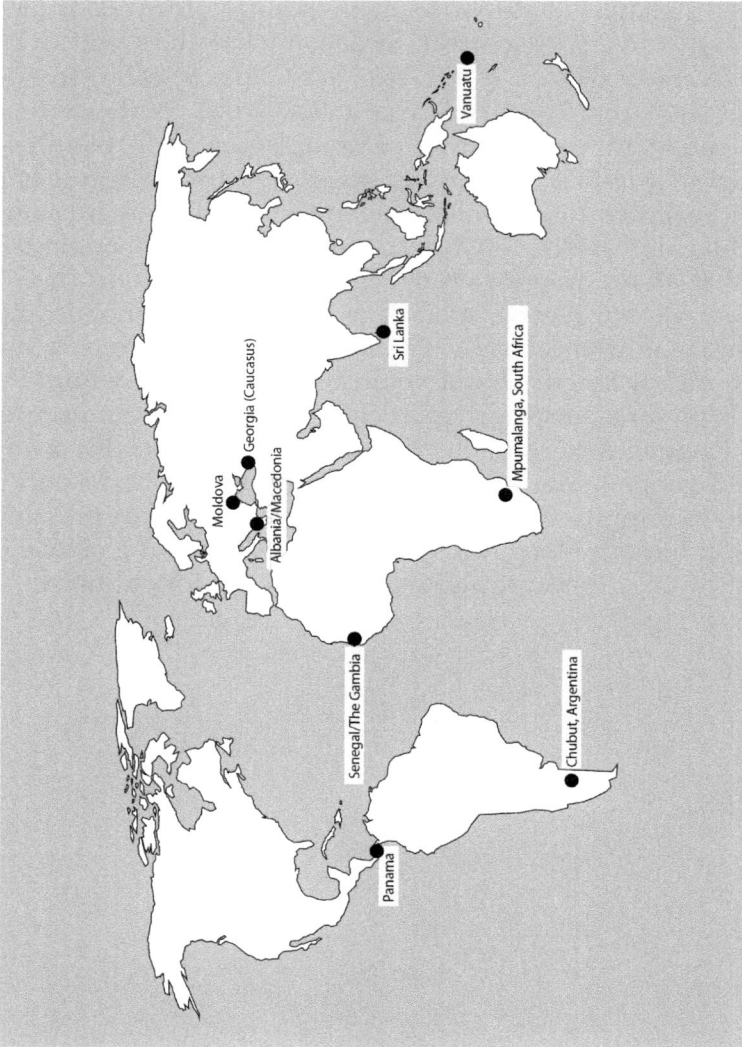

Figure 2: Places visited by the author for this research

CHAPTER 1
'NOISY NEIGHBOURS':
TRANSCENDING COLONIAL BORDERS
IN SENEGAMBIA

Political decisions are taken on a small bench underneath a baobab tree, the forces of law and order have never been here, sacks of marijuana are piled high against a nearby wall ready for export, and a line of disturbing pagan icons decorates the walls of the few shacks gathered around the tree. This is Kailo Island, in the mouth of a mangrove-flanked river deep in the Casamance region of southern Senegal, perhaps the quietest and gentlest anarchy in the world.

The 70 or so residents have their own language, understood by almost nobody else, and recognise no God. They are animists who fled from Islam as it advanced across West Africa in the Middle Ages, worshipping elements of the natural world, believing that every living thing has a soul and is interconnected.

The islanders spend much of the day in a state of repose: it is a fertile place with no need for frenetic action, particularly in the intense heat of November, when I visited, immediately after the wet season with rice fields high, coconuts and baobab fruit heavy on the branches. Indeed, the first thing I was shown was a sacred grove beneath a particularly huge baobab tree. The heavy fruits are never picked, never eaten, and must be allowed to rot where they drop. Below the branches, a series of scary looking knives had been stabbed into the bark, to represent a series of curses dealt out by the islanders. The precise mechanism by which the curses were supposed to work eluded me, although I grasped the unbearable poignancy of another principle, whereby small items belonging to a dead child had been left on a branch in the hope that they might one day be reunited.

'If you make a wish, if you believe it, it will happen,' said my companion Abdul, deadly serious, trying to explain the concept of wish fulfilment embodied by the items scattered below the tree. He was trying to be polite in front of the animists, and I understood the point he was trying to make about human psychology. He, a Muslim, did not hold with any of it. The vast majority of Senegalese are Sufi Muslims: and Kailo's remoteness and independent spirit is neatly illustrated by the fact that Islam was mobilised as a tool for resistance to French rule in colonial times. To hold out against those powerful religious, cultural and political forces is remarkable.

But hold out they had. And now, their 'graves' are unmarked pagan monuments, they resist the rule of the Dakar (and regional) government, and the imposition of modern infrastructure (although they do have solar panels powering one lamp). There are no roads, no cars or bikes, and they support themselves by selling those huge sacks of marijuana to boat-bound tradesmen who then distribute them around West Africa. How they arrange for this to happen in the ultimate 'off-grid' environment was not clear to me, because Abdul seemed reluctant to tell me. He had no real need to be tactful or cautious when describing their illicit economy or their belief system, however, as not only do the islanders not speak English, they do not speak French either – or Wolof, Mandinka, Jola or any of the other languages that characterise this diverse corner of West Africa.

Instead, they speak Karon, an ultra-obscure and critically endangered language that few people, even linguists, know anything about. In terms of its links, it is located somewhere along the Bak branch of the Niger–Congo language family. Abdul claimed to be the only person – literally, the only man on Earth – with the ability to speak the islanders' particular version of it, apart from the islanders themselves. I have no idea whether this is true or not, but I know that Abdul was the most remarkable linguist I have ever met.

'Noisy neighbours'

When a monoglot meets a multilinguist it is often a humiliating experience – but a few days spent with Abdul took this to an entirely new, humbling level of shame for me (my lifelong, largely unsuccessful attempts to gain fluency in Welsh, my paternal first language, are always thrown into sharp focus by such encounters). I first met him in Brikama, a Mandinka stronghold, perhaps the only large town in West Africa where that group predominate (although they are an influential minority group across the region and form a slender majority in The Gambia). It is a dusty, chaotic place – a linear settlement of ramshackle houses, scrap metal merchants and palm oil traders spread out across the main road taking travellers south from the Gambian capital Banjul towards Senegal and Guinea-Bissau.

I assumed Abdul (who made a living as a long-distance taxi driver – he had driven me to Brikama from Banjul) was Mandinka, as he held forth simultaneous shouted conversations with dozens of locals. But he was actually a Jola, whose grandparents had come from the Casamance, over the Senegalese border, where I was heading. 'Jola is my own language, my mother tongue, but I also speak English, French, Wolof, Karon, Mandinka – which is very different, quite good Fula, a little bit of German, and I am learning Portuguese Creole.' The latter was because, every summer rainy season, he made ends meet by travelling to Lusophone Guinea-Bissau from his Gambian home, buying multiple litres of palm oil (famously environmentally destructive – as indigenous forests are cleared to make way for the plantations) and transporting it back – via the crammed 'bush taxis' and *sept places*[iii] that ply these routes. He was a slim, hollow-cheeked man – with the distance running build of an East African despite his heritage – and an elegant dress sense

---

iii The characteristic 'seven place' taxis of West Africa, usually old Peugeots converted to include a row of exceptionally cramped extra seating.

that always included an immaculate pair of brogues (but never any socks).

By the time we arrived in Brikama I had arranged for him to take me across the border, where I would meet him later for the trip by pirogue (a long multi-person canoe) through the mangroves to Kailo. I had never heard of Kailo, and was only planning to visit the coast, but Abdul's description of it was enough to engage me – along with his remarkable claim that he was the only outsider able to communicate with them. I was a tad cynical: how did he speak this obscure language? He was a little evasive at first, but later said that he had 'lived with one of them for some time'.

The next day, we left Brikama by bush taxi to the border – crammed into a tiny space behind the driver as dozens of Mandinka and Jola people got on and off with assortments of goods, from live chickens to buckets of dried fish to bags full of old shoes. Abdul was a reassuring presence as I changed some Gambian dalasi for thousands of West African francs at a typical 'restaurant': three narrow benches propped up on oil drums around a man stirring a huge pot full of beans whilst simultaneously preparing mug after mug of instant coffee made mind-bendingly sweet by the addition of evaporated milk and huge quantities of sugar. The black-eyed beans are a characteristic feature of the food culture here – a filling and deeply flavoured breakfast, scooped up with a combination of the right hand and the West African version of a baguette called a tapalapa.

The money changer was a teenaged boy with a scar running from his mouth to his ear. He had a leather bag slung over his shoulder and a calculator in one hand, and he wandered round the bush taxis and lorries seeking trade. I handed him £30 sterling and a fistful of small denomination dalasi notes. He pulled a huge wodge of cash from the bag, several inches thick, with cardboard bookmarks separating the currencies – of which there were at least 10, maybe more, from euros and pounds to

Liberian dollars and Sierra Leonean Leones. A few taps on the calculator, with my mental arithmetic desperately straining to keep up, and I was liquid in CFA francs.

Over the Gambian border lies a long stretch of no-man's land, longer than anything I have ever encountered on my travels. It seemed strange given the relatively peaceful relationship between the two countries. Even when neighbours dislike each other intensely the no-man's land around international borders is not usually this big. In 2012, for example, I stood outside the monastery of Khor Virap, which lies in the shadow of Mount Ararat on the Armenian side of the Turkey–Armenia border. Below, the frontier between two countries that emphatically do not get along: it is a closed border, with a no-man's land between huge armoured fences, but Turkey is just a few hundred metres away, close enough to hear the call to prayer from mosques in the nearby villages.

The Gambia and Senegal get along fairly well: the more broad-minded residents concede they are 'the same people', and indeed the two were joined together in a short-lived confederation in the 1980s. But borders in this part of the world are frequently problematic. Tension and violence can spread easily, with linguistic and ethnic groups transcending national frontiers and the resultant cross-border loyalties exploitable by politicians. That, as well as the colonial realities of this Franco-British carve-up, is why it takes some time to get to Senegal across the broad neutral zone – with the border marked by a hidden trench dug into the dried mud, manned by two soldiers with machine guns. At the little hut that serves as the passport control office, two Senegalese soldiers scowled, in immaculate combat fatigues and Ray-Bans, their automatic weapons slung around their necks, fingers hovering over the triggers.

***

This seemed slightly unnecessary, but the weaponry illustrates the sensitive nature of this region. For over 30 years, rebels in this part of Senegal, the Casamance, have engaged in a low-level separatist conflict against the distant Dakar government: it is the longest running civil conflict in Africa, and that is up against some stiff competition. Its origins are many and varied, although interpretations often suggest a religious dimension, because the proportion of Christians (and animists, as in Kailo) in the south of Senegal is considerably higher than in the rest of this Muslim-dominated country. But that is too simplistic: this was not, and is not, primarily a religious dispute. It has much more to do with colonial history and the contemporary realities of political geography combined with differences in language and culture. The Casamance is separated from the rest of Senegal by the British colonial construct of The Gambia: from where I had just travelled. In the remote east, the land is connected, but to all intents and purposes the Casamance is detached, cast adrift from the main currents of Senegalese life.

The region is dominated by the Jola, who speak a Bak language from an entirely separate branch of the wider Niger–Congo family than the dominant Wolof to the north. The Wolof have long formed Senegal's elite; indeed they were primed to do so by the French colonists, and the Jola (sometimes spelt Diola) managed to unite other ethnic groups in the Casamance in opposition to that dominance – the Mandinka and the nomadic Fulani, for example. As a movement, the separatists immediately found themselves split on ethnic grounds – indeed the precise make-up of the groups provides a beginner's guide to the extraordinary linguistic complexity of this part of West Africa.

The umbrella organisation, known as the Movement of Democratic Forces of Casamance (MFDC), was formed in the early 1980s as a response to the perceived marginalisation of the region and the resentment provoked. By the early 1990s, the movement divided into two main groups along ethnic and linguistic lines: the 'Front Sud' was dominated by the Jola, while the 'Front Nord' encompassed a broader mix and tended to be more willing to compromise. In the mid-1990s, the conflict reached a peak, with thousands of people displaced. Since then, it has oscillated but remained relatively sporadic, with the history of attacks reading a little like the 'Troubles' in the Northern Ireland of the 1970s: an armed robbery here, an attack on an army outpost there.

In 2014, secret talks were held in the Vatican, of all places, and a cease-fire declared, with the Senegalese government of Macky Sali (enlightened by African standards) pursuing a decentralisation policy that most, but not all, have accepted.[18]

Serious tensions remain, and rose again before my trip in 2018. The planned exploitation of minerals in the large coastal dunes of the Casamance by the Dakar government, alongside US and Chinese firms, has caused resentment and even attracted the attention of the BBC, which carried interviews with MFDC leaders warning of a return to conflict if the project goes ahead.[19]

Worse still, 13 villagers were killed near Ziguinchor in a horrific ambush in early 2018, said to be an 'execution-style' act. The MFDC denied responsibility, saying it was connected to illegal logging in the region.[20] Tensions remain fairly high, with the odd roadblock and machine gun emplacement – although this part of West Africa has such a tranquil overall ambience, with lush tropical vegetation and laid-back fishing villages, that the casual visitor could be forgiven for not realising anything had ever been amiss: tension of any kind seems entirely absent.

***

At the border town of Seleti, we met our pre-arranged driver, Solomon, a smiling, round-faced Mandinka whose reserved personality was the polar opposite of Abdul's: he was a man of few words and a demeanour that bordered on the morose. Abdul knew him well, and almost immediately took to ridiculing his lack of English, as well as his poor Wolof – which is often used as a lingua franca, particularly in urban areas further north, and therefore has an air of sophistication attached to it. I found this rather uncomfortable, as I was clearly the intended audience, although Solomon seemed to take it in good faith. He took a dreadful, blurry picture of me standing next to the Senegalese border sign, safely away from the gun-toting soldiers, hidden behind an abandoned lorry from Conakry in Guinea, which looked like it had been there for months, rainy season rust colouring the body work.

We drove through a series of lively little towns with red dust pavements and beautiful mahogany trees, south through Dioloulou to the regional centre of Kafountine – where we got out to buy some snacks at a market full of fly-blown fish, stacked high with perfect fruit and vegetables. The road, so good up to that point, then deteriorates to a sandy track just wide enough for a vehicle to pass through. Kafountine itself then deteriorates from the vibrant bustle of the centre to the hellish realities of life for those scratching a living from the Atlantic Ocean, which crashes on to the beaches fringing this southern part of the town.

Long fishing skiffs, packed with locals, can be seen out in the ocean haze, ploughing through the dangerous surf. Hundreds of them are docked at any given time, and young men – those at the absolute bottom of the socioeconomic scale – run into the chest-deep waters carrying buckets. These are filled with fish, and the men, soaked to the skin, run back to the nearby 'factories', wooden huts where the fish are processed and dried. An appalling stench, with clouds of flies and smoke from wood-burning fires made it hard to see. Later, the last of the fish shacks are passed and all becomes tranquil, although memories of a violent past are still close – soon, the track passes a huge, multi-storey burned-out hotel with a decaying thatched roof that once housed dozens of French tourists but was abandoned during the violent early days of the separatist conflict in the 1980s: it is now frozen in time and dilapidation.

Beyond this lies the uninhabited bush. And beyond that, the mangroves and a long 'pirogue' – a 12-man canoe, usually with small motor – the only practical method of transport in these parts.

I was determined to avoid the obvious Conrad resonance of the subsequent journey, but failed. Sitting alone at the front of the pirogue, as its tiny motor spluttered away behind, the boatman taking us further and further down river, the echoes of *Heart of Darkness* refused to budge and my response to the journey descended into cliché. On either side, mangroves, utterly impenetrable and uninhabited, their tangled roots a barrier to any kind of riverside development. The heat and humidity built below a mackerel sky: this diffused the ferocious midday sun, just a bit, and made the gently rippling water shimmer, a dazzling shade of silver. The occasional osprey perched, a Senegal coucal launched itself across the river, pied kingfishers hovered. Apart from the barely detectable sound from the tiny engine, and the occasional ripple as a fish leapt out of the water, an absolute, unsettling silence reigned. Later, another big tributary joined from the left, the river changed colour as it widened, and royal terns flew overhead as we got closer to the open sea.

And then, finally, signs of human habitation. A wrecked shack containing the flapping inner sheets of an old dome tent, and a plume of smoke.

***

'The people on the island came here to avoid Muslims like me,' said Abdul, with a grin. 'They came for the sake of their safety and their freedom. When people were turning to Islam they found this place nice and good for them. They can do as they wish.'

He was not lying about being fluent in their version of the Karon language. The first islanders we encountered were a group of fishermen lying down in a prefabricated shack, avoiding the heat of midday as their catch stayed fresh in a large mesh bucket just offshore. They were taciturn to the point of hostility, but Abdul's natural charm and obvious fluency got them talking – a bit.

It is perhaps not surprising that the islanders are reserved, even in their own tongue, given the anarchic, lawless and unstructured nature of life on Kailo. Abdul claimed that the forces of authority had, literally, never set foot on the island: 'If they call the police about anything, it would be the worst thing they could ever do, they would have to leave the island, they would be enemies for life.' But what happens, I asked, if they have a disagreement? I could not help noticing that the men carried large machetes around for 'harvesting coconuts' and other more nefarious agricultural duties. 'The worst crime that happens here is a fight, maybe a bad one, but it's just a fight. They take care of things themselves.'

The single bench 'parliament' (which, I was told, is called the 'bantaba' in the local version of Karon) under the big baobab tree is the place where any notional punishment for misdemeanours is decided upon.

Time passes slowly in places which lack electricity: I spent a few happy, but long, hours getting scared by the alarming pagan icons painted on the side of the huts, and peering into the well the villagers used for drinking water ('if I drank it I would be sick for a year,' said Abdul. 'If you drank it you would die.'). I was not sure about that, but its murky green colour looked like a warning – it seemed incredible that anybody could drink this. The islanders have little choice, however, as the river here is essentially brackish, not far from the open sea, the mangrove-lined rivers opening out as the Atlantic is approached.

Behind, sacks of marijuana: each as big as a person. This year's crop was being planted when we were there. 'People travel by boat to buy the bags,' said Abdul. 'They are then taken up the coast.' I initially thought I had discovered a clue to the eventual destination on my return trip north through the Casamance, on a walk round the sleepy town of Abene, one of the strongholds of the Baye Fall sect of Senegal's dominant Mouride Sufi Muslims. The Baye Fall represent the outer reaches of the Islamic faith, the polar opposite to the fanatical Sunnis of the Islamic State. They dress in colourful rags, play music (the globally famous Cheich Lo is a Baye Fall), they wear beads and dreadlocks, and put me in mind of Indian Sadhus as they wander around looking wildly eccentric, asking for donations to help them live their ascetic lives. Abdul told me that they also often speak Wolof, unlike most of his fellow Jola in these parts, because of their sect's origins in the northern Senegalese city of Touba.

I could not help connecting the sacks of marijuana and the bloodshot, spaced out eyes of the Baye Fall I later encountered in Abene. Young backpackers, I was later told, often make the same mistake, wrongly assuming they are Rastafarians, with all that implies. Instead, they represent the wildest fringe of Sufi Islam, the quasi-mystic form of the religion hated by the Wahhabists of Saudi Arabia – indeed, the Baye Faal could be held up as a salutary reminder to those harbouring reductive views of Islam as a monolithic religion; a perfect illustration of the shades of opinion that still exist and thrive within it.

***

On returning to the south of The Gambia, I spent a few days birdwatching in the border area, all the way from Brufut (a largely Mandinka village further north where I was staying) right down to Kartong, which fringes the amorphous wetlands spanning both countries. Earlier that week, I'd visited Bijilo Forest Park near the tourist enclave of Kololi – this is a tiny slice of pristine West African forest, frequented by vervet monkeys and their audience of large groups of tourists from Britain, the Netherlands, Poland and Russia. Here I met Massameh, one of The Gambia's leading bird specialists.

Massameh hated working at Bijilo, spending his time pointing out the (rather obvious) monkeys to tourists wielding bags of nuts – a dubious practice that leaves the vervets dependent on the freebies. We got on well together in our more interesting search for pearl-spotted owlets and stone partridges, and later arranged to explore the remote and untravelled south-western border region together. As luck had it, he lived in Brufut, very near my accommodation – although like Abdul he was actually a Jola living among Mandinka and, again like Abdul, he felt at home almost anywhere in the region. Indeed, I later realised that their Jola heritage was a possible explanation for their liberal geopolitical outlook – as this linguistic group straddles the Casamance–Gambian border and has an equal footing in each.

He had travelled extensively throughout West Africa, quite unusual for a Gambian (Gambia remains one of the world's poorest countries despite its tourist industry – with a GDP per capita of $483, less than half that of Senegal[21]) and it struck me that his idealism was partly facilitated by his relative wealth as well as his linguistic ability (which did not quite match that of Abdul, but was still remarkable). 'You talk of "being the same people,' I said to him as we ate barracuda yassa in a filthy Lebanese-owned shack (with a broken electric fan) on the edge of Tanji. It was a question I had been wanting to ask for some time. 'So how far do you have to travel before things really change, before you really start to feel like a foreigner?' He thought for a moment. 'I would say the far side of Guinea and definitely Sierra Leone. Up to there we're the same people. After that, everything is different – not just the people and the languages, everything. We can speak English together but when I went there [to Freetown] I just wanted to come home.'

This is one of the many misconceptions about the colonial legacy in Africa. It is not so much that the European powers separated linguistic groups from each other by the dividing up of natural resources and features, more that entire regions – mosaics of ethnic groups and languages – have something in common with each other. The lines are indeed artificial colonial constructs, but they parcel up regions and language 'families' rather than just dividing linguistic groups and cultural affiliations. Senegal and The Gambia are classic examples. The Gambia's 'British' presence, which effectively split 'French' Senegal in two in the late nineteenth century, made conflict in the Casamance almost inevitable. The two countries are similar in many ways, but their respective colonial experiences made – for example – the short-lived Senegambian confederation in the 1980s unworkable for both practical and political reasons.[22]

The legacy of colonialism is perhaps the most disputed of all historical and academic topics: furious debates have raged for decades, spanning multiple perspectives from Edward Said's *Orientalism* to the positive interpretations offered by Niall Ferguson.[23] In Africa, the legacy of colonialism remains core to any discussion about geopolitics in the region. Postcolonialism, as a term of academic enquiry has been applied in multiple other contexts of course, even in Wales – although it will always be highly sensitive and potentially offensive to shift its focus (by multiple centuries) in this way. Numerous writers and academics have, however, felt able to at least raise the question in the Welsh context, even if merely to observe the fact that Wales was England's first colony and may well be her last. Aaron and Williams began their 2005 treatment of the topic with two rhetorical questions: Is it feasible to think of Wales as postcolonial? And in what ways, if any, does the concept of postcolonialism aid our understanding of Welsh cultural and political life?[24] Such questions now trace the edges of post-Brexit debate about the nature of Britishness and the resurgence of a hard-to-define English patriotism.

In a widely quoted speech, Plaid Cymru AM Adam Price (now leader of the party) called Wales 'a post-colonial country still waiting to be decolonised … a hybrid state living in the cracks between a dependent past and an independent future'.[25]

The vision for the future expressed in this 2009 speech was subsequently shattered by the 2016 EU referendum, which saw Welsh voting patterns essentially mirror those of England.[iv] But regardless of the sensitivities of mobilising varying degrees of postcolonialism as some kind of 'determinant' for present-day issues, it retains immense power in all the varied geopolitical environments which deem it at least partially relevant to their contemporary existence and experience.

**

New connections between Africa's present and its past are continually being made by politicians and academics in Senegambia. The political, cultural and economic realities of postcolonial development connect in multiple ways with the preceding centuries of foreign occupation. Language simultaneously unifies and divides the broad region of Senegambia. If West Africa as a whole is second only to the Melanesian South Pacific in terms of its linguistic diversity, then Senegambia is a typical slice of the larger whole.

Languages like Wolof, Fulani and Serer share common elements as a branch of the Niger–Congo family, but other common languages in the region – like Mandinka and, to a lesser extent Jola – spiral off in extraordinary complexity across different parts of the region. The two people I spent most time with in West Africa – Abdul and Massameh – were both Jola who spent most of their time conversing in other languages, slipping seamlessly between them. And although they were both unusually talented linguists, they were by no means atypical:

---

iv Although by digging deeper they (and the 2019 General Election results) also revealed something of the continuing, culturally-driven internal diversity of Wales: see, for example, S. G. Roberts (2019). A pit we have dug ourselves: Brexit and the Welsh democratic deficit. In F. León-Solís, H. O'Donnell, & F. Ridge-Newman, *Reporting the Road to Brexit: International Media and the EU Referendum 2016* (pp. 75–92). London, UK: Palgrave Macmillan.

many West Africans share the same sense of multilingualism as a foundational principle of national and even multinational identity.

So the inherent diversity of the region is not a barrier to cooperation or a sense of shared endeavour and identity – linguistic diversity is generally celebrated. One can be proudly Gambian and proudly Jola at the same time.

A Mandinka homeland, or even a Wolof homeland, would never really be possible – the boundaries would be too complex, the linguistic groups too fragmented. Instead, it is best to view the complex linguistic map of West Africa as broadly 'regional' rather like, in Europe, the nations grouped as 'Slavic' are on one side of a cultural and linguistic divide that separates them from the nations grouped as 'Germanic' or 'Latin'. Ultimately, language is at the heart of this – the lodestone of culture.

A further European comparison (never a wise thing to do) might be the way in which the Yugoslavian regime viewed Bosnia-Herzegovina before the conflict of the 1990s – as a melting pot of different peoples, scattered in a complex kaleidoscope pattern with Serbs, Croats, Bosnian Muslims and Albanians living together. Unlike 1990s Bosnia, however, the Mandinka, Jola and Wolof generally rub along well, and regard themselves as having something in common rather than seeking out ethnically cleansed and linguistically pure 'homelands'.

And there are wider elements of the culture, most obviously music and food, that loosely trace the edges of similar boundaries. Kora music, for example, transcends borders in this part of Africa and matches the linguistic contours of the arc of countries dropping down from Mali in the north east to Guinea-Bissau in the south west. The kora is a complicated 21-string version of a harp that is played by the Mandinka people across all those countries. Its players – who are among the most skilled musicians on the planet – traditionally come from jali families. In Mandinka culture, the jali are bards, roving story-tellers.

Language is central: the jali are Mandinka, and used to be known as griots under French colonial rule. The indigenous term is now preferred although their role essentially remains the same – they are seen as a repository of culture, of stories, a way of linking the present with the past. As such, the jali/griot tradition finds echoes elsewhere with such stories often mobilised in the preservation of fragile languages and cultures. One immediately thinks of the Welsh bardic tradition in this context: privileged members of the wider society who were required to maintain that sense of grounding and history that lends a culture integrity and power.

Alongside music, food is a good measure of this combination of commonality and diversity. Take, for example, the characteristic and deeply satisfying peanut-based stew called 'maafe' by the Wolof. It is known as 'domoda' in The Gambia, or 'durango' by the Mandinka, or 'tigadeguena' in Mali. The more famous Jollof rice is an even better example – spiralling off into multiple regional versions depending on tribal and linguistic group: from 'benachin' in The Gambia to 'thieboudienne' in the Casamance to 'chebu jen' and Jollof rice further afield.

Massameh's comment about Sierra Leone and the outer limits of his 'home' region was strangely prescient, because we soon reached a busy T-junction in Serrekunda, The Gambia's largest town, as we cut across country on the search for birds. As we waited for a line of cars to cross, a mutilated man came across to us, thrusting his arm, which was cut off below the elbow, through the open window of the battered old Peugeot we were travelling in. 'May I hear your voice Sir,' he said to me in perfect, almost plummy, English. I answered, and he responded in the same weirdly accented English, as if impersonating Jacob Rees-Mogg. 'I am a migrant from Freetown, Sierra Leone. I cannot work. Would you be kind enough to help?' he said, pushing the stump on to the top of the window to prevent me from closing it. The flow of human misery across Africa, which we often view in Eurocentric terms, is actually far more complex and multi-faceted: if you are a mutilated victim of conflict in Sierra Leone, unable to even contemplate the journey north towards Europe, then begging at a chaotic Gambian road junction is a 'good' option.

***

Later, as we walked along the wetlands marking the coastal stretch of the border between Senegal and The Gambia, I found time to pose another question I had wanted to ask for some time. I was intrigued by the conversations Massameh had whenever he approached a shopkeeper or café owner, or even the policewomen manning the frequent roadblocks (here, these are less for military reasons than to stop huge sand-mining trucks from speeding and carelessly ploughing into bush taxis and pedestrians – a frequent event judging by the number of wrecked vehicles in ditches).

'How do you know what language to speak when you meet a stranger, like a policeman?' I asked. 'You just know – sometimes it is the village or the area, sometimes it is the jobs people do, sometimes it is the way they look.' I was later told that this is innate, and genuinely hard for outsiders to grasp – the signals are so subtle. The impression I got from Massameh's conversations was that it was a perfect example of code-switching: instantaneous adaptation occurred until a common tongue was found, and this took just seconds – it seemed to be an entirely natural process, a normal part of life in this multilingual environment. It is paralleled in the way Welsh is sometimes negotiated in areas where the proportion of speakers is reasonably high, but not dominant: Denbigh perhaps, or Aberystwyth.

As I often experienced in other linguistically diverse areas during the research for this book, everybody in Senegambia was delighted to talk about language – it is central to life, culture and identity in West Africa in much the same way as it is in the South Pacific, the Balkans or Central America. People are not reluctant to discuss their linguistic heritage, they do not need to have their thoughts on its significance teased out of them: they are proud of it, and they absolutely understand its significance in a globalised world and the way in which the negotiation with global languages like English or French is conducted. In West Africa, almost nobody speaks English or French except as a last resort: perhaps to foreigners, or less commonly if that seamless code-switching negotiation process does not throw up an alternative lingua franca (it usually does, with Wolof often serving this function in Senegambia).

As we walked through Tujereng woods in the malevolent heat of mid-afternoon, searching for violet-backed sunbirds and whistling cisticolas, Massameh was continually fiddling with his phone, keeping in touch with his friends back at Bijilo. 'What language do you text in?' I asked. 'I'm not texting, I'm using WhatsApp', he replied. A more remote location could hardly be imagined; the Welsh equivalent, in Cwm Eigiau perhaps, would undoubtedly render my phone useless, unreachable by any network. But here, and right across West Africa, people's chosen methods of communication are messaging services accessed via Africell or whatever network they can afford. Mobile communication supplanted traditional landlines in much of Africa, as a standard infrastructure never developed. Messaging services, and social media as a whole, lend themselves to aural cultures: indeed Massameh then showed me his messages, in an intriguing blend of Mandinka and English, reminding me of the way in which colloquial Welsh is used on Facebook and Twitter. It is imperfect but pragmatic and realistic. Thus language evolves: with social media both threat and opportunity.

Massameh wore an old black Manchester United away kit incessantly. Inevitably, we finally got on to football. I had been trying to avoid it. In my youth, I was a keen Manchester City fan, following them around the country during the wilderness years of the 1990s. Now, as just another global megabrand, the team is a worldwide symbol of obscene wealth and sporting excess: as such, conversations about allegiance can be awkward and misinterpreted by enthusiasts who understandably just see and know the modern brand. Massameh's response to my admission was instant, as he quoted Alex Ferguson's famous early dismissal of the threat City posed to United's dominance: 'noisy neighbours'.

The perfect antidote to my idealistic take on the regional unity of West Africa came later that day, when I asked him whether he'd supported Senegal in that summer's World Cup. He looked at me, mock aghast, and with exquisite comic timing said: 'Definitely not. I would never support them. They are *noisy neighbours.*'

CHAPTER 2
'MOUNTAIN OF TONGUES':
THE CAUCASIAN POLYGLOSSIA

Arab travellers in the early Middle Ages called the Caucasus *djabal al-alsun*, the 'mountain of languages', in an attempt to encapsulate its extraordinary polyglossia, the multiplicity of tongues in a single region. And they were far from the first to make that observation: one thousand years before, the Greek historian Strabo wrote that 'in Phasis, there are people speaking 60 different languages'.

Ancient Phasis is present-day Poti, on the Black Sea coast of Samegrelo, astride the route of the Silk Road and still the main Georgian port. While conversations on its surprisingly broad streets (rather elegant) and black sand beach (an acquired taste) now tend to be held in Mingrelian or Georgian, the Caucasus as a whole still has more than 50 extant languages tucked away within the folds of its spectacular topography.

More recent travellers have resorted to justifiable hyperbole: 'ethnological mayhem' was Tony Anderson's take as he travelled through Georgia in the late 1990s.[26] The entire region is still characterised by the most extreme form of linguistic diversity, which reaches a peak in the north-eastern corner of Georgia, where that country abuts the Russian republic of Dagestan. Here, on both sides of the border, distinctive communities live in bewilderingly complex, geographically discrete units which are almost impossible to pin down accurately. One valley contains the Ginukh, another the Bats, another the Bezhita, and on and on through groups of Tindi, Khwarshi, Chechens, Ingush, Kists and Karata. Some villages contain one clannish group, others are part of a wider community with scattered outposts across the Caucasus. Most, if not all, speak their own languages: some, like the Lezgins, numbering hundreds of thousands, others, like the Hunzib, a few hundred.[27]

'Mountain of tongues'

There is something life-affirming about this superabundance, something analogous to the rich, yet fragile, biodiversity of the rainforest. The area is not without its problems, and we will come to that, but there is also a mutual respect – and even an interdependence – that extends across these mountain peoples despite their desire to protect their own languages and customs. A detailed description is superfluous and utterly unfeasible, but consider – by way of example – the Bats people, who retain their language, 'batsbur mott', which uses a smattering of Georgian loan-words but cannot be understood by Chechen or Ingush people, who speak related languages from the Nakh family. The relationship between the three is, according to Joanna Nichols, analogous to that between Czech, Polish and Russian: it is obvious that there is a close relationship, some phrases can be understood, but that is as far as it goes. Like many of the Caucasian languages, Bats is 'frighteningly complex', with multiple verbal genres meaning that (to take one random example) the imperative 'come' can have eight different versions depending on the gender and precise number of the people being addressed. It is, perhaps unsurprisingly, endangered.[28]

Cultural practices, geopolitical loyalties, and even religions, vary dramatically from valley to valley. The Kists, for example, may be Christians, Animists or Sunni Muslims, or a syncretised version of all three in varying combinations depending on their precise geographical location. Most of them live in the Pankisi gorge, which became internationally notorious in the 1990s for sheltering radical Chechens – many of whom were protected by the Kists, who are closely related, although even that (and the alleged 'sheltering') is a reductive and disputed observation.[29] The point is that the region is almost impossible for outsiders to grasp accurately; as the indigenous population often disagrees about loyalties and the exact nature of the relationship between the different linguistic groups.

***

35

It is the combination of dramatic physical geography and a uniquely liminal global location (it is the ultimate cultural crossroads, poised between Europe and Asia) that forms the point of departure for any subsequent attempt to capture the region's remarkable linguistic complexity. The long tradition of decentralisation and fiercely-guarded independence – that expresses itself politically and culturally in different ways across the region – is intrinsically linked to the landscape. To take Georgia as an example, the people of Svaneti and Tusheti, high up in the mountains, were barely linked to central rule from Tbilisi until recently, which goes some way to explaining the prevailing idiosyncrasies of these mountain hideaways.[30]

The medieval Arabs were right: and there is still nowhere else with quite the same scenic and cultural variety – a blend that gives it a magnetic appeal for the small number of curious foreigners that manage to penetrate what can initially seem problematic destinations. I first visited the Caucasus in 2011, when I travelled to the Georgian capital Tbilisi and the surrounding Mtskheta-Mtianeti region. In 2012, I made a more ambitious trip to neighbouring Armenia, meandering south from Yerevan to mountainous Jermuk, its market stalls and cafés buried under three metres of snow in late March. Jermuk is hard-up against the border of disputed Nagorno-Karabakh, and the road passes through former Azeri exclaves as it winds its way up into the mountains. The road to Iran passes this way too, marked by dozens of roadside stalls full of two litre 'cola' bottles filled with the local red wine, for ease of smuggling past the border guards as coachloads of partying Persians head home to the Islamic Republic.

Both those trips proved an obvious point to me: the Caucasus is the only place in the world where the biggest geographical cliché of all – that of 'East meets West' – is really apposite. It's an overused phrase that has been applied to all sorts of places over many centuries – anywhere that might be said to represent some kind of crossing point, or merging of cultures: Venice, Istanbul, Cyprus, Sarajevo.

But the Caucasus is where that cliché becomes genuinely relevant, indeed the only way to accurately describe its blend of language and culture.

The size and scale of the mountain range – there are numerous peaks above 5,000 metres, considerably higher than the Alps – means that only four driveable roads cross its entire length. To the north of the high peaks lie seven autonomous Russian republics, most of them broadly Islamic, all of them culturally diverse, almost impossibly so in some cases (Dagestan, for example). To the south, the somewhat more tourist-friendly countries of Georgia, Armenia and Azerbaijan.

If pushed, most people place those latter three in Eastern Europe. Look at a map, however, and that illusion is hard to sustain, with Georgia east of the outer margins of Turkey, and Armenia bordering Iran. Continental boundaries are a little arbitrary at the best of times, but most authorities draw the Europe–Asia line at the Caucasus itself: under this interpretation of continental geography, the Islamic Russian republics are, theoretically, Europe – whilst Georgia, Armenia and Azerbaijan are, theoretically, Asia.

Georgia and Armenia are perhaps the two most robustly Christian countries on Earth – their Orthodox religion is core to their sense of identity in a way that has disappeared from most of Europe and even Latin America. The fact that Georgia, in particular, 'feels' European, is at least partly down to its Christian heritage. Along with Armenia, it is the oldest Christian nation on Earth, adopting the religion in the fourth century, and bordering on aggressive in its assertiveness of that status.

But it is not fully Europe, nor is it Asia, or the Middle East – it is somewhere else, somewhere in between. Before we get on to language, consider the food as another obviously analogous way of illustrating that cultural liminality, hovering between worlds. To take one example among many possible candidates, 'Badrijani Nigvzit' is a popular Georgian dish of thinly-sliced fried aubergine wrapped round a paste of walnuts, garlic, coriander and fenugreek. It is usually topped with pomegranate seeds and fresh dill. You do not need to be a particularly well-informed gastronaut to grasp the influences there, and to see how they relate to Georgia's geographical position at a cultural crossroads. The walnuts and pomegranates are often associated with Persian (Iranian) cookery, the fenugreek and coriander from further east, the dill and the frying from Russia, the stuffed vegetable technique linked to the 'dolma' of Turkey and Greece. But to see Georgian food only in terms of its external influences is to do it a disservice: it is also entirely distinctive, undoubtedly one of the world's most underrated cuisines, an endlessly fascinating reflection of those wider cultural trends and linked to the region's overarching diversity.

Indeed, German anthropologist Florian Muehlfried argues that rituals of the table were one way for Georgians to separate themselves from their Russian rulers in the Soviet era. Because they shared a religion, the 'self-othering' of the Georgian nation had to be based on folk culture and language. The 'supra' soon became a symbol of that cultural otherness, a manifestation of Georgian hospitality based on a distinctive way of eating, drinking and feasting. Anybody who has experienced a Georgian breakfast knows this, although the supra is a more specific traditional feast, always hosted by a designated 'tamada' (toastmaster) who coordinates the drinking with various elaborate toasts, each of which builds on the previous. It is poor form to drink between the toasts, which leads to much unpleasant guzzling and is not really conducive to an appreciation of the subtle flavour of rare Georgian varietals. I was told, however, that so-called 'democratic supras' are now a thing with the young and the urban – allowing for the radical concept of drinking at leisure, between toasts, and occasionally even putting the glass down.[v]

On my first morning in Kutaisi, after multiple different dishes (more than a dozen) had been placed on the table (at 8am), Zaza, the owner of the hotel, asked if I would like some wine to go with it. 'Thank you, but not really', I said, clutching my stomach to indicate satiation. The wine was the usual greenish-brown home-brew, not overly appealing. 'How about a chacha then, my own bottle, just a small one?' he said, thumb and forefinger squeezed tightly together to indicate just how inconsequentially tiny it would be. I knew from my previous trip to Georgia that 'chacha' is an unusually powerful Georgian version of grappa or eau de vie, a home-brewed moonshine that can reach a devastating 65% proof. I felt obliged to accept, as Zaza – rightly, I think – outlined its benefits: 'It is very healthy, you must drink chacha for breakfast, it helps the digestion, it keeps you slim. Just one, though, just a small one,' he added, pouring a gigantic measure, right up to the brim of the glass. 'I like food too much, it's my big problem,' he said later, watching me work through slices of the celebrated cheese bread, 'khatchapuri', patting his enormous belly and gesturing to the groaning table whilst downing his own chacha. Nothing unusual in this, of course: the French 'trou normand' ('Norman hole') is the same concept, a stiff calvados to ease digestion, although it isn't usually taken at 8am.

The traditions of the supra are paralleled by language. After Georgia's national church was subsumed by the Russian Orthodox Church in 1811, 'Kartuli' (the Georgian tongue) became the focus for self-identification – any attempt to downgrade it or

---

v Georgian food and restaurants have long been popular across all the countries of the former Soviet Union. Their role, as purveyors of interesting and exotic flavours in countries less noted for their cuisine, is analogous to that of Indian or Thai restaurants in 1980s/1990s Britain: a welcome oasis of stimulating food in a desert of stodgy blandness.

replace it with Russian met fierce resistance. Moscow's threat to remove the status of Georgian within the SSR (Soviet Socialist Republic) in 1978 is now a legendary moment of Georgian history, which ended with a humiliating climb-down in front of protestors in Tbilisi carrying placards saying 'Ai ia' ('Here is a violet' – the first line in a popular Kartuli language primer distributed in the nineteenth century). Since 1990, the day on which this happened, 14 April, has been celebrated as the 'Day of the Georgian language'.[31]

The Georgians call their country 'Sakartvelo' ('a place for the speakers of the language of Kartuli'), revealing the centrality of language to their identity, written into the country's very name, in much the same way that 'yr hen iaith', the old tongue, is the focus of the Welsh national anthem. The celebrated, rousing final line of which, 'O bydded I'r hen iaith barhau', translates to something like 'long may the old language prevail'. Kartuli is the main representative of a distinct family, unrelated to any other languages apart from Mingrelian, Svan and Laz, which we will come to shortly. It is characterised by explosive 'ejective stops' and clusters of consonants, which outsiders often describe as 'unpronounceable' (Welsh is deemed similarly 'consonant heavy' and 'unpronounceable', entirely reductively, by people who do not take the time to find out the logical and phonetic pronunciation rules).

Kartuli has something Welsh does not, however: its own alphabet, which like the Armenian alphabet is unique, beautifully artistic, and at least 1,500 years old. It makes marshrutka (minibus) travel problematic at times, because place-names are rarely 'translated' into the Roman alphabet – on more than one occasion I was forced to hold my guidebook, which had Georgian-script place names, next to the front of the bus to check that what to me are just a beautiful set of elaborately curled symbols matched up.

***

My third trip to the region illustrates the point that, in the Caucasus, you only need to travel tiny distances to experience the astounding diversity of the region. The gorges and mountains form multiple impenetrable barriers that have historically allowed sequestered communities to develop in relative isolation and this becomes clear even on a relatively short overland journey.

Kutaisi styles itself as Georgia's second city (although Batumi has a bigger population). It is the capital of Imereti, an ancient and modern region of Georgia which was once an independent kingdom, and feels very different from the capital of Tbilisi further east. From Kutaisi, I took a typical Soviet-era marshrutka to Zugdidi, no more than 100 kilometres to the west, and the capital of Samegrelo region (also known as Mingrelia). The east–west split in Georgia is historic. To a certain extent, it reflects ancient history, Ottoman (west) versus Persian (east) spheres of influence, still just about detectable in food culture and aspects of the architecture and language.

The Mingrelians speak a language that is related to Georgian, but incomprehensible to the people of Kutaisi a short drive away. Zugdidi is just a few kilometres from the Abkhazian border, where everything changes again, but far more dramatically in this case. Abkhazia was, and is, a major post-Soviet flashpoint – one of those phantom states that is stoked and supported by the Putin regime. Like Transdniestria (covered in the Moldova chapter later in this book) and South Ossetia (subject of the 2008 war between Georgia and Russia), it is a region that found itself on the wrong side of history after the collapse of the Soviet Union – and subsequently found itself something of a pawn in a larger geopolitical game revolving around spheres of influence, Putin's Russia versus the 'West'. Abkhazia's history is complex (even by the standards of the Caucasus), but Zugdidi now houses thousands of ethnic Georgians who were forced to flee their homes in the 1990s after the Abkhaz regime, supported by Russia, expelled them from its territory. For their part, the Abkhaz had complained for many years about the enforced 'Georgianisation' of their nation and culture.[32]

From Zugdidi, I travelled along the Abkhazian border north-east into Svaneti, the archetypal isolated mountainous land, and home of the Svans, another ethnic group speaking an entirely different Kartvelian language.

And this is just a single journey, just a tiny snapshot of the bigger whole.

***

To properly unpick the 'mountain of tongues', the extraordinary linguistic complexity of the Caucasus, takes some time, but it is necessary, if only to come to some understanding about the contemporary geopolitics of the region. A caveat is necessary in advance: the region is so complex that over-simplification is inevitable. A comprehensive guide would be impossible without specialist knowledge and a great deal of space, so the following potted summary must be viewed merely as a superficial illustration of its linguistic complexity.

Firstly, the region has to be divided in two – the North Caucasus and the South Caucasus, separated by the high peaks of the border regions. Taking the South Caucasus first: there are three superficially dominant ethnic and linguistic groups – Azeris, Georgians, Armenians – all of whom have a sovereign state to call their own, albeit all with problematic boundary issues of one kind or another. But within those three countries are numerous smaller nationalities and linguistic identities: these include Ossetians, Abkhazians, Kurds (Muslim and Yezidi Christian), Talysh and Lezgins. Then, like a Russian doll, each of these nationalities tends to have significant linguistic diversity within: the overarching Georgian identity is real, but masks further complexity, with the Mingrelians and Svans having their own languages, which are related to the dominant Kartvelian tongue but distinct from it, and not mutually intelligible. This does not mean that they want independence, but it does mean that there is significant linguistic diversity that goes well beyond the regional, let alone national, political boundaries.

The North Caucasus is considerably more complex, and a much harder region through which to travel – less stable, problematic transport links, awkward visa requirements. It is made up of seven autonomous regions, all of which are nominally Russian – and a mainly Muslim mix of nationalities (though that is, of course, a simplification). The sheer scale of the Caucasus mountains (many peaks above 5,000 metres) means that there is little crossover – although some linguistic groups, like the Ossetians and Circassians, have footholds on either side of the mountains, and there has been intermittent interaction between groups for centuries.

There are seven branches of the North-East Caucasian language family – all of which are further subdivided into mutually unintelligible tongues. Some of these have hundreds of thousands of speakers – the Avar for example – while others are much smaller, like those within the Tsezic, Dargin and Lak branches. The region reaches its complex apotheosis in the previously-mentioned Russian republic of Dagestan, a land of such bewildering linguistic abundance that it only really makes sense when viewed in map form. It is extraordinarily heterogeneous, with 13 official languages (three more than superdiverse South Africa, but with a tiny fraction of the population) and numerous unofficial languages.

Immediately west are the speakers of the Nakh languages, which include Chechen and Ingush, perhaps the best known North Caucasian nationalities to the outside world. Further west again lies a different macro-region, the North-West Caucasus, which is a little less complex than the North-East, but such a term should be viewed relatively, with the Abkhaz, Abaza, Circassians and Kabardians dominating.

Lenin realised, even in the early idealistic days of the Soviet Union (1922) that its cultural and linguistic diversity (well over 100 nationalities) potentially contained the seeds of its downfall: 'It would be unforgiveable opportunism if … we should undermine our prestige … with even the slightest rudeness or injustice to our own minorities.'[33] The Soviets oscillated between oppression and celebration of their multiple minorities, but kept an authoritarian lid on self-determination until the ideology began to unravel in the late 1980s.

Lenin's fretting proved prescient, of course. The Baltic States, Central Asia, and other countries on the margins of that vast empire all rebelled against Moscow's rule when its centralised control began to weaken in the 1980s. But the Caucasus was always likely to correspond most closely to Lenin's doubts, given its diversity. And three decades after the Soviet Union's collapse, there remain numerous unresolved flashpoints and conflict zones across the region, where coexistence has proved problematic. The four that have the biggest global traction, those that have at times attracted the attention of the world's media are Chechnya, Nagorno-Karabakh, South Ossetia and Abkhazia.

***

Zugdidi is a bustling little town, not without its problems (partly as a result of an influx of Mingrelian Georgians, refugees from war-torn Abkhazia, which is so close you can actually see it from the top floor breakfast balcony of the Hotel Grand, where I was staying).

Just outside was a Soviet-era mural – made out of iron – above a row of small shops with pictures of Marlon Brando and Bob Marley advertising 'flights to London' and tobacco. Signs of the Soviet past are always interesting, with their rather opaque political messages, but they are becoming endangered in places that once formed the outer reaches of the Empire. I stood back from it, on the other side of the street, trying to discern its meaning. Eventually it became clear – it depicted the history of transport, from a prancing Mercury with winged feet, through to horses, locomotives and space flight.

Directly opposite were the offices of a radio station, Radio Atinati, broadcasting in Russian and Georgian, partially funded by the US, and deliberately located here to beam over the border to Putin-leaning Abkhazia.[34]

That evening, as I devoured a huge bowl of skhermuli chicken – which swims in a thin milk and garlic sauce, a waiter asked where I was from. I told him, and he cleared his throat before theatrically declaring: 'to be or not to be'. He then paused, nodding towards me, until I grasped I was supposed to add 'that is the question'. I did so, and he then went on, in a fruity English accent: 'Whether 'tis nobler in the mind to suffer the slings and arrows of outrageous fortune' and managed at least six lines of the Shakespearean soliloquy, reaching 'thousand natural shocks' before his memory failed.

Davit was a Zugdidi native, a rare English speaker, a proud Mingrelian, and something of a scholar. He had a degree in literature and had lived in Tbilisi, but was now at the parental home, looking after elderly relatives. 'Mingrelian has many books, a real literature,' he said. 'And we have our own newspapers too.' In the 1930s, at least six newspapers were published in the language, but its relationship with Georgian is complicated, and it was not clear to me whether any media is now produced in it. In 1999, books by the Georgian poet Murman Lebanidze were burned in Zugdidi after he made a series of rude remarks about Mingrelian, and its speakers, the implication being that it was a debased form of Georgian, or a threat to the centre.[35] Davit was a living riposte to this: 'There's a German–Mingrelian dictionary, and a Georgian one, but we're all Georgians, we always will be, and we're proud of it. Did you know that Gamsakhurdia came from here?'

Zviad Gamsakhurdia was the first President of independent Georgia and a figure that still divides opinion within the country. He was a proto-populist, a typical example of the kind of intellectual nationalist that emerged across the post-Communist world at that time, reading the runes, sensing the direction of travel with all the old certainties gone, garnering support by unleashing the forces of identity politics, emphasising the threat posed by the 'other'. If it sounds horribly familiar, it should, as some of our own politicians get in on the same unwise act 30 years later (although I am not, of course, making a direct comparison).

In Georgia's case, it all had the obvious effect of destabilising the regions that spoke different languages (especially those from different language families) and felt threatened by the growing tide of nationalism: the Circassians of South Ossetia and the Abkhazians being the pre-eminent examples. Their subsequent experience echoes that of the Transdniestrians discussed in the Moldova chapter: they looked to Moscow for support, and now exist as phantom states, propped up by the Putin regime, eternally opposed to the pro-Western states they find themselves, *de jure* at least, trapped in.

As in the Balkans, the convulsions of the post-Communist era mean that the region has become somewhat less diverse than it used to be. Certainly, that is the case in the big cities, which were once famous for their melting-pot ambience; the romance of the Silk Road. As Thomas de Waal points out: 'A century ago, neither Tbilisi, Baku, nor Yerevan had a majority population of Georgians, Azerbaijanis, or Armenians, respectively.'[36] Gurdjieff, in his uncategorisable book *Meetings with Remarkable Men* describes 1930s Tbilisi as a happy polyglot city, where speaking five or six languages was not uncommon. Gurdjieff claimed to speak 18, his friend Abram Yelov a staggering 30.[vi]

vi Author, mystic and philosopher G. I. Gurdjieff was himself a Greek-Armenian who grew up in Kars (then a famously diverse

But that has all gone, swept away by the realities of the post-Soviet era: Tbilisi's population is now largely Georgian. There are numerous well-documented examples of the effects – but the one that has always stuck with me is that of the Chess Grandmaster Garry Kasparov, born in Baku, Azerbaijan, to an Armenian mother and a Russian-Jewish father. That was 1963, when the Soviet Union kept a relatively effective lid on identity politics and ethnic tensions. By the time the Kasparovs fled in the early 1990s, as the three south Caucasian republics moved towards independence, it had become virtually impossible for Armenians to live in Azerbaijan, and vice versa, and that has not changed since. Kasparov has never returned to the city of his birth. The reverse is true of the Qarabag football team, which often appears in European competition. 'Qarabag' is an Azeri team from the ruined town of Aghdam in Nagorno-Karabakh, dubbed the 'Caucasian Hiroshima' by some, which gives some indication of its post-conflict appearance. Its name, crest and colours make reference to its origins in Azeri Karabakh, as does its 'refugee' nickname – because Qarabag is the mirror-image of Kasparov: the club moved to faraway Baku when Azeri-dominated Aghdam was destroyed by Armenian troops in the early 1990s conflict. Aghdam remains a ghost town, uninhabited and dilapidated.

***

From Zugdidi, I traced the Abkhaz border along the River Engudi, to the town of Jvari. We passed close to the tiny settlement of Sachino, which achieved a modest level of global fame in 2012, when the 'world's oldest person', Antisa Khvichava, died aged 132.

---

city on the edge of the Russian Empire, now at the outer margins of eastern Turkey, near the Armenian border) and encountered scores of linguistic communities in everyday life. *Meetings with Remarkable Men* is a celebrated work from the 1960s Soviet Union, which blends fact, fiction and philosophy. G. I. Gurdjieff (1991). *Meetings with Remarkable Men: All and everything* (2nd series). London, UK: Penguin.

Khvichava held a Soviet passport (which, by definition, must have been acquired well after her supposed birth in 1880) so her age was always a matter of conjecture. The Georgians do have a reputation for longevity, however, and despite the fact that she was almost certainly younger, there is a much more interesting detail about her life, which did appear in some of the news reports albeit not contextualised as an illustration of the complex realities of Caucasian identities. Khvichava spoke only Mingrelian and did not understand Georgian, never mind Russian.[37]

It is, of course, compulsory for centenarians to put their long lives down to some form of hard liquor. And if they don't, journalists will push them until they finally crack. Khvichava was no exception; predictably enough, a sneaky (and small) chacha at breakfast is the apparent secret to 13 decades of life.

At times, this road comes close enough to the Abkhaz border to allow views across into the disputed territory. The border is not sealed, as the Georgian state regards it as a fundamental part of the country, but it is very tricky and complicated for foreigners to cross. Across the broad Engudi river lies the embattled landscape around the town of Gali – an area some have described as a twilight zone, with its exclusively Mingrelian population forced to either adapt to the de facto Abkhaz reality by abandoning education in their native language, or move out entirely.

Language has always been central to the Abkhaz–Georgian conflict, perhaps because Abkhaz – unlike Svan or Mingrelian – comes from a different language family, unrelated to its Kartvelian neighbours. The questions are the eternal ones: what should be prioritised, what should be the language of governance, of education? Who has the right to speak? Inevitably, it is highly contentious, with the Abkhaz claiming the issues date from a history of forced assimilation, when teaching in the Abkhaz language was suppressed, Georgians were encouraged to settle, their alphabet imposed, and place names given Georgian endings.

This was rooted in Soviet history and, some say, relates to Stalin's own Georgian heritage (he came from Gori, not far from Tbilisi, bore an archetypal Georgian surname, Jughashvili, and grew up speaking Kartuli). One of Stalin's acolytes, Akaki Mgeladze, wrote in his memoirs of a lunch where Stalin said: 'They [the Abkhaz] are closer to Georgians than the Svans, but it does not occur to anyone that Svans are not Georgians. Everyone who knows their history well ought to understand that Abkhazia was always part of Georgia. The customs and beliefs of the Abkhaz basically don't differ from the customs of western Georgians.'[38]

Now, the Soviet era's prejudices have been reversed, with a long history of post-Soviet conflict (including a full-blown war in the early 1990s), and most Georgians long since expelled from Abkhazia. The Mingrelians around the town of Gali were allowed to remain, a recognition of their 'minority' status (the Abkhaz did not consider the Mingrelians to be fully Georgian) but with their language compromised. All other Georgians were forced to flee.

As so often happens, the wheel has now turned full circle. Mateu reported a new language policy in Abkhazia in 2016, and outlined the history of that turning wheel. It is an illustration of the ways in which minority languages can be politicised and mobilised in the pursuit of an illiberal cause. In November 2007, the de facto authorities of Abkhazia adopted a new law 'on the state language of the Republic of Abkhazia' that mandated Abkhaz as the language of official communication. After that date, all meetings held by the president, parliament and government had to be conducted in Abkhaz (instead of Russian, which is often the de facto language of choice). In 2015, the scope of this was extended, to insist that all state officials are now obliged to use Abkhaz as their language of everyday business.

There was a problem, however: Abkhaz is not universally spoken within Abkhazia, even among the Abkhaz themselves. Some argued that the implementation of the law was unrealistic, suggesting it will drive non-Abkhaz speakers away from Abkhazia and hurt the independent press, the teaching profession and others due to the number of non-Abkhaz speakers among ethnic minorities as well as the Abkhaz themselves. But the law is an attempt to amend a situation where up to a third of the ethnic Abkhaz population are no longer capable of speaking their native language, and even more are unable to read or write it;[39] instead, Russian is the language most commonly used in public life at present. This sort of measure is not unusual: the Baltic States deliberately marginalised Russian speakers post-independence as they attempted to enforce their own tongues on the large Russian-speaking minorities in those countries. And in Wales, of course, measures to promote and protect the Welsh language have often been deemed illiberal by English speakers. It is a very tricky conundrum: how to protect a fragile culture and a language in decline, a language threatened by something bigger, without adopting illiberal and potentially alienating policies? How do you balance the desire to protect with the need to remain open and inclusive?

In Abkhazia, the plan is to have everything in the minority tongue until the later years of education, when it switches to Russian – an illustration of the role of language as indicator of wider trends, in this case the Russian political influence on the breakaway state. As Mateu says 'this new language policy seems to be more of a political statement to emphasise the political detachment of the breakaway region from Georgia. This in turn will harshly affect the Mingrelian-speaking population in Gali, as they will lose the chance to learn Georgian, the language of their *de jure* country, leaving the generations to come unable to communicate with their relatives and friends on the other side of the border.'[40]

***

The marshrutka driver refused to accept the tiny bus was overloaded, attempting to squeeze an elderly lady into the absurdly inadequate space between the sliding door and the middle seats. 'Come on, you're too lazy to take the bags off the roof, there's no more space, no more people, chop-chop, let's go,' said a German backpacker to him, clapping impatiently, keen to get to Svaneti. We were trying to leave Jvari, a town near the Abkhaz border at the gates of the vast Enguri gorge, a twisting valley that leads ever upwards towards the hidden, mystical land of Svaneti – a place that has loomed large in my imagination for decades. The driver was a huge bear of a man, shaped like a cube, with a thick neck, obsidian black eyes, and an outlandish cap with limp visor, which he constantly had to push upwards in order to properly see through the cracked windscreen. He wore a royal blue tracksuit bearing an unlikely football crest: not Dynamo Tbilisi, or Torpedo Kutaisi. Not Barcelona, or Manchester United, but 'Havering Borough FC, established 2012'. It raised so many intriguing questions, shame we did not share a common language – he spoke Svan, Georgian and Russian, but not a single word of English.

Svaneti has a distinctive status within Georgia. It is seen as something of a repository of Georgian culture, the essential lodestone, rather like the concept of 'La France Profonde' (Deep France), despite the obvious reality that it has its own language and cultural practices which frequently predate those of the 'centre'. In that sense, its status struck me as analogous to the way the Welsh were often treated by Victorian travellers – George Borrow's *Wild Wales* being an archetypal example, or perhaps just an easy target. Borrow travelled the country having taught himself a version of Welsh – his approach was largely respectful, but inherently colonial, as he unwittingly describes the natives' bemusement at what is very likely to have been his rather outré pronunciation (he lived in Norfolk). The Welsh were, at the time, seen as the authentic 'Britons', co-opted into a convenient national story, with the Arthurian myths (for example) re-packaged as allegorical tales of British heroism and repulsing of the invader, regardless of the Brythonic versus Saxon narrative that came to prominence in the twelfth century (Arthurian legend has always been distinctly 'customisable' in order to suit varied agendas). In a further parallel, my landlady in Mestia told me that art treasures were moved to Svaneti from Kutaisi and Tbilisi in times of national crisis, reminding me of Manod Mawr's role in World War II, when hundreds of priceless paintings from the National Gallery in London were moved to quarries under that mountain near Blaenau Ffestiniog for safe-keeping away from the Luftwaffe's bombs.

The Svans do consider themselves Georgian, but they do so rather like the Sicilians or Genoese consider themselves Italian: the regional identity comes first, the national a distant second. The sheer remoteness of Svaneti had multiple effects – the most visible lasting legacy being the medieval defensive towers that dot the landscape, with every village having numerous examples, almost all still standing. The towers are paralleled in certain Tuscan towns, like San Gimignano, the villages of the Mani peninsula in the Greek Peloponnese, and the medieval mudbrick 'skyscrapers' of Shibam, Yemen: almost always, they indicate a lack (or distrust) of central authority. They represent the need to defend your own family, in areas remote from conventional justice. And Svaneti, particularly its upper reaches, almost defines remoteness.

Unlike Tuscany and the Peloponnese, however, Svaneti retains its medieval feel throughout as a partial result of that remoteness. In that sense, it reminded me of parts of Nepal or the less accessible valleys of the Atlas Mountains of Morocco. This related to the lack of metalled road access, the almost complete absence of modernity or renovation, and in particular the fusing of ancient paganism with a version of monotheism, in this case

Orthodox Christianity. The names given to the Svan Gods of hunting conjure up an impossibly romantic world, redolent of Tolkien or *Game of Thrones*: Dal, Apsasd, Sgim-Bermodzgvar.[vii] These had to be placated, with sacrificial oxen cooked in a giant 'leighen' cauldron. I was shown one of the original cauldrons, retrieved from an abandoned farmhouse near the village of Tsvirmi; it was the size of a small car, a Fiat 125 perhaps. Its function as the focus of rituals and feasts – essential bonding for these isolated communities – could easily be imagined, the giant vessel feeding the community, the quiet observance of timeless cultural practice cementing family ties and societal cohesion.

Mikheil Chartolani, at the ethnographic museum in Mestia (the rapidly changing 'capital' of Svaneti) suggests that the 'coexistence of pagan and Christian rituals and practice of offering various objects in sacred places played a significant role in the preservation of the cultural heritage of Svaneti'. I was particularly taken by the 'sheepbird'; hybrid creatures are common in folklore but this unlikely combination is rare, possibly unique to Svaneti. The museum has multiple carved silver images of a mythic creature with the body of a large bird, the head and neck of a sheep. Public feasts dedicated to the cult of ancestors or fertility, rituals celebrated near the window of the eastern wall, it all echoes similar syncretised religions that manage to preserve older cultural practice in developing countries from Latin America to Africa (and often preserve archaic languages in passing). Cuba's 'Santeria' is an obvious point of comparison, blending as it does Yoruba-derived paganism with Catholicism, with the Lucumi language its sacred tongue.

A few of the old Svan towers are open. In one, I was shown a primitive 'central heating' system that I had never encountered before, although it seemed obvious in its almost comic simplicity.

---

vii Svan names rendered in the Roman alphabet, transcribed by me from a display of hunting paraphernalia at the Svaneti Museum of History and Ethnography in Mestia.

Livestock – sheep, pigs, goats – were stuffed into numerous open stone 'kennels' round a central living room. Their body heat then warmed the room around the central table: the resultant fug and pungency can only be imagined. I climbed two of the towers (known as 'kor' in Svan) – five or six floors with rickety wooden ladders leading to tiny holes in the roof and the odd bit of rock climbing (as a lifelong climber, I would refer to the final footless haul as a 'mantelshelf' move, above a big drop). The oldest tower still stands in the tiny hamlet of Chazhashi, 2,200 metres up at the end of a twisting valley; the tower, surrounded by ancient stone houses that all look equally old, dates back to the tenth century and it – along with the rest of this particular hamlet – is an arresting sight, apparently unchanged for 1,000 years.

From Mestia, I was determined to continue the journey to Ushguli – a place so extraordinary, its location so otherworldly, that it is not surprising that two iconic films have been shot here – almost a century apart. The first was *Salt for Svanetia*, directed in 1930 by Mikhail Kalatosov. It is a classic slice of early Soviet propaganda, saturated with the supreme ideological confidence of that era. It begins with another quote from Lenin: 'Even now there are far reaches of the Soviet Union where the patriarchal way of life persists along with remnants of the clan system', and is essentially an ethnographic study of the Svans filtered through a distinctly political Soviet perspective. It is silent, and limited by its technological context, but manages to capture something of the lifestyle and scenery of Ushguli. It revolves around the Soviet effort to build a road up to the highest villages in Georgia, in order to transport much-needed salt to the remote community, and for the blighted peasant community to embrace Communist ideals: there are lots of pickaxes and oiled torsos as Soviet heroes carve out the road (which, almost a century on, remains a rutted gravel track, perilously exposed to the screes of the tight Engudi gorge in places, as well as the fact that Ushguli is cut off for six months of the year, buried – along with the road – under several metres of snow).

There is still a legacy that relates to the historic shortage of salt in the region. A local speciality, 'Svanuri Marili', or 'Svan salt', is sold by elderly women in the villages – it is salt that has been padded-out, made to go further, with blue fenugreek, garlic, 'gitsruli' (wild Caucasian caraway seeds) and marigold flowers, lending it a yellowish-orange colour. Its pungent aroma is transporting: redolent of the east, of Iran, India, Pakistan, and another perfect illustration of Georgia's liminality. I bought four bags from an old lady who sits in a tiny wooden stall at the edge of Mestia, finding quite quickly that it was almost impossible to contain the smell, no matter how tightly it was wrapped. Every time I moved, wafts of fenugreek and garlic were released. The scent followed me around the humid Georgian lowlands, all the way back to Luton airport, where it continued to attract a considerable amount of attention.

Much more recently, in 2015, the second of the two films was shot in Ushguli: *Dede*. I watched this sitting on a beanbag in a tiny arthouse cinema in Mestia, the day before travelling onwards to Ushguli in a tiny battered marshrutka. *Dede* is set in the recent past, 1992, and uses the region's stunning scenery and cultural practices as appropriately dramatic backdrop to a slightly hackneyed – but uplifting – story of a spirited woman rebelling against the strictures and customs of an isolated, conservative community.

That film's dialogue is a mixture of Georgian and Svan, which is still widely spoken in the remoter parts of this mountainous region. Svan is endangered, however, with its 30,000 or so speakers living in atomised communities and young people – in time-honoured fashion – leaving for opportunities elsewhere. It has no literature, and has never been properly recorded. Like many of the Caucasian languages, is not easy for outsiders to pick up; several writers have described the 'terrible complexity' of the languages just across the Russian border. One analysis of Tsez detected 42 different locative case markers which can describe precisely which kind of space someone or something is in, at, under, by, near, away from.[41] But, like Svan, its unwritten status combines with its complexity and the realities of out-migration from isolated, poverty-stricken mountainous regions to render it threatened by the slow creep of modernity in the Caucasus. The obvious analogy with biology seems apposite again: the impractical, the slow to adapt species, are inevitably endangered – I was reminded of the highly specific habitat requirements of the ultra-rare slender-billed curlew, which insists on breeding only in the peat-bogs of the Siberian Taiga. The north Caucasus language Archi is dying, so is Hunzib. Once gone, they cannot be revived in the Cornish sense, as without a literature they have left no historical trace. Ubykh, which was formerly celebrated for its 80 consonants, is already dead. Tabasaran, spoken by 90,000 people, has eight genders, leading Soviet-era linguists to amuse themselves by introducing unfamiliar items to the community, waiting to see which of the eight genders the object would be assigned.

'Sounds very modern to me', was my wife's instant response when I mentioned the genders of Tabasaran to her. After some thought, I had to agree: it may sound unwieldy and impractical, but it would surely cope much more effectively than English with the contemporary debate around gender fluidity and sexuality.

CHAPTER 3
MAMA TADA: LANGUAGE AND LANDSCAPE
IN THE NGABE COMARCA OF PANAMA

You do not expect a riot in a retirement community, but that was exactly what this was turning into. I was in the most genteel town in Central America, Boquete, famous for its perfect climate of perpetual spring. A large proportion of its residents are American pensioners, attracted by that climate and some attractive tax breaks. They live in sprawling pastel-shaded mansions, with tropical flowers in the gardens, hummingbirds above the marble patios, and expansive views of the cloud forest: all very chichi.

But this was a booze-fuelled brawl of a kind not untypical in 'rougher' parts of Central America. Its origins were obvious, even to me as a casual observer. It had started as a fight between two drunken young men from the Ngabe 'tribe', who were still at the epicentre stripped to the waist, but it was now becoming a little more serious as their friends and family took sides and joined in.

I first noticed the disturbance as I passed a dingy bar on a side street, well away from the main Boquete drag with its artisanal shops, single source locally produced coffee and craft beer bars. Here, just a few feet away, two bloodied indigenous men were knocking twelve bells out of each other. With every minute that passed, their respective groups of friends became more and more involved, and increasingly agitated. As the noise got louder and the violence more obvious, some tourists and mainstream Boquete residents did start to notice, but few gave it more than a second glance: indeed, it seemed to me that the shopkeepers made a point of ignoring it, the subtext being: typical Ngabe behaviour.

The Ngabe are the archetypal marginalised group. Almost any statistic of deprivation has them at the bottom of the

Panamanian development scale: unemployment, for example, is over 90% and the majority of Ngabe adults are illiterate.[42] If there is violence on the streets of Boquete, it is likely to be the Ngabe. If there is poor housing on the nearby hills, it is likely to be Ngabe.

Despite this, the community is in better shape than it has been for decades. Its language is now formally protected and after many years of political pressure, the community was granted a 'comarca' (autonomous region) in the late 1990s. Now, unified to an extent by new technologies – even social media – the Ngabe present a relatively coherent, politicised face to central government in Panama and, to a lesser degree, neighbouring Costa Rica. Some have solar electricity, although more choose to stay away from contact with urban Panama. When they are in town, in Boquete or David (a much larger city, around an hour 'downhill' and a staging post on the Pan-American highway towards Costa Rica), they keep themselves to themselves, moving around in extended family units and frequenting particular zones in which they feel comfortable (or so it seemed to me).

There has been significant progress with regard to the protection of indigenous languages and culture right across Panama, but in the case of the Ngabe an undercurrent of violence, particularly drunken violence, persists. The 'Balseria' is perhaps the best example of this, and does little to endear the nation to the increasingly affluent Panamanian mainstream which has otherwise travelled some distance on the journey towards accepting and celebrating its minority communities. In essence, the Balseria is a four-day festival of violence and drunkenness, although the Ngabe themselves would claim, with some justification, that this is overplayed by the Spanish-speaking majority and that it is primarily a misunderstood celebration of a fragile indigenous culture.

Any sport that revolves around attempts to temporarily maim your opponent by throwing large sticks at their legs seems likely to attract a degree of opprobrium, however, and the expat

Americans I met in Boquete were particularly scathing about the practice. Unsurprisingly, the local firewater – a form of palm leaf liquor called 'Seco' – plays a considerable role in the festival and presumably numbs the pain caused by four-foot long balsa logs being hurled into unprotected shins.

Although I was unable to witness the Balseria first hand in my Panamanian journey, the violence implicit in the festival did seem to be echoed in the brawl I was now watching. One American told me that the worst fight he had ever seen resulted from an infringement of Balseria conventions, when a stick was hurled 'above the knee' of an opponent. Such an infringement always results in a full-blown fist fight and, perhaps, the riot that was now unfolding also had its origins in a perceived slight or rule infringement of some kind: betting disputes, often quite minor in origin, are common in Central American bars. It might have been that, or it might have been something else, something trivial or something important: pure speculation on my part, and the bar owners that I later spoke to about it (all of whom claimed it would 'ciertamente' have been a betting dispute).

It felt unpleasantly voyeuristic to watch, and the brutality of the fighting became genuinely disturbing after a while; I retired to a nearby café, somewhat unnerved. When I finished my coffee and returned to the scene of the brawl, less than an hour later, there was no sign that anything untoward had happened. The street was relatively clean, plastic chairs were back in their usual place on the street, there was no blood and, most remarkably, there were no Ngabe, not even inside the bar, which was now completely empty.

***

I had no idea what had happened – I had not heard any sirens and later asked the café owner about it. He said that fights like this were fairly common, but the Ngabe tended to act as one when certain community leaders were in command. 'The guys in charge are good guys,' he said. 'At least the ones who live near town are. When they hear that something bad is happening in town, they come down to sort it out.' There was, he said, a lot of respect for them: which I took to mean that the Hispanic residents of the town liked the fact that the tribal leaders acted as a kind of informal police force.

Much of the Ngabe's more recent unified face stems from a bizarre religious cult called Mama Tada. This derives from an incident in the early 1960s when a Ngabe woman claimed to have received a visitation from the Virgin Mary. Stories of illiterate peasants being visited by Mary are, admittedly, ten a penny, and global in scope – she certainly gets around. But in the case of the Ngabe the strict (and occasionally seemingly paradoxical) commandments given served to unify the community and lend it a sense of political purpose.[43]

There was more than a hint of bog-standard racism about the Virgin's commandment to avoid contact with mainstream Latino (that is, Hispanic Panamanian) society – but by abandoning feuding and attempting to limit alcohol consumption, the commandments also had the positive effect of preserving Ngabe language and culture (even if those commandments are not always strictly observed). As the tenets of Mama Tada were outlined to me by the stereotypically friendly American, Tim, who ran my guesthouse, I was put in mind of the role of Methodism in the preservation of the Welsh language. A certain narrow-mindedness and reverse bigotry against the dominant group, while distasteful, insular and self-defeating in the long-term, can sometimes play an important role in minority language preservation. This was particularly the case in less enlightened times: the nineteenth century in the case of Wales, the 1960s in the case of Panama.

***

Community leaders are well aware that insularity of this kind cuts both ways. On the one hand, it offers a simple route to preservation, a seemingly obvious solution with an appealing sense of purity accentuated by the attractive notion that the dominant culture is somehow a contaminating force. On the other hand, it can lead to misunderstandings and false perceptions. The kind of drunken violence I had just witnessed, no matter how rare it might be, can lead to a patronising and simplistic view of indigenous marginalisation and hopelessness, rather like the narrative sometimes applied to the aboriginal population of Australia. But, as is usually the case with easily-digested narratives applied to those who lack the will or ability to respond, it obscures the multi-faceted and complex reality of Ngabe life.

My first direct contact with the Ngabe had been a few days before, as I descended from Volcan Baru, an extinct volcano that is Panama's highest peak. Usually wreathed in cloud, my dry season visit coincided with a spell of crystalline clarity which lasted well into every afternoon before the clouds finally gathered. The cloud forest, famously misty, mossy and dripping, looked odd: weirdly bleached and desiccated in the sun-drenched conditions, and my run to the peak and back in this weather led, inevitably, to dehydration.

I have been a mountain runner, rock climber and Alpine mountaineer for over 30 years, so any nearby peak is likely to call me strongly, particularly one that dominates the surrounding region in the way that this still-active volcano does. But the steep and rutted jeep track up Baru, 15 kilometres long, was mostly through dense cloud forest and so, even for me, interest began to wane. I happened to be in marathon training at the time, so it worked as an unconventional 'long run'. And, despite the rather boring track, I saw long-tailed silky flycatchers, tanagers, sooty thrushes and other wonderfully obscure and colourful birdlife:

then, towards the top, views opened out as the ancient caldera is breached. The unusual conditions I had enjoyed since arriving in Boquete now provided a spectacularly fortunate dividend. The summit is famed for its simultaneous views over the Pacific and Caribbean, an obvious function of a big peak's position in the centre of a narrow isthmus in the heart of Central America. Young backpackers were already making their way down the mountain, bleary eyed after spending the night with their guides, bivouacking at the summit in an attempt to ease the pain of the climb and give themselves a chance of clear dawn views over the two oceans. They need not have bothered, because it was still perfectly clear as I jogged across the caldera to the summit, feeling rather smug (I had spent the night in a comfortable hotel bed) but gasping in the thin air (the summit is just below 3,500 metres). Tendrils of mist had gathered over the nearby cloud forest, and cloud was bubbling up on the Caribbean side, but apart from that the views stretched across the border to Costa Rica and the oceans on both sides.

Central America was at my feet, or so it temporarily seemed: the pleasure I derived from the view was short-lived and tempered by unease. I know from decades of experience that there is always a compromise between weight and comfort when running in the mountains and my water was running out – time at the summit was therefore severely restricted, I knew my water would be insufficient for the long way down. The final descent, after 30 kilometres of running up and down the 3,500m peak, turned into a dry-mouthed nightmare, sandy footsteps, clouds of dust and not a drop of water to be found. At the bottom of the track, legs beginning to sway, vision beginning to blur, I remembered that there was some kind of very modest park ranger's house, the only possible source of water and the only building for miles. It was deserted, but I found a plastic tap at the back of the house. Turning it on, like a cliché from an old Western, led to a low gurgle, then a long pause, until a cloud of dust vomited out – not a hint of moisture, even though I was in the middle of the cloud forest, noted for its damp fecundity.

After reaching the roadhead, I looked around for taxis: nothing. The air was still, the midday heat intense and, as is usually the case in the tropics, the birdlife sensibly disappears by late morning, leaving an eerie silence which can be counter-intuitive for those expecting an abundance of life and biodiversity. I am no stranger to dehydration, but the situation was becoming a tad desperate and, despite my tiredness, I started to jog downhill in the general direction of Boquete, convinced I could smell water.

After a couple of miles, I jogged past a Ngabe couple and exchanged greetings. Then a ramshackle farmhouse appeared by the side of the road with – to my intense relief – some kind of standpipe spurting water into a drainage ditch by the side of the road. I filled my empty bottle with apparently clear water and was just about to drink when the male from the Ngabe couple I had just overtaken rushed forward to grab the bottle – again, rather like a movie scene – just before it reached my lips.

'*Aqua non potable*', he warned, '*es per los porcos*'. Glancing up, I saw those pigs lurking in the roadside bushes, and with that, my saviour from porcine swill took my bottle inside to a kind of courtyard, which seemed to be a communal farm for Ngabe people. The communal feel was heightened by the building: a sprawling single-storey structure, almost like a stable, whitewashed, built in a square around what I soon realised was less a courtyard, more a convenient and perfectly-designed space for adults to sit and chat, and children to play. The square was lined with washing. I thanked the couple for their help (they filled my bottle) and asked about the dry season in my rudimentary Spanish, the subtext being: surely this is unusual, it feels more like a desert than a cloud forest? It had indeed been unusually dry, they agreed, but – indicating the washing drying in the warm sunshine – said that was a good thing: 'normalmente muy humedo' (most of the time it is very wet).

We were, both of us, struggling to express ourselves: the language of choice in these communities is not Spanish, but Ngabere; and a peculiarly distinctive form of Ngabere at that. This relatively small area around the foothills of Volcan Baru, although dominated by the Ngabe away from Boquete and the big coffee plantations, is separated from the rest of the Ngabe-Bugle comarca. This is not untypical for minorities in Central America, and it seemed to me that the experience of living in atomised groups characterises the contemporary Ngabe experience with groups of speakers living across a large area of western Panama. The danger with this kind of fragmentation is that large numbers of already-marginalised people, carving out a fragile existence and speaking a threatened language find themselves in separate 'enclaves' divided by topographical or political barriers: the result, often, is that the weaker enclave finds itself cut off from the centre and gradually, imperceptibly, withers away and dies as the dominant group pushes in and its influence spreads.

The British Isles experienced the same phenomenon in the early Middle Ages, as Anglo-Saxon influence split the indigenous Brythonic Celts. The sheer cultural dominance of the 'incoming' group, combined with the scale of their confidence and ambition, then directly threatens an increasingly marginalised indigenous community. Indeed, I always think that the history of the British Isles can be encapsulated in a single (admittedly slightly reductive) linguistic fact: namely, that Welsh is German for 'foreign'. In modern German, for example, 'Welschriesling' means the non-native and inherently inferior version of the famous Riesling wine grape. In old German, 'Welschtirol' referred to Trentino, the region of the South Tirol in which Romance-speakers predominate (Trentino remains Italian-speaking in contrast to the German-speaking Südtirol/Alto Adige immediately north), and there are multiple other examples of this word being applied to all kinds of non-Germanic strangers across Europe.

Consider Brittonic, the ancient form of Welsh formerly spoken in present-day Cumbria and Strathclyde, 'yr hen ogledd' (the old north) of Welsh legend. Those alternative strains of Welsh culture were unable to maintain their precarious existence, separated from the lodestone of that culture and pushed further towards the margins by the advancing Anglo-Saxons (worse still, they were squeezed in a pincer movement, with Gaelic culture pushing down from the north). As well as Strathclyde, we might also make a comparison with Cornwall, although here the place name evidence remains a more vivid, obvious and accessible reminder of past times, of that older cultural reality.

In southern Scotland and Cumbria, you have to search further for that evidence: but not all that far. Cumbria itself has obvious resonance with 'Cymru', but my personal favourite is Ecclefechan in Dumfries, just a few miles from the English border, a well-known village on the main road to Glasgow, and weirdly 'Celtic' sounding at first acquaintance. You only need a rudimentary understanding of Scottish history to know that it cannot possibly be Gaelic, it is far too southerly for that. Its real origins become obvious to anybody with even a basic knowledge of Welsh after a few moments of thought and unpicking: Ecclefechan, 'Eglwys Fychan', smallest church. A little less obvious, although perhaps better known, is Glasgow's derivation from 'Glas Cau' and Lanark from 'Llanarth'. Indeed, the earliest recorded written Welsh scripts have been found in Strathclyde, another indication that it was once the centre of a vibrant Brythonic culture.

But unlike 'yr hen ogledd' or Cornwall, Ngabere, as a living and breathing tongue, does not seem in danger of splintering, or experiencing the withering of isolated exclaves (although there are lots of these; it is not just this distinctive community above Boquete that is separate from the rest of the comarca, existing in an isolated bubble, the map of the comarca looks like a Jackson Pollock painting; a series of separate blobs and dots).[44] The Ngabe might be hindered by topography and geography, but they are helped by the fact that they are, by far, the most numerous of Panama's numerous indigenous communities and by the fact that language remains a crucial part of their identity. Further, modern forms of media technology, even a growing use of social media, allows fragmented communities to connect with the centre, the rest of the core linguistic community. By contrast, the Brythonic 'Welsh' of Strathclyde and Cumbria might as well have been on the moon, so distant were they from mainstream Brythonic culture. It is hardly surprising that culture withered and died.

My initial encounter with the Ngabe was a little surprising because they are also known as being considerably more hostile to outsiders than other indigenous Panamanian peoples: for example, the Guna, who live on preposterously scenic islands dotted along the tourist-friendly white-sand coastline of the eastern Caribbean. The Guna also have a distinctive traditional costume that is both commonly worn and – like the beaches – perfectly calibrated to appeal to the modern 'adventure' tourism industry.

It would be unwise to push the point too far, as the Guna are also protective of their customs and wary of outsiders, uncomfortably aware of their lifestyle's appeal to the outside world as well as its relative accessibility, much closer to Panama City (and the Ngabe themselves are also intertwined with the dominant Hispanic culture and, sometimes, with the Panamanian tourism industry). In very general terms, however, the Ngabe have a less picturesque but more 'real' culture – protected to a great extent by topography, the awkward and impenetrable mountain terrain and cloud forest that characterises their home region of western Panama and makes roadbuilding, for example, a complex task.

Instead of the beads and nose-rings of the Guna, Ngabe women wear gown-like dresses which are colourful but not remotely traditional: rather, they are a consequence of intensive missionary work in the 1950s and 1960s. The dresses extend down to the ankle, although they generally expose the arms, and have that classic shapeless modesty-preserving look associated with missionary ideals.

All the women in the courtyard were wearing those dresses. I had seen a group of Canadian tourists taking photographs of Ngabe women in the centre of Boquete earlier in my stay, presumably thinking they were an entirely authentic expression of indigenous culture. In the courtyard, the garments were quite practical, easy to wash, cool but giving a degree of protection from the sun: they just happen to be colourful, which gives them an aura of authenticity, however inaccurate that might be. Most important of all, the different colours render the costumes distinctly 'Instagrammable', hence the Canadians' enthusiasm. The men are considerably less photogenic: they tend to walk round in Wellington boots, or a version of them, which looks odd at the height of the dry season. The man who had filled up my bottle also brought out a tray of dried plantain chips, another act of kindness no doubt provoked by my gaunt and slightly desperate appearance. It was pretty obvious that I had just been up Volcan Baru, as there was no other reason to be up here in this isolated spot above a single-track road leading nowhere, a giant cul-de-sac. The courtyard was pleasant and sunny and the unexpected encounter all the more welcome for being so relaxed and apparently natural: I ate the plantains and gradually rehydrated.

To indulge in a spot of misplaced Eurocentrism, an imaginative observer might discern a similarity between the Ngabe and the Welsh, and the Guna and the Irish.

The Ngabe, taciturn and reserved, pushed to the fringes of their mountain hideaways yet able to preserve their language (almost all the 250,000 Ngabe still speak the language, which is known as Ngabere or Guaymi). The Guna, more open and colourful, more immediately appealing to the outside world, yet somehow too obvious, too prepared to offer up a neatly packaged and easily digestible version of that culture.

Where does this lead? To a quick buck, to a kind of global fame, but also to a sense that something is lost in this process of marketing, the commercialisation of a culture for the sake of mass tourism. Again, in that sense, the brittle fragility of Ngabe culture parallels that of traditional Welsh speaking communities in the north and west: both are hard for outsiders to penetrate, less amenable to neatly packaged global tourism and marketing soundbites. The imaginative observer would be advised to be cautious at this point, of course, because this is deliberately reductive, framing four distinctive cultures in very simplistic terms. There is plenty that is genuine about Irish and Guna culture, and much that is packaged about Welsh and Ngabe culture: but sometimes such comparisons are just too neat not to indulge in, just a bit, and always with tongue sufficiently lodged in cheek.

***

Days in Boquete pass pleasantly, and it is not surprising that many visitors to highland Panama remain insulated from the linguistic and cultural diversity of this tiny country. That is not to criticise, because it's an entirely logical and delightful place to spend some time (indeed, many Americans never leave, and the hillsides directly above the town are dotted with homes that would not be out of place in Key West or Southern California). As is often the case with these kinds of informal enclaves settled by 'westerners', Boquete still hums with local life *outside* the main tourist-centric drag, and you are never far from the vibrant presence of the Ngabe.

In contrast, the capital of the country, Panama City, is a world apart: the Dubai of Central America (not a tourist-board slogan, but an obvious comparison that immediately occurred to me as, I suspect, it occurs to most first-time visitors) soaked in money from the canal (to name just the most transparent source of cash). It is a city that bridges two worlds: in a sense, it links North and South America, the two continents, more effectively than anywhere else in Central America, including the touristy parts of Mexico. Partly, this is because it feels so distinct and separate from the rest of the nation, almost like an independent free-wheeling city state. Capital cities rarely have much in common with the rest of the country that they dominate: London being a very obvious example. But Panama City takes this near-universal truism to a different level. Indeed, residents of this sprawling city dismiss the rest of the country as 'el interior': the implication being that it is hardly worth bothering with, inhabited by bumpkins ('interioranos') closer to Hondurans and Salvadoreans in income, culture and lifestyle when compared with the capital's urban sophisticates.

After my time in the Highlands, I flew in to Panama City on a tiny internal aircraft, still sipping beer in a glass full of ice-cubes as we landed at the tiny 'Albrook' airport just over the Panama Canal, finding the city an ear-splitting and frenetic contrast to the tranquillity of the cloud forests and volcanoes further west. An eight-lane highway curves around the edge of this airport, encircling a shopping mall and giant bus station as it sweeps round the urban mountain of Cerro Ancon. Up there, three-toed sloths and keel-billed toucans live in close proximity to the city centre, but down here the noise is constant and intense: the usual clamour of a developing country combined with the extreme wealth apparent in certain aspects of some Panamanians' lives.

The scale of the capital, and that sense of extreme contrast, does not do much to mitigate the runaway egos of some of the locals, either: it is not too controversial to observe that the residents have a slightly inflated sense of their own importance. It seemed to me that the non-too-subtle dismissal of el interior carried with it colonial, or semi-colonial, baggage: it seems to encapsulate the notion that Hispanic culture retains full dominance over the indigenous communities, and there is an inescapable, if not always overt, racial element to this characterisation too. The interioranos are mainly mestizo people (with mixed European and indigenous heritage), often speaking indigenous languages, of which the Ngabe are merely the most numerous.[45]

This lofty dismissal of indigenous culture also finds echoes globally, not least in the Celtic world: consider the Scottish 'teuchter' and its undercurrent of distaste for Highland culture, a word once familiar in the urban Central Belt and only recently airbrushed out of polite conversation. The Irish equivalent, culchie, is perhaps even better known. All carry with them an implicit disdain for diversity and the rural, Gaelic-speaking margins of their countries. 'Hick', in the English sense of a backward rural resident, does not really carry the same cultural baggage, perhaps because the linguistic dimension to the insult is missing. Neither, interestingly, does 'Gog', the only comparable Welsh term. Gog (northerner – from 'gogledd' – but also, by extension, often implying a Welsh speaker from Gwynedd or Anglesey) does not have the same implications, and the fact that there is no Welsh equivalent for 'teuchter', 'culchie' or 'interiorano' could be taken as a significant indication of the centrality of – and respect for – language, to the broader sense of Welsh identity.

The Panamanian version of this common phenomenon is thrown into sharper focus by the fact that the government has been rather liberal in its treatment of its indigenous minorities in recent years, certainly by Central American standards.[46] The comarcas, and the associated protection of indigenous languages, marks the country out as something of a flagship in the region and is beginning to be copied, rather like the Welsh approach to language preservation was widely replicated across Europe after the successes of the 1960s. As always, the key is that the initial building blocks underpinning any concept of preservation must be tangible, grounded in ordinary lives. An obvious comparison would be the way that the Mudiad Meithrin movement, which focused on the provision of Welsh-medium nursery education inspired the Breton *Diwan* concept in the 1970s.[47]

The comarcas, at the moment, are more to do with protecting indigenous land rights and political autonomy than language preservation, because the concerns of the Ngabe remain more fundamental in nature. But language underpins Ngabe identity, echoing nationalist 'badge of nationhood' claims in other international contexts, and voices are now raised against the tendency (not uncommon in Hispanic society, or indeed any linguistically dominant group) to refer to indigenous Central American languages as 'dialectos', presumably in a deliberate attempt to devalue and marginalise them. Resistance to these tactics continues to increase, which is not surprising given the importance of preservation in this context.

It is almost a cliché to say that all languages express the identity of the people who speak them, which is why the Ngabe, for example, increasingly resist any attempts at marginalisation. For those who find themselves to be 'a small part of a large community', as David Crystal puts it, the role of language is especially important. All speakers of minority tongues, he says, want to see their language treated with respect by the dominant culture, they want opportunities to use their language in public and see it valued.[48]

Several estimates now put the number of Ngabere speakers close to 200,000. By global standards, not especially small, but – as is often the case with 'tribal' languages, even those that are widely spoken – it has historically been entirely oral. There is no canon of literature to draw upon. Unlike Welsh, the heritage of the language, its literary past, cannot be mobilised or even referenced for political reasons, because it does not really exist. This tends to limit the wider potential of the language to act as a means of unifying a people (unlike Welsh, Basque or Breton, where it is central). An associated 'problem' with preserving oral cultures is an obvious one: that it has often been difficult for linguists, ethnographers and anthropologists to study them, and Ngabere is an archetypal example.

All these factors are frequently cited as reasons for the fact that language extinction on an enormous scale has now been occurring for decades (centuries, actually) and has sped up dramatically over the last 100 years. But there are also grounds for optimism. If we consider the classic cycle through which languages are lost: where a period of dominance (by an incoming 'colonial' language which becomes a powerful force in a region) is followed by bilingualism (where people become proficient in both 'native' and 'colonial' languages) through to monolinguilism (where younger generations are proficient only in the 'colonial' form), then European exemplars like Welsh provide a kind of model to escape that cycle, where the crucial second bilingual stage is negotiated in such a way that the indigenous tongue survives and is celebrated. The slide towards the monolingual final stage, in which the indigenous minority tongue is a source of shame for younger generations, is halted.

This all requires funding and intervention, of course, and is not necessarily practical for languages like Ngabere. But there are further grounds for optimism if we accept that the power of such languages lies in their ability to frame a specific landscape, to provide a distinctive and irreplaceable framework for the understanding of a particular environment. Robert Macfarlane points this out in the context of the Scottish Hebrides, observing that well into the twentieth century most inhabitants of the Western Isles 'did not use conventional maps but relied on memory maps, learnt on the land and carried in the skull.[49] These were facilitated by experience and crucially, language, the specific features of Hebridean Gaelic that allowed them to distinguish between subtly delineated features of the landscape and weather: they were a specific response to the environment, which simply cannot be captured by English.

Specific linguistic heritage of this kind is replicated thousands of times globally. The Ngabe have hundreds of names for the abundant plant and animal life of their particular segment of Central America – which cannot easily be replicated or even rendered in Spanish. The Welsh notion of the 'milltir sgwar' (square mile) encapsulates the relationship between human being and micro-environment; as do dozens of words for the natural world that either have no real English equivalent, or that have a workaday and prosaic English version that fails to match the precisely observed character of the Welsh. Examples are abundant, but consider the bird name 'crec yr eithin'. Unlike the English translation 'whinchat', the onomatopoeic 'crec' perfectly captures the characteristic call of this species, with 'eithin' (gorse) its favoured habitat. It is a bird of open country, perching on elevated bushes, typical of the Welsh landscape.

With the concept of the milltir sgwar, and the Ngabe's rich lexicon, language defines the human relationship to place and it is this additional factor that potentially holds the key to salvation for languages like Ngabere. Macfarlane quotes the ethno-linguist K. David Harrison, who suggests that language death means the loss of 'long cultivated knowledge that has guided human-environment interaction for millennia ... accumulated wisdom and observations of generations of people about the natural world, plants, animals, weather, soil. The loss (is) incalculable, the knowledge mostly unrecoverable.' It is, however, this awareness of loss that provides additional grounds for optimism. It is not just that new forms of media are being mobilised to encompass distinctive forms of minority language, as my man in Struga demonstrated, but it could also be argued that another counter-intuitive feature of a truly globalised media is that it tends to shed new light on the value of diversity. We are, in short, made *aware* of what we stand to lose.

As it happens, I was on something of a side quest for a highly specific and localised feature of the Western Panamanian biosphere whilst I was staying in the heartland of the Ngabe. I have always had an interest in birds, and since I was a small boy I have wanted to see the resplendent quetzal, one of the world's most distinctive and beautiful species. I have a vivid childhood memory of seeing it on a Guatemalan stamp, aged perhaps five or six, and thinking: one day I will see it for real. The bird is native to the cloud forests in this part of Panama, and it was February, breeding season, the perfect time to see this normally reclusive species displaying. One morning in particular seemed ideal: I got up early, took a bus to the end of a trail that was noted for its quetzal sightings, and set off through the cloud forest in the half light of dawn. Everything was set up perfectly: how could I fail? I waited, and waited. I walked, and walked, always with a view to the suitability of the habitats – I had read endless tips and hints about quetzal-spotting tactics. But as the sun rose, and the heat of the day with it, without so much as a glimpse of an emerald tail feather, I started to lose hope. The immediate environment was beautiful: a stony track above a tiny Ngabe settlement with drystone walls, rushing streams and native flowers. Above, tendrils of mist rising from the cloud forest. But there was no sign of the quetzal. I gave up, driven down by hunger, and was walking along the track when a huge dark bird landed, completely silently, in a bush just a few metres in front of me. It was not the quetzal; that would have been too neat. It was a black guan. A frugivorous and silent bird, almost as large as a turkey, with black feathers and a luminously contrasting blue face, it moves through the forest canopy eating berries while remaining utterly silent; and it only lives in a specific band of high-altitude forest on the fringes of Panama and Costa Rica.

It seemed a weirdly appropriate metaphor. The gaudy quetzal had failed to show, but in its place came something more subtle and interesting. The black guan was less obviously attractive, far less likely to feature on a stamp, but a perfect expression of place, of a bizarre adaptation to landscape. It is also, perhaps unsurprisingly, a species threatened by habitat loss. Because it is restricted to this very specific cloud forest environment, a tiny and diminishing range, any degradation of that environment, any tree felling, immediately threatens it. Its sheer size, and its impractical and highly particularised requirements resonated immediately with my thoughts on Ngabere and similar indigenous Central American languages. It may not be adaptable, it may not be widespread, it may be limited to a fruit-rich high-altitude habitat, but it is irreplaceable.

I was struck by something I was told as I sat on the rickety bus which leads from Boquete down to the stifling heat and dust of David, a veritable metropolis by comparison to the nearby highlands and cloud forests. I got talking to a 'Hispanic' Panamanian, sitting next to me, who was on his way back to his home in David having spent a month working in a Boquete bar. Although he liked the Ngabe he had met and felt that they were often unfairly demonised by certain elements in Panamanian society, he was not quite so liberal about the language. Ngabere, he said, is impossible to learn because 'all the words sound the same'. My Spanish was not good enough for me to tease out what he meant by this, but on returning home I did some reading and found that it does indeed have an unusually high number of 'polysemic' words, those that carry multiple meanings depending on context. Among the many eye-wateringly confusing examples, one in particular appealed to me. The single word 'tare' can mean 'pain', 'difficulty', or 'love': if there is a word, globally, more loaded with potentially disastrous misinterpretations then I have yet to find it.

CHAPTER 4
INVISIBLE LINES IN THE BALKANS:
GOGS AND GHEGS, HWNTWS AND TOSKS

It was turning into one of my more embarrassing navigation failures. Getting lost is one thing, but being unable to find an international border seemed to plumb new depths of incompetence. The worst part was that I had gone to the trouble of retracing my steps to the Macedonian monastery of Sveti Naum specifically in order to cross the Albanian border on foot. It struck me as a good and rather romantic idea at the time, as I had been told that a footpath led along the banks of Lake Ohrid: a spectacular turquoise even under the leaden skies of early April. Crashing through the undergrowth after walking past the ancient monastery buildings, it quickly became obvious that the footpath was either entirely fictitious or hopelessly overgrown.

Instead, twisted and unusually dense woodland, moist ferns and fronds, blocked my onward route along the lakeside and took most of the already-dim light away: the idea of walking to the border seemed unwise at best, impossible at worst. Inland, the only feasible escape route led to an abandoned caravan site, so strange and out-of-place that I felt obliged to investigate.

This apparently illicit act saw me – by now, utterly disorientated – stray close to the unmarked border well before the official crossing point. An urgent shout tipped me off. Then a Macedonian soldier, lurking unseen in a small shelter, emerged to reprimand me: he was as taut and slender as the sentry box he was hidden in, dressed in combat fatigues, visibly armed, and surprisingly angry given the tranquillity of his posting.

I was marooned in the middle of the site, not sure which way to go as the guard came towards me, an angry facial tic rippling under his left ear. I had transgressed: that was obvious, although quite how was not entirely clear to me. Hundreds of orange and white caravans stretched away on all sides, their vivid kitsch instantly reminding me of my 1970s childhood and holidays on the Ceredigion coast in Cei Bach. There was even a hint of brown amidst the peeling interior décor – a dead giveaway in terms of the era, almost as accurate as carbon dating. I thought: 1973, maybe 1974.

The caravan site was truly incongruous, weirdly located in a dark hollow, and unusual because of its astonishing scale and the precise uniformity of its dereliction, as if every van had been evacuated on exactly the same day, reminiscent of the infamous Pripyat – the Soviet town in Ukraine left in a permanent time warp after Chernobyl's meltdown. It had that same disconcerting sense of abandonment frozen in time, and its disturbing atmosphere was heightened by its sunken location, set back from the main lake, hidden from view, hemmed in by thick woodland.

All the caravans were still intact, but moss grew across the exteriors and vegetation had devoured the small plots around them. The site exuded that distinctive ambience of 1960s and 1970s Yugo-socialism: it wasn't just the garish colours and the adventurous approach to architecture, but it seemed to my untrained eye to go further, to relate to something fundamentally ideological about the planning of public space. The caravans were arranged in concentric circles, around a collapsing playground and a black, rubble-filled hole – perhaps a former swimming pool. As with Pripyat, there is something particularly spooky about an empty, silent facsimile of something that once embodied a deliberately communitarian idealism.

This was, presumably, once a Yugoslav holiday resort: Marshall Tito famously encouraged domestic and foreign tourists to most corners of his varied and beautiful supranational country from the 1950s onwards, keen to generate income after breaking ties with the Soviets. But this just seemed too obscure even for

Tito's ambitious tourism policy, it was surely too close to what has often been a contentious and problematic border for that to be entirely feasible. In fact, right up to the 1920s Sveti Naum – a remarkable 1,000-year-old monastery founded by ascetic Bulgarians – was on the Albanian side of the border. And in the more recent past – particularly the 1970s and 1980s – Albania was famously isolationist, with Macedonia,[viii] very briefly, the only country to offer a highly constrained short break from that isolation. Even today, as my ludicrous perambulations were proving, it is not the simplest border crossing to make, and no buses (and very few cars) travel between the two countries down this obscure road.

The guard and I had few words in common, but his body language and demeanour was more than sufficient. He stopped short of confronting me directly, and his weapon remained safely stowed: that was good, but the air of hostility was not so good. The caravan site, as well as the border, was clearly out of bounds, to him as well as me (I was later told, by an Ohrid taxi driver, that its sensitive location was indeed the reason for its abandonment: this border represented an ideological chasm in the 1970s, at the height of Albania's self-imposed isolation and Yugoslavia's liberal version of socialism).

He stood at the edge of the outermost circle and indicated very firmly that I should head back in what I now knew to be the Macedonian direction; so I reluctantly left the site and walked through the birch trees, following the noise from intermittent cars, trying to find the road to the official border crossing. A tiny path led through the woods, indistinct enough to make me reluctant, like something out of a Grimms' fairy tale, leading down a dark scrubby tunnel into moss-covered birches. It was the first week in April, and the trees in this cold spot, miles

viii Formally renamed Republic of North Macedonia in 2019, after a long dispute with Greece over the name 'Macedonia' (which is also an administrative and geographic region of northern Greece).

from the open sea, were completely bare and particularly uninviting. After a long walk through the woods, feeling like a fugitive, I vaulted a crash barrier and finally emerged, with some relief, at a narrow and entirely deserted final stretch of Macedonian road. On a hunch, I turned right – although I had no compass and no real way of knowing whether I was moving towards the border or back into Macedonia.

Either by innate wisdom or pure fluke, I got it right, and finally crossed the border in glorious solitude under threateningly dark skies. After crossing the Macedonian side, a mile-long walk through no-man's land brought me to the entrance to Albania which was marked by a characteristic caved-in military bunker, and a lone taxi tout smoking a roll-up in front of an equally characteristic beaten-up Mercedes (old Mercedes and concrete bunkers being two integral elements of the Albanian *genius loci*). To my surprise, I found myself agreeing to his offer of a five-euro taxi ride into the nearby town of Pogradec. This was clearly extortionate, but I was the ultimate captive audience marooned at a very quiet border post. The journey went past a few more bunkers (one of which had been painted to look like a ladybird in a doomed attempt at levity), then skirted the small lakeside town of Tushemist, before continuing at breakneck speed through the centre of Pogradec to drop me outside the amusingly named Guesthouse Bimbli on the lakeside road.

The driver, Bujar, spoke a bit of English and told me almost immediately, apropos of nothing, that he was 'not a taxi driver' but a vinologist from Tirana. In the blasted agricultural wilderness of this part of Albania, it seemed akin to declaring himself an astronaut. But over the next few days I got to know him quite well, and it was true. He had graduated with a degree in vinology from a university in the capital, had an in-depth knowledge of the subject and its economic potential in the region, but was reduced to touting at the border and working in a friend's hotel to make ends meet. He detested Pogradec, but found its status as tourist town gave him more opportunities than the capital. Looking around at the desolate lakefront and deserted hotels, I found this impossible to believe. How many tourists came to Pogradec? 'Thousands – from all over the world,' he claimed, suddenly rather defensive after dismissing the town as 'boring' as we entered the outer suburbs just minutes ago.

It was intriguing. The town certainly had the hotel capacity to cope, but it was just a week before Easter and after walking around for several days I strongly suspected I was the only foreigner in town, save for two or three American Mormon missionaries. So I pressed him: where do they come from? Russia? Albania? 'Yes, yes. Russians, Greeks, Dutch, English, everywhere – and lots from Tirana, like me. Drinking, having fun, music.' The sorriest waterpark I had ever seen graced the lakeside in Pogradec, apparently the jewel in its tourism crown, next to an abandoned building site with piles of cement and upturned wheelbarrows. The 'waterpark' was a black slide with a single twist and rusted iron steps: revellers were presumably discharged, from a great height, directly into the lake. Perhaps it was just the unseasonal cold (and occasional sleet showers) of early April that made it look so unappealing, but I struggled to imagine travelling Dutch holidaymakers squealing with delight as they plunged in.

After dropping me off, Bujar joined me in the vast hotel reception for coffee. He was, he said without me asking, proud to be a Gheg, with family from the north of Albania, and did not have much time for the Tosks of the south. This is the great fault-line in Albanian culture, and one I had encountered before when travelling among Bujar's fellow Ghegs in northern Macedonia and Kosovo in 2014.

There would be time to muse on the Gheg/Tosk divide later, but in the meantime Bujar knew the owners of the Bimbli and led me in to what proved to be a rather extraordinary hotel. As far as I could tell, it was completely empty and remained so throughout my stay, but it employed numerous staff and was, presumably as a result, absolutely immaculate throughout its six floors. I was shown to my room, bizarrely located on the most isolated wing of the uppermost floor, by an extravagantly moustachioed assistant. My quarters were palatial, above five empty floors, with two balconies: one overlooking the whole of Lake Ohrid (which is stunningly beautiful from every angle) the other overlooking a wasteland inhabited by some Roma gypsies, their ageing donkeys, and a row of makeshift tarpaulin tents. I could instantly move, if the desire took me, between abject squalor and scenic splendour just by walking through the room. Above the town, the land climbed immediately to high forested ridges and bare mountains.

Pogradec is a bustling place, quite sizeable, with lots of cafés and small shops. It is all fairly down-at-heel, as might be expected in provincial Albania, and a considerable contrast with the relative glitz and glamour of Macedonia's Ohrid, visible very distantly across the huge lake. This is not necessarily a negative, however, and the Roman alphabet, simple after Macedonia's Cyrillic, aided navigation. Even better, I changed a few 10-dollar bills that I had left over from previous trips and became instantly liquid in this very cheap destination – my first time in Albania 'proper'.

***

I have been travelling in the Balkans for 25 years. This, the start of my sixth trip to the region, had started rather like all the others: the cultural and linguistic diversity of this corner of Europe renders it full of life and interest. It may not be the easiest place to navigate, but it is hugely rewarding: the diversity and variety of the landscape easily matched by the diversity and variety of the people who live here.

I was particularly keen to explore this region of southern Albania, having travelled in Albanian-dominated regions of

Macedonia on previous visits, as well as Kosovo, both areas dominated by the Ghegs. The reason I was so keen to cross the border to Pogradec and the south was because such a journey would take me into the domain of the Tosks for the first time.

An invisible linguistic and cultural divide splits the Albanian people: and this divide, between Gheg and Tosk, also transcends the border to take in Albanian-dominated regions of Macedonia and Kosovo. From a Welsh perspective, the divide, and even the names, have echoes of 'Gog' and 'Hwntw', the semantic divide between north and south Wales. And the invisible boundary itself finds echoes in Pembrokeshire's 'Landsker Line', the cultural divide between its Welsh-speaking north and the 'little England beyond Wales' to the south. But any similarities are rather eclipsed by Albania's more serious cultural fault-lines, which have had wider implications over centuries.

Most of the Albanian regions of Macedonia, through which I had recently passed, along with the brutal mountainous landscape of the north, and neighbouring Kosovo, speak versions of Gheg (versions being the operative word, as they are not always mutually intelligible having developed and evolved in isolated valleys over centuries). The divide between Gheg and Tosk is multi-faceted and complex, hard to generalise about and hard for outsiders to grasp. Gheg, for example, was at one time the language of the elite, of the literary classes, but it also encompasses the wildest, most isolated regions of northern Albania, characterised by a taste for blood feuds and tight-knit family clans.

South of the Shkumbi river, the Tosks are essentially the Albanians of the plains, and the Communist regime made Tosk into the language of the upper echelons, the literary form of Albanian in which business was to be done. This, unsurprisingly, caused resentment which lingers and which has often provoked problematic communal divisions in Albanian politics: rendering the country, at certain times in the recent past, closer to parts of sub-Saharan Africa than Europe in terms of governance. Bujar's views were the mildest manifestation of this divide, hardly surprising as a Gheg working in the heartland of the Tosks. Diplomacy, in such circumstances, is paramount.

Overlaid on top of this split is the much broader concept of Albanian irredentism, or a Greater Albania, bringing together all the regions in which the language is spoken, a potentially explosive Balkan ideology which transcends almost all the otherwise awkward realities of physical geography and culture. In essence, one of the few things that unites the otherwise divided Albanian people is their hatred of the Serbs and their occasional calls for a Greater Albania. Albanian irredentism has, from time to time, come to international prominence: one example being the drone carrying a flag calling for such an entity to be established, which was flown into the Serbia versus Albania European Championship qualifier in 2014. This caused an immediate riot involving players, supporters and officials, and the game was abandoned. This fixture represented the ultimate sporting security nightmare; Cardiff versus Millwall is like a crown green bowls match by comparison. The match was obviously problematic and ripe for a deliberately provocative act: which was precisely what happened. It also illustrated to the outside world that the tensions in the former Yugoslavia may have eased, but they have not disappeared, and that the Serb–Albanian culture clash is as potent as ever.

Bujar's take on this was instructive: 'Our politicians play games.' The implication being: this is all a useful distraction from the real problems that face us. My take on it was that, as so often in the Balkans, a geopolitically specific version of populism still dominates the public sphere. 'You could say that we are told to hate the Serbs ... but you could also say that they're *taught* to hate us.' The Balkans hardly have a monopoly on xenophobic populism, of course – as recent events further West prove – but there is a specific and unusually damaging version of the phenomenon that has characterised politics in the region since Slobodan Milosevic let the genie out of the bottle following a Serb demonstration against Albanian harassment in 1987 (plenty of footage exists online of this incident in Kosovo Polje, the exact moment that he chose to mobilise identity politics, albeit indirectly, with his 'no one has the right to beat you' speech: the rest is history). After this brief conversation with Bujar, indeed, I heard the word 'Kosovo' from his companions, and a conference ensued: this topic, an open wound, is inescapable in any discussion about Serb–Albanian relations, and it is rarely a good idea for foreigners to join in.

Aside from this (admittedly very powerful) unifying factor, the Albanian people are hopelessly divided by topography, by the complex geographical realities of the Balkans, so it is hardly surprising that diverse dialects evolve and flourish in this region. Tosk and Gheg is just the start of it: with both forms of the Albanian language then splintering off into literally dozens of distinctive sub-forms, all spoken in intricately sequestered corners of the country.

***

On an earlier journey through Albanian lands, in September 2014, I had met a remarkable man called Lum Citakyu, very obviously destined for bigger things, on a bus journey from Pristina, the capital of Kosovo, to Skopje, the capital of Macedonia. It is not a long journey, but it is a fascinating one, and by the end of it Citakyu, no more than 25 years old at the time, had convinced me that I had just met a future politician, perhaps even a future president of his tiny country. It did not quite work out like that, or perhaps I should say that it has not yet. But his charismatic and deeply thoughtful take on the realities of life in this border zone, where the boundary between Kosovo and Macedonia has phantom qualities – in the sense that it isn't much of a 'border' at all – stayed with me. The liminal nature of the land through which we were travelling, which could variously be considered Serbian, Kosovan, Gheg, Northern Gheg, Eastern (Northern) Gheg, or generic Albanian, depending on who you are talking to, lends itself to reflections on the nature of nation and identity. For Citakyu, and all those on the bus, the land on both sides of the border is unambiguously Albanian: but he put me in touch with linguists who see things slightly, subtly, differently.

The Albanian population who make up a slender majority in the northern edge of Macedonia, along with almost all of Kosovo, is Gheg. That much is straightforward. Beyond that, however, things start to get complicated. The border marks a significant boundary between the northern Gheg subdialect and its southern equivalent. Not only that, but on the northern (Kosovo) side, there is a major east–west split within this subdialect (making it, I suppose, a sub-subdialect). South of the Macedonian border, and we are into the domain of the southern Gheg subdialect – and, to be more specific, the central variant of this.

For linguist Robert Elsie, these varied Gheg dialects are 'usually intelligible *for those with an ear for language*'.[50] The implication being that those who do not have such an ear might struggle, even if they are fluent speakers of one of the other forms of Albanian. This, certainly, is the message I absorbed from Lum Citakyu. On the one hand, he has an idealistic vision for his country (he is a Kosovar Albanian). On the other, it was clear that a degree of misunderstanding arises whenever Albanians, especially older ones, from different sides of the linguistic divide (or national frontier) get together. On the short journey to Skopje, a group of young men got on at one village just over the Macedonian border. Then, minutes later, two old women got on – evidently just beyond the invisible border between the two Gheg dialects. Although I could follow none of the ensuing conversation, the tone, the facial expressions, and the basic delight taken in the wordplay and relationship between generations and linguistic groups was obvious. There was a lot of banter: one of the old women was clearly a 'local character' and had groups of young men almost weeping with genuine unforced laughter as she regaled them with deadpan anecdotes. I had never seen anything quite like it in terms of the relationship between generations. Part of it was based, I assumed, on the subtlety of linguistic variations and the fun they were deriving from that on what was a 'cross border' bus, despite its exclusively Albanian (indeed, exclusively Gheg) passengers. But it was the deep respect, simultaneously formal and informal, between the generations that was so distinctive and attractive. Citakyu told me he had been exiled to Skopje as a small boy during the early days of the 1990s conflict, sent to stay with elderly relatives, just like this woman, while Kosovo tore itself apart just a few miles away and his parents stayed in Pristina.

My presence, as an unusual foreigner on the bus, was, I think, part of the reason for the interaction and the general buoyancy of the conversation. Like a rare bird, fleetingly sighted, I proved to be a talking point, and a provocation for reflections about the war and the variety inherent in Albanian life and language. The latter is a subject that will always inspire cyclical discussion without meaningful conclusion. Are we talking about dialects, or languages? Where should the line be drawn? Robert Elsie suggests that there has never been any full agreement on the classification of Albanian dialects, or much agreement about their precise definition, or even that bigger question: the extent to which they conform to recognised definitions of 'dialect' or 'language'. Tellingly, he admits that 'the definitive word on the subject has yet to be written'.[51]

When we arrived in Skopje, that day in 2014, I felt that I had seen an insight into a universal ideal model through which generations and dialect groups might relate to each other: the combination of respect (but not too much) and warmth (but not too much), among non-relatives, away from the family setting, all underpinned by gentle humour, was new to me. Pulling up in the centre of Skopje, with its monumental new statues – symbolic of the government's aggressive form of Macedonian nationalism which some suggest is deliberately antagonistic to the Albanian minority – removed any residual idealism, however. And I concluded, after spending so much time with the Ghegs trying to engage with the complexity of their world, which transcends so many international borders, that time spent with the Tosks of the South would provide some necessary 'balance' and a different perspective on the realities of contemporary Albania.

***

Entering the Tosk zone here in Pogradec brings a further surprise for students of cultural diversity: the lakeside town is also an Orthodox stronghold, far removed from the Islamic culture of most of Albania (although also containing an intriguing Bektashi community of Sufi Muslims, detested and considered blasphemous by many Sunni Muslims). As a partial result of this Orthodox tradition, and the cultural links with neighbouring countries it implies, the residents of Pogradec were among the first in Albania to be granted temporary release from the extreme isolation of the Hoxha years when they, and only they, were granted 32 hours in Macedonia in April 1992 after the new (post-Communist) Berisha regime introduced immigration quotas into EC countries.

Macedonia was the only country to extend an invitation, and even then in the most limited way imaginable, with Pogradec's small Muslim population also invited as long as they could prove they lived in the town. In the words of Miranda Vickers, the day-trippers were the first Albanians to leave the country legally since 1948 and 'returned to tell awestruck relatives and friends of the amazing consumer goods they had seen'.[52]

The next day dawned wet and gloomy, the town took on a depressing air accentuated by the Hoxha-era architecture, and even a quarter of a century on it wasn't hard to envisage how stunning the contrast must have been for those Pogradec residents allowed across the border in 1992. I went downstairs through the empty hotel building, curious as to whether breakfast was a possibility. It was, though as the only guest in a cavernous and empty dining room I was required to randomly stipulate my requirements as I was attended to by yet another member of staff, this time an elderly man in an immaculate suit. He seemed to be acting as waiter and spoke some German, presumably the reason he was sent out to deal with me, but in common with the rest of the staff (apart from Bujar, who seemed to have a nebulous role as itinerant 'fixer') spoke no English at all. 'Omelette?' I ventured, as tentatively as possible in these rather awkward circumstances. He grunted with an almost imperceptible nod of the head and left the room. Soon, an excellent ham and cheese omelette arrived with some more excellent Albanian bread and a very good cappuccino (the much vaunted, but often undetectable Italian influence on Albanian culture).

Fortified, I headed out into the murk and attempted to negotiate the Albanian public transport system. This is, let's say, not typically European and is much more akin to travelling in the developing world. Informal 'furgons' (minibuses) all serve specific destinations and all leave in seemingly haphazard fashion. Actually, however, the system – which appears chaotic and impenetrable initially – is logical and very efficient, and I was immediately ushered into a Korce furgon after identifying the correct street. All furgons have specific destinations and all will leave from a specific street, even if this is not formally identified (it is never formally identified). Five minutes later we were hurtling through the potholed streets of outer Pogradec, south towards Korce.

If the Albanian landscape is known for anything in the outside world, it is for the hundreds of thousands of defensive bunkers which litter the landscape, all of them built during Enver Hoxha's Communist dictatorship. They are not quite as insanely paranoid as popular myth suggests: and were actually a response to the Soviet invasion of Czechoslovakia in 1968, after which Albania withdrew from the Warsaw Pact. They can, in other words, be interpreted as a fairly logical response to the extreme isolation Albania found itself in at the time (its lone ally, China, was not really in a position to help for obvious geographical reasons).

By the late 1970s, Albania dropped the Chinese link and was reduced to a degree of self-imposed ideological and political isolation for which there is hardly any modern parallel, globally, let alone within the boundaries of the European continent. Present-day North Korea is perhaps the best comparison, but even Kim Jong-un's regime has allies of a sort. Some of the select band of adventurous travellers able to penetrate its borders at this time have since cited the country's total seclusion during this era, forgotten behind its formidable, lonely mountains.

Those mountains are far less formidable in this southern land of the Tosks, compared to the savage wilderness of the northern frontiers. Nevertheless, a long and twisting road climbs over the hills that surround Pogradec. The road was terrible initially, potholed and very rough. On the way back, I noticed that it was scheduled to be resurfaced by the Saudis, who are gradually extending their influence across Muslim-dominated parts of the Balkans: in a 2013 trip round Bosnia-Herzegovina I was struck by the brand new mosques dotting the landscape between Mostar and Sarajevo, a once-mixed region that is now almost entirely Muslim since the appalling 'ethnic cleansing' of the 1990s conflict (the mirror image of parts of the Bosnian Serb 'entity', in which the same disturbing processes occurred in reverse).

The Saudi influence, such as it is, must be seen as historically anomalous. Indeed, I fell into conversation with a fellow furgon passenger who saw me take a picture of the Saudi funding sign. I was embarrassed that he had noticed, and annoyed that my customary incognito travelling style had warped into that of 'obvious foreigner'. He instantly understood why I, as a visitor, had found the Saudi funding sign of interest, and immediately cited the Bektashi influence on Albania, using it as a way of dismissing any idea of political Islam that may have been germinating in my mind. 'The reason we Albanians are Islamic is because the Bektashis made us so', he said in near-fluent English. And it is true that the headquarters of the modern Bektashi community are in Tirana, not Turkey. My travelling companion was keen to make this point: 'I'm not a Sunni, *we're* not Sunnis.' Although he was speaking for himself, his distaste for Saudi influence was clear, and I was later told that around a quarter of Albanian Muslims identify themselves as at least partially Bektashi, their famed self-deprecating tolerance and vague spirituality rendering them distasteful (to say the least) in the eyes of the Saudis and other Sunnis. The Bektashi community, perhaps unsurprisingly, also found itself targeted by the polar opposite form of reactionary regime, that of Enver Hoxha's Communism: religious practice of all kinds, let alone the wilder reaches of Sufi Islam, were completely banned by the late 1960s, babas and dervishes summarily executed.[53] He fell silent for a while, before launching into a lengthy, and often lurid, summary of Pogradec's nightlife. I presumed this was another attempt to distance the town, and Albanian identity in general, from any notion that may have been germinating in my mind about creeping Islamism.

After cresting a mountain pass, a very fast straight road allowed the driver of the furgon to go fully insane, plummeting towards the next valley with the speedometer maxed out. A densely populated region with lots of little villages, new mosques, dilapidated farmhouses and the distant Morava mountains emerging from the mist. And always those bunkers: usually compact and family sized, but sometimes jumbo versions, looking like landed flying saucers and seemingly capable of accommodating entire villages. All are made of the same dense and indestructible grey concrete: indeed, the designer was supposedly torpedoed inside one to prove they worked, although it is a good idea to be a tad sceptical of such stories, which tend to be associated with Communist 'excess'.

Soon, we entered the suburbs of Korce, if such a descriptor can be applied to a shattered wilderness of abandoned factories and goat farms. We pulled up among hundreds of other minibuses in another Albanian 'bus stop' – no timetable, no signs, but a functional logic making it all work. Although it poured with rain for the rest of the day, Korce is a surprisingly attractive town with a restored Ottoman quarter characterised by cobbled streets and small craft shops, and side streets leading up to the large and historic mosque: the oldest in Albania, dating back to the fifteenth century. It survived the Hoxha regime, as did some of the other most important architectural sites in Albania, again contrary to popular belief.

Korce is a fascinating place, which enjoyed a stint as a fully-fledged independent republic between 1916 and 1920. Robert Carver argues that 'in the strange jigsaw of modern Balkan politics perhaps nothing is more bizarre than the short-lived French Republic of Korce'. In the midst of World War I, the city came under French control. An Autonomous Albanian Republic was established by the French rulers, who introduced French and re-introduced Albanian as the joint official languages. A new flag was flown, with the double-headed Albanian eagle flanked by the Tricolour, and an independent gendarmerie launched, with a mysterious 'roving' role. French schools, one of which was attended by a young Enver Hoxha, were set up, an attempt to introduce some kind of stability and permanence after years of upheaval in the town.[54]

The French Republic was, at least in part, a response to the linguistic and cultural complexities of this part of southern Albania, a region traditionally known as 'Northern Epirus', and populated not just by Albanians, but by a blend of peoples: Aromanians[ix] and Greeks in particular. So, Korce is not only distinguished by its Tosk character, and the divisions between north and south Albania that implies, but also by its historically multi-ethnic and diverse character – with a complex mosaic of languages in and around the town. It is a super-diverse mixture of peoples, each subdivided by varied cultural loyalties, languages and religions, not unlike Sarajevo before the Bosnian conflict. It is also the home of a distinctive folk music culture (described, not entirely accurately, as 'Saz'iso' when it was modestly marketed in the West by a CD release rejoicing in the title 'At Least Wave Your Handkerchief At Me' in 2017),[55] which is rooted in the diversity of the immediate region, and of place and peasant traditions, unashamedly emotional, complex and polyphonic.

The result of Korce's linguistic make-up and geographical location was an extraordinarily tortuous and chaotic early twentieth-century history, with the town and region passing from Albania to Bulgaria to Greece to France over the course of a few short years. One of these entities, the Autonomous Republic of Northern Epirus, propped up by Greece, lasted for a mere three

---

ix The Aromanians speak a Latin language similar to Romanian and live in scattered pockets throughout the Balkans. They are also known as Vlachs, although this is an exonym directly analogous to 'Welsh'. Both Vlach and Welsh derive from the same source – the old German Walhaz/Welsch, indicating a 'foreigner', a speaker of Celtic or Romance languages, also explored in Chapter 3. There are also echoes of this in Walloon (French-speaking Belgians) and many other exonyms (external names for places and peoples) across Europe.

months in 1914: a historical curio unlikely to figure in the most challenging pub quiz.[56] Even by Balkan standards, Korce was and is an unusually diverse place with a tragic history partially emanating from that diversity. Now, like the rest of the region, an uneasy accommodation of that diversity is developing. The issues are not over, far from it, but some mutually acceptable solutions are emerging as ways to negotiate that complexity and history. For example, there are now 17 Greek schools in Korce. That is significant, given that the Greek language was banned for 60 years in the region.[57]

***

From a cultural perspective, this area – and others like it in the Caucasus, Central America, the South Pacific, West and Southern Africa – have always struck me as akin to the extraordinary biodiversity of the rainforest. Languages and dialects, protected by awkward geography, topography and terrain, survive relatively unscathed by homogenised modernity. There are obvious parallels globally and historically: Switzerland was once like this, for example, characterised by distinct dialects spoken by people who rarely left their home valleys. Partly, this was because of a natural insularity and a natural lack of intellectual curiosity among subsistence farmers. And partly, it was a result of the sheer physical hostility of the terrain.

From a Welsh perspective, of course, the survival of a language is also intrinsically linked to landscape and topography: pushed to the mountainous terrain of the west by the invading Anglo-Saxons, the Welsh were able to protect their fragile culture and language until (a happy coincidence) the breaking down of those topographical barriers by the power of technology and engineering arrived simultaneously with a more enlightened awareness of the value of diversity and the desirability of its preservation. This is to strike a deliberately positive note, as I have been travelling in the Balkans for a quarter of a century now, and have seen an evolution from the tension and distrust of the early 1990s to the situation we have today – far from perfect, but better than it was, and looking to exemplars, like Wales, of how fragile cultures and languages can be protected without resorting to exclusivity, hostility or the 'othering' of those seen as threatening to that culture.

I am not a linguist, and on these travels to 'superdiverse', multilingual parts of the world I was not really concerned with the mechanics of the languages themselves. Instead, the cultural geography of these regions and the diversity within them strikes me as something worth celebrating in a world in which the notion of 'identity politics', often so central to the survival of fragile cultures and languages, as the Welsh experience proves, has suddenly morphed into something that can be mobilised by dominant groups who – for the first time perhaps – feel that their own cultures are under threat. The process of Brexit and the election of Trump are the most obvious manifestations of this.

But travels in the most diverse regions of the world almost always suggest that protecting a culture need not be combined with introspection or notions of purity: quite the opposite, in fact. Wales is a model, not perfect but not bad, for the way in which an overwhelmingly dominant culture can be accommodated whilst preserving and celebrating a fragile minority revolving around the centrality of language. And if, further to that, the experience of living with that dominant culture actually helps these processes, because it reveals something about the value of diversity, the value of preserving that which is distinctive, then there are signs that this model, or a version of it, is being adopted elsewhere.

Contrary to popular opinion, technology can help, not hinder, this process. In Struga, near the Macedonian–Albanian border, I met a man who uses Twitter and Facebook to celebrate the distinctive local version of Macedonian. He told me that he tries to frame comments in such a way that they revolve around the features of his dialect that are unique – but which might in other circumstances be in danger of being lost. There is nothing exclusive about this – he also tweeted in standard Macedonian and English – but the vibrancy of the local form is something worth celebrating and social media is the perfect vehicle for doing this as it reflects the oral nature of these kinds of regional dialects while simultaneously extending their reach and 'proving' their contemporary relevance. This use of technology, and particularly social media, as a vehicle for celebrating and therefore preserving minority languages is one to which we will return (and, as the man in Struga proves, it can involve distinctive dialects too – the use of Dundonian and other versions of the Scots language on Twitter is an example of this from closer to home).[58]

***

My time in Korce was characterised by the worst imaginable April weather. Despite its proximity to Greece, and the time of year, the rain was not only continuous, but cold – an unholy blend of sleet and hail lent some variety to my suffering but eventually its persistence ground me down, as did the rough accommodation. A return to Pogradec seemed in order, and I retreated to the immaculate (and still empty) Bimbli – where I was determined to sample some Albanian wine with Bujar.

As I had anticipated, he was there in the gigantic dining room when I arrived in the early evening, soaked to the skin again after briefly drying off in a tortuous (and vomit-inducing) furgon ride around some of the more obscure corners of southern Albania. Bujar, along with all the other staff, was lounging around watching Turkish football on a giant TV screen without much enthusiasm, almost the definition of the word 'listless'.

I was greeted enthusiastically. Not, I fear, because of any great impression I had made, or any intrinsic charisma, but because they were bored out of their minds by the 'Super Lig' match they were watching (between Trabzonspor and Rizespor – still goalless after 70 minutes). After a beer and a sandwich, I handed Bujar a $10 note and asked him to use his vinologist's expertise to get something interesting from what looked like a fully functioning wine fridge. He talked me through the wines, some grown from 'international' varieties – Merlot and the like – but more derived from indigenous grapes, and therefore considerably more interesting. 'Lots of our grapes are similar to European ones,' said Bujar, misreading my intentions. 'Serine is like Syrah we think. I've had an Australian Shiraz and I think it's got the same big character.'

That was not quite what I had in mind, so we ended up with Shesh I Bardhe, which, I reflected, might have to rebrand if it is ever to gain an international audience. It was an excellent white, floral and apple-scented. If there had been any fish from the lake (Ohrid trout is endemic and famous) it would have been perfect. As it was, I had another cheese sandwich, for want of a single alternative in the still empty hotel, and had already finished it by the time we opened the bottle.

It is hardly an original thought to discern a similarity between the winemaker's concept of 'terroir' and the roots of language and culture. I had no idea that Albania had a serious wine industry – I would have assumed that the mountainous terrain, combined with the climate, was too harsh. But, of course, this assumption was ripped apart in a matter of minutes. Like Italy, with which it has something in common, Albania is characterised by numerous unique indigenous grape varieties, some good, some bad, some distinctive, some echoing more famous international varieties. 'You've seen how hard it is to travel round here,' said Bujar. 'Well that's why we have so many grapes I think, each corner of Albania is different. One valley is warm, the next one is cold.' It seemed a useful way of thinking about linguistic diversity, each valley sequestered and protected from bland uniformity, developing unique characteristics in glorious isolation. And now, emerging into the wider world at just the right time: aware of its distinctiveness, eager to preserve it, but also able to place it in its appropriate context. To put it another way, there is nothing insular about selecting 'Shesh I Bardhe' instead of an ersatz Australian shiraz. It can be enjoyed for what it is: something unique that has developed in a specific place for specific reasons, now ready to take its place in global wine catalogues, like an Amazonian explorer adding an undiscovered beetle to the taxonomy of species.

***

From Albania, I re-crossed the border into Macedonia. Although I had been to Macedonia before, I was keen to explore the south-western corner of the country because of its famous diversity – so famous that it gave its name to a French fruit salad, the range of ingredients ('Macedoine') intended to echo the linguistic melting pot. The Macedonian language, which many linguists (and most Bulgarian nationalists) consider to be merely a version of Bulgarian, splinters into multiple dialects and reaches a kind of super-abundance in these western fringes of the country, where the remote frontiers of the former Yugoslavia bleed into the wild mountain peaks of Albania.

Macedonian, according to linguists, currently has around 30 distinct varieties: distinct to the point that they are, at times, mutually unintelligible, containing fundamental differences including those that revolve around the rudiments of tense and gender.[59] To give a few indications of this diversity, after travelling from Skopje in the spring of 2017, I fetched up in the village of Pestani among the speakers of the Upper Prespa form of the language, having already stopped in Gostivar (where they rejoice in a command of the Upper Polog dialect, characterised by its use of masculine forms and various other unique features), and Struga (with its own unique dialect, restricted to this one town, with separate words for clothes, shoes, melons, people, towels, small girls). Even touristy Ohrid, the main town on the shores of the beautiful lake that shares its name, has its own distinctive version of the Macedonian language.[x]

***

The weather was turning again, and I was trying to multi-task, simultaneously avoiding both the driving sleet and the predatory taxi drivers by sheltering beneath some pine trees fringing the lakeside. Beyond the Albanian border, Pogradec was almost hidden behind a dark curtain of rain. But here, a few miles away across the Macedonia border, nothing stirred, and I strained my ears for the sound of the bus, willing it to arrive before I succumbed to hypothermia.

A wryneck, a cryptic member of the woodpecker family, sang its one note song from a tree near the shore. Some reed beds danced in the light breeze. I strolled along to the monastery to keep warm and kill time, passing the perfectly clear spring which flows into Lake Ohrid from a verdant tree-fringed pond. A long pedestrianised walkway stretched out to my right, full of stalls selling religious icons and Macedonian flags, but the lack of activity and painfully obvious lack of tourists lent a dispiriting ennui to the place. There really was nothing to do here, and the wait for the bus seemed a particularly appalling prospect in this grim weather. Eventually, after what seemed like hours, two old men playing backgammon near the monastery gates shouted

---

x Not just dialects, the region also has numerous important minority languages. On the road to the capital Skopje, I stopped in Kicevo and Krusevo. The latter town formally recognises the Aromanian minority language, which, as we have already established, is similar to Romanian but borrows heavily from Greek. The Aromanians, who constitute a significant minority in the town, are known as Vlachs in Macedonia, a word cognate with Welsh (and Walloon), again derived from the proto-German Welsch for stranger or foreigner, as previously explored in Chapter 3. Kicevo has a much-graffitied quadrilingual 'welcome' sign in Albanian, Macedonian, Turkish and English, a reflection of its diversity.

that the bus was on its way, clearly more attuned to detecting slight changes to the profound silence than I was.

I paid a nominal fare to Pestani, about 10 miles away, and the bus began its tortuous journey along the steep lakeside hills below the Galichicha Mountains. By now, it was mid-afternoon and I was starving. However, Pestani – a very modest (tiny, in fact) Yugoslav-era lakeside resort – seemed just as deserted as Sveti Naum, and my chances of a meal non-existent. I wandered the streets, looking out to the black lake, finding every restaurant and café either locked or boarded up: the familiar melancholy of an out of season resort and powerfully redolent, for me, of the North Wales coast in early spring.

One place had an open door. It faced the lake with a faded sign marked 'Dac' in gothic lettering. It was completely unlit, and completely empty, but I could hear voices and people moving around in what I presumed to be a kitchen so gave a polite little cough. I queried 'food', with the imbecilic international gesture of invisible soup bowl and spoon to mouth, as a tiny man in his late sixties came out of the kitchen. Yes, he said in German, he could do me something, indicating a couple (literally) of possibilities from his menu, which was characteristically Balkan in the sense that it was unfeasibly long and largely fictitious (after numerous trips to the region I knew better than to select at will from the menu). Sounds of furious frying soon emerged from the kitchen, 10 minutes later his invisible wife shouted, and he came back carrying a huge plate of 12 freshly cooked kebabs (the renowned 'cevapi', common across the Balkans), a mound of perfectly fried potatoes, and a deep bowl of Macedonian salad with olives, excellent tomatoes and roasted green peppers.

I then had the problem of finding 'Vila Magda', my accommodation. As it was £7 a night, I did not expect much, and suspected it would just be a private house with rented rooms. This was indeed the case, but none of the houses had names and few had numbers, and all the streets in Pestani were just dirt tracks winding up the hillside. I asked an old lady tending to her garden: she looked blank, had clearly never heard the name before, and did not even recognise the picture I had of the house (and this despite the fact that the village was tiny). She asked a young girl, who thought she knew, and gave some vague directions in the piercing local form of Macedonian. Eventually, I found it at the end of an alley near a small school at the top of the village, and was immediately accosted by the elderly lady owner who took eccentricity to an additional level of Balkan intensity, hugging me, possibly even squeezing my cheek at one point. We had no words in common, but she was very keen to point out the blankets in the clean but tiny room. I nodded, rather puzzled as to the emphasis she seemed to be placing on them. I realised why shortly afterwards: there was no heating of any kind and with the early April weather clearing, a very cold night was in prospect. On the plus side, I had a small balcony with stunning views over the village to the lake and the distant Albanian mountains: to the left, I could see the top of the highest peak in the Galichicha range, Magaro, now glistening white after the earlier snowfall, and framed against a deep blue evening sky.

After a walk through gnarled and mossy woodland above the village, I bumped into the man of the house – in his eighties, tiny, with a crooked back, 'chairman Mao' overalls and a blue beret – on the stairs back to my room, and he invited me in to his 'basement' (a moonshine brewing den) for what he described as 'schnapps'. A memorable half hour ensued. I had two or three glasses from his huge vat of homemade raki (the characteristic Balkan version of fruit brandy) which was pure and good, and not at all dissimilar to Austrian schnapps. I paid my £7 in Macedonian dinars. He broke a crystal glass, to his intense embarrassment and annoyance. And we had a long chat in very broken German (to be more specific: broken in his case, almost non-existent in mine). This was somewhat farcical as I constantly repeated one of my very few German phrases, 'Schönes Blick' ('beautiful view'), and we tried to work out what his house would be worth in the UK (half a million pounds was my considered opinion, given its size, garden, and views of lake and mountain). He had a multilingual guide to the area which spent some time focusing on the Drekavac, a mythical creature central to folklore across certain parts of the southern Balkans, which here takes the form of a one-legged wailing banshee (Drekavac translates to 'the screecher') with dark red eyes, which emerges after dark to 'taunt and scare people'. Not conducive to a good night's sleep.

Pushing the Drekavac to the back of my mind, I scampered back to my quarters for a memorable 'balcony drink'. The sun set over a long hour directly in front of me, casting its rays over the whole of Lake Ohrid and the Albanian mountains fringing it to the west. The sky retained that distinctive pallid blue of winter, fading to white as it met the horizon, but the direct sunshine retained a hint of warmth. I sipped my beer and enjoyed the immense peace, expansive views, and evening birdsong. As soon as the sun dropped, the sky turned orange and then a vivid shade of purple, and the temperature plunged extraordinarily quickly – presumably because of Pestani's location, trapped between steep mountains and the lake, a gigantic sink of cold air. I still had another beer to finish, and it was taken through a slit in my balaclava as I held the can with Dachstein mittens. It was, as the owner had been right to predict, an outrageously cold night in my unheated room, and I spent it with my frozen nose poking out of the heavy blankets: every one of them on top of me, provoking nightmares of slow, stifling suffocation, the one-legged Drekavac never far away.

CHAPTER 5
'MORE THAN A LANGUAGE':
THE TAMIL MINORITY IN
CONTEMPORARY SRI LANKA

The 'dosa'[xi] is perhaps the ultimate marker of Tamil identity, even if it does originate in Karnataka. Food is central to culture across south Asia, and the consumption of dosas epitomises Tamil life, especially at breakfast time. Which makes it all the more surprising that the best dosa I ate in Sri Lanka was in Kandy, the spiritual heartland of Sinhalese Buddhist culture, at the Balaji Dosai Tamil restaurant directly opposite that culture's most sacred site: the Temple of the Sacred Tooth.

It seemed a particularly striking example of a journey from conflict to coexistence. This is not to be naïve: around 100,000 people from both Sinhalese and Tamil communities were killed in a 25-year period in Sri Lanka.[60] This cannot be swept aside in a tourist-friendly simulation of total harmony: accusations of government-sanctioned pogroms during the conflict persist, and inter-ethnic tensions are far from over.

But, consider the fact that in 1998, when Tamil nationalist violence was at its height, an appalling but largely forgotten portent of IS-inspired terror tactics struck the Temple of the Sacred Tooth, directly opposite the Tamil restaurant in which I was enjoying my dosa. Three members of the militant Tamil Tigers group drove a truck containing 400kg of explosives through the roadblocks around the temple and aimed for the entrance, firing automatic weapons indiscriminately as they went. It was a suicide attack using a vehicle as weapon, long before the wider world became fully versed in the technique, and perpetrated by Tamil Hindus, not Sunni Muslims. It resulted in the deaths of 16 people (including the three attackers).[61]

---

xi A rice batter pancake originating in southern India.

To have a Tamil restaurant operating so close to the site seems to encapsulate the tolerance which significant elements in Sri Lankan society now do a great deal to promote. 'Multi-ethnicity is our strength', read a sticker on the window of the central bus station's enquiry office and although this again masks a complex and sometimes difficult reality and legacy of conflict, the sentiments are real enough.

The dosa, stuffed with the classic 'masala' filling of potatoes spiced with fenugreek, mustard seeds and chilli, was predictably ambrosial – this dish almost always is, whenever it is encountered in Sri Lanka or southern India (and, of course, it is not exclusively Tamil, as it is far too good to be restricted in its range). It would, no doubt, be dismissed as 'double carbing' by the joyless British health police, but on a wet day in Kandy, after a long and uncomfortable bus journey, it lifted my spirits (and, in reality, it is not remotely unhealthy). The Balaji Dosai restaurant itself is extremely basic, but lined with pictures of luminaries who have supposedly called in after visiting the temple (Bill Clinton and Morgan Freeman among them, although I couldn't help noticing that the backdrop was a tad indistinct in some of the shots). It is always full, and it is always occupied by a genuinely diverse mix of customers, from a handful of adventurous Western tourists through to enthusiastic Sinhalese diners feeding on emblematic Tamil food.

As I left, another downpour began, and by the time I had reached the corner of the street I was as wet as if I had fallen into the famous lake of Kiri Muhuda, the Sea of Milk, that provides the foreground to the Temple of the Tooth for a million tourist photos. I peered at the piece of paper my guesthouse owner had given me, which rendered the destination I needed in both Sinhalese and Tamil: the buses now have a mixture of both languages above the driver's seat, wherever they are in the country, regardless of which language dominates. The paper was soaked and already congealing, the rendering of both of the beautifully decorative and complex alphabets entirely illegible. So I got on a bus randomly, hoping for the best, finding myself surrounded by Sinhalese schoolchildren on their way home. None of them had heard of my guesthouse (although all spoke excellent English) and I was eventually forced to jump off at the last landmark I recognised, a muddy road bridge, and plot my way up the maze of flooded paths winding their way up a steep hill that (I told myself) looked vaguely familiar from when I had arrived, by tuk-tuk, in an identical apocalyptic deluge the previous evening.

***

The Tamil language, long suppressed in Sri Lanka, is now everywhere, even on the front of the chemist shop later visited for a cold cure in this, the Sinhalese heartland of Kandy. This is a relatively new development, as former Tamil militant Suresh Premachandran pointed out when he spoke, a few weeks later, in Colombo: 'This is basically a historical grievance for us,' he said, referring to the politics of the Tamil language's acceptance across the island. 'It's one of the national languages, but Tamil's applicability was always confined to the areas where Tamil-speaking people are the majority.' In other words, Tamil signage and visibility has historically been restricted to parts of the north and east of the island, generally those parts that the outside world rarely see.

Consider this from a Welsh perspective: imagine if Welsh only appeared on signposts in areas where the language dominates, in the north-west and west. Imagine if Caernarfon was bilingual but Holywell was not. If Cardigan had its name translated on road signs but border towns like Mold did not. The status of the minority tongue is immediately diminished by such measures: it seems reduced, irrelevant and archaic. It is also very difficult to know where to draw some kind of arbitrary line which will always, inevitably, be disputed. Where, in Wales, might it be drawn? The Vale of Clwyd? Gwent? It

105

would be an impossible decision and an obviously unhelpful divide (although a similar line *does* exist in Scotland, for entirely logical reasons – Gaelic road signs suddenly appear as one drives north and enters the zone where the language was historically spoken, essentially the start of the Highlands around Loch Lomond). But in countries with a less clear-cut linguistic and cultural history, characterised by less predictable geographies and flows of population, it is hardly surprising that language campaigners refuse to entertain the notion of 'relativity' or compromise the drive for full and precise equity. For Wijedesa Rajapakshe, a human rights lawyer, 'language parity is one of the biggest challenges to Sri Lanka's peace and reconciliation efforts, and indeed its future'.[62]

The reason for this approach, which seems quite 'European' at first glance (notably similar to the language and signage policies we see in Wales, Catalonia, Ireland and the Basque County) is because language remains central to Tamil identity, and Sri Lankan government policy towards it used to be far, far worse. And you don't have to go back too far to find examples of what, on the face of it, seem to be deliberately divisive or provocative measures. A Sinhalese-only language law was passed in 1956, for example, echoing more recent policies in the Baltic states which marginalised the sizeable Russian-speaking minorities in those countries (these were post-1990s nationalist-inspired measures which continue to cause tensions). Or, even closer to home and even more recent, the Slovakian language law amendment in 2009 which saw the speakers of Hungarian 'criminalised', according to its opponents.[63]

A further obvious analogy is that of the infamous 'Welsh Not', the nineteenth-century practice of hanging a piece of wood around the shoulders of schoolchildren who persisted in speaking Welsh. Regardless of how often this was actually used in Wales, it remains a cause célèbre, a useful rallying point and a powerful way of conceptualising the sins of the past. This can be used to mobilise support for the politicisation of the language, a means of accentuating its value and stressing its fragility.

In Sri Lanka, the divisive 1956 law was never fully implemented, and as in Slovakia its motives are disputed, but whatever those motives were, it had the unsurprising effect of instantly fuelling tension between the two communities, with many Tamils citing linguistic (rather than religious) discrimination as central to their sense of disenfranchisement.

Now, it has all changed: even in Sinhalese dominated areas, Tamil translations are almost universal. Stickers and slogans celebrating diversity and multiethnicity, like the one in Kandy station, are common. And in areas where that diversity reaches its apotheosis on the island, the accommodation of that diversity is often remarkable.

***

From Kandy, I headed up on the impossibly scenic train journey to Haputale, a small town built on a spectacular ridge, high up in the tea plantations, that encapsulates ethnic and linguistic diversity.

This is because Haputale's small population is divided into four almost exact quarters: 25% of its population are Sinhalese (and therefore largely Buddhist), 25% are Sri Lankan Tamil, 25% Indian Tamil and 25% Sri Lankan Muslim. The Islamic call to prayer is one of the loudest I have ever heard, even louder than it tends to be in remoter parts of Muslim majority areas – the Jordanian desert or the Atlas mountains of Morocco, for example. The lower key but more persistent chants from the nearby Buddhist and Hindu temples mark the daylight hours, and mist tumbles down from the montane forests and tea plantations with startling suddenness and unpredictability. It is an extraordinary place, both physically and culturally. When the mist clears, as it often does in the early morning and late evening, the view stretches for hundreds of miles across the plains and remnant rainforest to the east coast of Sri Lanka and the Bay of Bengal beyond.

The Indian Tamils were brought in from the south-east of that country in to work in the tea plantations because they were felt to be more amenable than the native Sri Lankans to the kind of 'hard labour for small reward' that the work involved. Since then, the development of the plantations in the hill country of Sri Lanka has created – since their inception in Victorian times – what may well be the most beautiful 'man made' rural landscape on Earth. I spent my days in Haputale walking or taking short bus journeys up to the plantations, mingling with the Tamil pickers as tendrils of mist rolled over the green bushes.

Working the tea plantations is still the primary role of the Tamils in this area, and the hillsides above Haputale and Ella are dotted with their settlements and gaudy Hindu temples. The picturesque nature of the plantations masks a hard existence, long days for the Tamil women who then become the subject of a thousand tourist photos. It is hard to think of a more emblematic symbol of global inequality and the strange dynamic thrown up by modern tourism than a group of Western tourists moving into position for the most Instagrammable shot of the Tamil tea pickers who may already be hours into a physically exhausting day. My first trip up to Lipton's Peak was marred by a group of five Belgian tourists arranging themselves strategically in order to get the best shot of the Tamil women; it felt hugely intrusive and inappropriate, echoing the way in which people move around to take shots of wildlife on safari. But it was presumably a daily occurrence for the pickers, who continue their work without halting or paying the slightest attention to the tourists.

***

My hotel in Haputale was a peculiar sprawling venue, seemingly far too big for such a small town (particularly as the vast majority of visitors to the 'tea country' head to the backpacker's haven of Ella for chocolate brownies and good WiFi). Two huge buildings were separated by what looked like allotments, which were frequented by one enormous and very determined ruddy mongoose – I could look down on him (or her) from my balcony, watching as he (or she) scurried through the vegetation looking for prey. Balconies come cheap in provincial Sri Lanka, and for a few pounds I had a view stretching down to the Bay of Bengal (or just as far as the mongoose, if I preferred). The rain, low cloud and howling wind that frequently enveloped the town made the balcony a tad less appealing, although it did make me feel at home – it was powerfully reminiscent of Llanberis or Blaenau Ffestiniog.

When it cleared, I felt the urge for a drink or two to accompany the view, the quest for which brought me into inadvertent contact with another element of Tamil life in the town: those marginalised from all forms of work or community involvement, and addicted to arak, the local brew. All alcohol in Sri Lanka is sold in little wooden booths, not unlike the rougher parts of British cities, with barred windows, and a small slit through which money is passed. There is, as with the 'chemist shop' liquor dispensers of Scandinavia, a distinct and presumably intentional feeling of transgression, of something squalid in the transaction, with purchases packaged up in a brown paper bag.

And within those shops, a pitiful scene, as mainly Tamil alcoholics in rags beg for cash to buy arak (which is a painfully rough firewater distilled from the sap of coconut flowers – at least it is in Sri Lanka, but the word is also used in many countries to describe various forms of strong liquor). It is, without question, the quickest and cheapest way to oblivion. I watched as a man with no shoes, literally dressed in rags, downed a miniature bottle (presumably all he could afford) immediately, still standing inside the shop. In fact, the shop, tiny as it was, formed a kind of focal point in a town without bars or pubs: the equivalent of Wetherspoons. All the alcoholics gathered there; I noticed the same phenomenon on the next night, and the one after that, as I passed my money through the hatch, just to get a couple of beers.

**

One morning in Haputale dawned clear as a bell (in stark contrast to my post-Arak head), which saw me scampering off along the ridge towards Adisham, an incongruous colonial lodge turned even-more-incongruous Benedictine monastery. On the way back, hungry, I stopped in a bizarre empty hotel café, an appendage to the large and jarring Hotel Olympus, which brings a touch of 1980s glamour to the town. It looks, literally, like a Colwyn Bay nightclub from that era. As I gave my order in the empty café, the bored waiter heard my voice and perked up: 'Are you from Leeds?' he asked, excited, I can only presume, by my non-standard pronunciation. Somewhat taken aback, and mildly offended, I said that I was sorry to disappoint him, but the answer was a firm 'no'. He was called Muthal, a student, and a Sri Lankan native Tamil, slightly unusual in this part of town, where Indian Tamils predominate. Why did he think I was from Leeds? 'I play cricket,' he said. 'We played a team from Leeds and you sound like them ... you look a bit like them too,' he added after some consideration, indicating with a meaningful glance (it seemed to me) my bald head and less then elegant shorts.

Ah, cricket, that explained it. Although I remained mildly offended by the comment, I was less surprised and consoled myself with the thought that Muthal was probably just trying to start a conversation about his favourite subject. The devotion of Sri Lankans to the sport is without parallel, even the Indians seem like dilettantes in comparison. If there is no cricket to watch, if the season is over for example, television channels will screen endless repeats, in full, of recent (or even not-so-recent) matches.

Time was clearly not pressing on Muthal, so I asked him about the relationship between Indian and Sri Lankan Tamils up here in the hill country. There was, he implied, a clear distinction between the older community and what he described

110

as 'migrants', meaning a much more recent wave of Tamils moving from India to Sri Lanka. 'Younger Indian Tamils seem like Sri Lankans, mainly because of the way they dress. It's only their accent that gives them away.' He meant, I assumed, that the older community tends to wear the colourful saris that sets them apart. The unifier, as so often, is language. For Muthal, 'language is what it means to be a Tamil, that's all, we all love our mother language'. Echoes of Gwynfor Evans again and the early days of Plaid Cymru: with language viewed as the 'badge of identity'. In Wales, this has always been a problematic and contested notion, for obvious numerical reasons. But for the Tamils, the language remains, justifiably, central – with the emphasis more on perceived notions of 'purity', another slippery and divisive concept. Muthal went on to claim that Indian Tamils often observe that Sri Lankan Tamils speak a purer form of the Tamil language. David Shulman's Tamil 'biography' makes a similar point while stressing the constant flux of the language, the fact that it is a 'living entity' intrinsic to the wider culture.[64]

In much the same way as the Patagonian Welsh speak an idealised, slightly archaic version of the language, untainted by English imports, the Sri Lankan Tamils, according to Muthal, preserve certain features of the language away from the domineering influence of Hindi. The centrality of language to the culture and unity of the Tamils is fascinating, and the great antiquity of the tongue is frequently invoked by its enthusiasts – a tactic that bears obvious comparison with Welsh and Basque. The great age of the languages acts partly as a riposte to what can then be framed as the gauche arrivistes of the dominant cultural group – whether they speak Hindi, English or Spanish – and this can be done with the comfort and certain knowledge that it is based on historical fact.

Tamil is spoken by 80 million people, and is genuinely of ancient Dravidian origin, hence its mobilisation as a political tool. It is also, according to those that really know these things, complex, highly distinctive and hard to learn. People often say this about old languages, perhaps as a way to marginalise them or diminish them (it is commonly heard in relation to Welsh and Basque) but there is some agreement that Tamil has evolved into an unusually distinctive way of not just speaking, but thinking and singing. Shulman attempts to encapsulate this by arguing that Tamil, more than a language, is 'a body of knowledge'; suggesting that the word itself can simultaneously mean 'knowing how to love' and 'being a civilised person'.[65]

***

Negombo is the first taste of Sri Lanka for most visitors, as it is just a few miles from the airport. But its rather tawdry seafront, a row of restaurants shielded from the Indian Ocean by dilapidated buildings and palm trees, masks a fascinating cultural profile. This is entirely unexpected, as Negombo seems to typify west-coast Sri Lanka, with its Sinhalese majority and tourists looking in vain for a stereotypical white-sand tropical beach. It is far removed, at first glance, from the diversity of the hill country, let alone the Tamil heartland of the north and east.

Beyond the touristy patina of the coastal strip, however, the town's history partly revolves around a particular, highly distinctive form of Tamil identity. It does have a Sinhalese majority, but most of these are Catholic, not Buddhist (a result of its colonial past, with centuries-old links with Portuguese culture) and – more surprising still – the Catholic Sinhalese live alongside a distinctive community of Tamils that have been here for centuries.

These Tamils, sometimes called Puttalam Tamils, are native to this part of western Sri Lanka (unlike the Tamils of nearby Colombo, most of whom are internal migrants). Their dialect is distinctive to the point that it is almost a separate language, an inevitable result of their geographical location, immersed in, and surrounded by, Sinhalese culture; far removed from the famous

Tamil communities in their heartlands in the north and east of the island.

I found a guesthouse down a maze of narrow streets half a mile inland from the seafront. Potholed sandy roads swilled monsoonal mud around, and the canal (characteristic of the town – built by the Dutch) gave the appearance of a squalid tropical version of Venice, in the sense that it had a practical function: goods could be moved more easily on it, as opposed to the chaotic roads.

The guesthouse backed on to the canal at the end of a long dirt cul-de-sac: its inaccessibility lent it a tranquil atmosphere, its essential peace only broken by the occasional motorised barge transporting a startlingly diverse range of products 'up river'. Most of the time this was bricks, enormous bags of rice, or barrels of fuel. But I also saw what looked like a four-poster bed chugging up the canal late one evening, the barge struggling to stay afloat, its small motor straining with the effort. Birdsong and the rustle of eucalyptus leaves in the breeze were the only other sounds in the hotel garden.

Or rather, they were. Until one evening, as I relaxed with a guava juice next to the tiny, but very pleasant, hotel pool (unaccustomed luxury for me). I heard a raised voice coming from what passed for a reception area (not really necessary as the venue cannot have had more than six rooms). The voice immediately jarred, partly because it was so unusual to hear anything in that quiet place, let alone a raised human voice, and partly because the accent was so familiar and so unexpected. A British woman, with distinctive estuary tones, nasal and insistent, that began to rise in volume exponentially. At first I couldn't make out the words, but as the volume increased with the level of her consternation, it reached me: she was exercised about some fault with the guesthouse (or error with her booking) and was taking it out on the skinny young local man who manned the front desk on the rare occasions it became necessary.

Remarkably quickly, the argument escalated to an extraordinary level of abuse. 'THIS is the place we booked, and YOU know it,' she shouted. His response was mumbled, indistinct. 'You're just taking our money and sending us to a shithole up the road, aren't you?' Another mumbled response. 'Are you laughing? You're a CHEATING shit, that's what you are.' Then, after a long pause, another voice, male this time, same accent – I later discovered it was her teenaged son. Near hysterical: 'Don't you threaten her you little shit', then another pause and another indistinct mumble from the poor chap, the subject of all this abuse. 'What did you say? WHAT DID YOU SAY? Say that again, say it to her face.'

It is a truism to observe that many bourgeois Brits deliberately choose to avoid their fellow countrymen and women when travelling abroad. Itineraries, specifically designed for this purpose, trace a route through Umbria or the Lot in a deliberate attempt to circumvent Tuscany or the Dordogne. White-washed villages in the Andalucian interior are chosen for their mountain views, backs deliberately turned to the vulgar coastal resorts with their full English breakfasts and real English pubs. It wasn't something I had often thought about before (although I was well aware of the phenomenon) as holidays in provincial Moldova, eastern Ukraine and Kyrgyzstan do not generally involve much contact with 'home'. This, then, was a novel experience, and I was not too sure what to do.

Morally, I wondered if I should intervene as it sounded like somebody might get hurt. Personally, I felt disinclined to get involved, partly because somebody might get hurt (and that somebody might have been me). I tussled with this dilemma for a few minutes, realising I was much closer to the dramatis personae than I had initially realised – they were on the other side of a fairly narrow dividing wall. The argument briefly died down, but this was temporary: soon, the sound of a glass, or plate, smashing – and then another, louder this time, followed

114

by more angry shouting. Wearing only shorts, and with some trepidation, I thought I should at least check that nobody had been injured, although I had no idea what to do, or who to call, if they had been.

I peered round the dividing wall. Nothing. Then I walked through to a kind of muddy porch-cum-courtyard immediately outside. Here stood the skinny young man, holding a small bottle of fruit juice. By his feet, a crate of fruit juice with a third of the bottles missing. In front of him, the alley, strewn with broken glass and sticky juice. The two Brits gone. Still waters run deep, I thought, imagining this quiet little man throwing bottles at his interlocutors. I was inclined to think he was in the right, but also felt it might be a good idea to check out next morning, just in case.

***

I knew I was in for an expensive tuk-tuk ride next morning, from the guesthouse to the bus station, but did not have much choice. It is common for the drivers of Asian three-wheelers to sleep in the sheltered, canvas-lined passenger areas of their vehicles so, indecently early next morning, I approached one randomly (actually, not entirely randomly. I was attracted by the slogan on the back of one of the tuk-tuks. Unlike the usual Bob Marley or Che Guevara or Buddha profiles, this one had a slogan – 'Politics is a wild animal, don't let it bite U').

'Six-hundred rupees boss' was his considered response to my request for a price to the station. An outrageous figure, but I was too tired to bargain – or not much, anyway. I got him down to 400, which was obviously still a pretty good result for him as he began to flatter me immediately. After a chat about why I was here alone, which always leads to a discussion about family, he saw his opportunity. He claimed to be surprised by the age of my children (they are 14 and 16). He turned to face me, ignoring the road in front, eyebrows raised in astonishment. 'How old are you? You must be 31, maybe 32?' I am 49, and let us just say

I am rarely complemented on my unblemished complexion or youthful looks.

We got on well after that: he was a clever man, and I am not used to flattery. I got him a cup of chai at the bus station because he had no change for my 1,000 rupee note, or said he did not. His English was superb, so I asked him about the Negombo Tamils. 'They're fishing people – my own father was a fisherman. That's what we call the language, fishermen's Tamil,' he said. I asked him whether he spoke it, but he shook his head. Just Sinhalese and English, and I noticed he never referred to himself, or his father, as Tamil. The distinctive form of Tamil spoken in Negombo traces its distinctiveness, again, to its location – it has adopted so many Sinhalese words and structures, over centuries, that it has morphed into a near-separate language.

Sri Lanka is often portrayed in ethnic terms: it is widely understood that Tamils dominate the east and north of the country, with the Sinhalese dominating the rest. But this is a real misrepresentation of the complex reality. It is not just unusual hill towns like Haputale that have a mixed population for historical reasons, as the realities of Negombo prove. In Negombo, many of those identifying as Sinhalese are actually Tamil, and often even speak Tamil. Given the long history of conflict on the island, this fact is perhaps surprising but tells us something about the processes of hybridity and assimilation that often underpin these environments – and act as a riposte to those citing notions of 'purity' or advocating some kind of monoculture.

Given the realities of conflict on the island, it is hardly surprising that this isolated community of Tamils in the west began to call themselves Sinhalese after the dominant group. There are dozens of global parallels with this process – but let's just view it from a Welsh perspective, from the remnant Brythons of Cumbria and Strathclyde, whose culture was cut adrift and became untenable, to the Welsh of Pennsylvania, those 'good Americans' who integrated into the dominant culture far more quickly than their Irish or Italian counterparts, who were more determined to hang on to elements of their own identity.

The conflict in Sri Lanka also had the effect of increasing diversity in the dominant capital, Colombo, which surprises even casual visitors by its multi-ethnicity. I had assumed, before arriving from the hill country, that Colombo would be mono-ethnically Sinhalese with small numbers of migrants from other parts of Sri Lanka. If you'd pushed me, I might have assumed that those migrants from the conflict might have been Sinhalese people displaced from Tamil-dominated areas of the east and north. But this assumption was wrong, and essentially applied my understanding of the ways in which 'ethnicity' has been tragically negotiated in parts of the Balkans.

In Colombo, despite the cultural dominance of Buddhism and Sinhalese symbolism, only around 40% of the population are Sinhalese. Well over a quarter of the population are Sri Lankan Tamil, and native Muslims are only a shade less numerous. There are Sri Lankan Malays, and Burghers and Chetties too. And this in a teeming city of five million people. There is often an element of what Edward Said famously called 'Orientalism' about the way in which foreign tourists often assume that Asian cities, in particular, are somehow immune to the processes of migration that have altered the character and supercharged the dynamism of cities in the 'developed' world.[66] The idea that cities like Colombo, or Bangkok, or Delhi, are monoethnic and timeless, is hopelessly outdated. In reality, both internal and external migrations have shaped most Asian cities for decades, and these processes have accelerated in recent years to the point that a city like Colombo is almost as diverse as London, Paris or New York.

A near-universal rule characterises global entrepôt cities of this kind. All, or almost all, come to some kind of accommodation with the numerous minorities that lend them their diversity. They become far more liberal and tolerant places than – often

– the hinterland of the countries they dominate. An illustration of this came in early 2018 when Alex, the owner of the house in Kandy I had stayed in, emailed me to say that tensions were increasing in the town. A few days later, Kandy erupted in violence, but this time the clashes were not between the Buddhist Sinhalese and the Hindu Tamils, not that historic dividing line that has haunted Sri Lankan geopolitics for decades. Instead, the dominant Sinhalese community in the town attacked properties belonging to the Muslim minority, after rumours spread of an attack on a Buddhist temple in Abathanna. There were, said Alex, depressing echoes of the past in the sense that it seemed to represent a return to the old feeling that the Sinhalese consider Sri Lanka to be 'theirs' and the other communities 'arrivistes' whom they tolerate. Hardline Buddhist nationalists were blamed, along with social media (later blocked), for spreading rumours and coordinating protests. And it was not just a return to the past: it was also, sadly, a reflection of global currents, a growing tendency to distrust the Muslim minority, damagingly mirrored, sometimes, in that minority's own sense of exceptionalism (see postscript on p. 121).

Implicit within the protests seemed to be the notion that the majority Sinhalese residents of Kandy see themselves as guardians of Buddhist culture on the island – there was an apparent connection between the town's portrayal of itself, with some justification, as the epicentre of Buddhist culture on the island, home of its most sacred sites, and the kind of othering of minority groups that form of racial superiority often becomes associated with. The subsequent tensions were addressed by the influential former captain of the Sri Lankan cricket team, Kumar Sangakkara, in a Tweet which was widely shared domestically and internationally.

'No one in Sri Lanka can be marginalised or threatened or harmed due to their ethnicity or religion. We are One Country and One People. Love, trust and acceptance should be our common mantra. No place for racism and violence. STOP. Stand together and stand strong.'[67] There was a fairly obvious irony in the imposition of a state of emergency, given the island's contemporary status as a peaceful tourist-friendly nation emerging from conflict: it was the first time since 2011 that Sri Lanka has imposed such a measure, and this time it was a reflection of an entirely different set of inter-ethnic tensions.

***

My impressions of the relationship between the Muslim minority and the rest of Sri Lanka could hardly have been more different, and revolved around a striking encounter with a Sri Lankan 'moor' bereaved in the most tragic of circumstances, the Boxing Day tsunami of 2004 which hit the country particularly hard and resulted in devastating fatalities.

From Colombo, I travelled on to Galle, at the south-western tip of the country, more or less the furthest point away from Tamil culture. Given this geographical reality, it is not surprising that Galle is dominated by the Buddhist Sinhalese and has only a very small number of Tamil residents: but a quarter of its residents are Muslim, descended from Arab traders and sailors who settled here centuries ago when the city passed between the colonists of Portugal and the Netherlands. Sri Lankan Muslims (generally, and officially, identified by the rather archaic-sounding 'Moors' in the country, redolent of medieval Iberia) are far more numerous and long-established than most outsiders realise. Their influence is particularly notable in Galle, where it combines with a fascinating colonial heritage and seaside location to render the city immensely appealing to tourists; simultaneously impossibly exotic with its coconut trees and purple-faced langur monkeys, and strangely familiar with its Dutch and Portuguese architecture and historic city walls.

Today, Galle is packed with tourists enjoying that intrinsic exoticism and the vibrant restaurants in the old town. But its success masks an underlying sadness that soon becomes apparent with just the briefest attempt to scratch away at the superficial surface of the town. The reality is that very few Galle residents emerged entirely unscathed by the 2004 tsunami; and even those that were physically unharmed almost invariably had relatives who were killed.

In fact, the busy coastal railway line between Colombo and Galle that I travelled on alongside thousands of locals and tourists was the scene of the worst rail tragedy in history, when the 2004 Tsunami destroyed a packed train near the tourist hangout of Hikkaduwa. There were at least 1,500 passengers on board as the wall of water knocked the train sideways. The force of the wave and the subsequent flooding was compounded by the fact that the line threads a route between the Indian Ocean on one side, and mangrove swamps on the other. The train was effectively pushed into lying water and therefore flooded very rapidly from both sides as it rolled over. The power of the water was devastating in its effect, and yet another compounding factor was the understandable decision taken by local villagers to board the train, seeing it as a potentially safe haven as their houses flooded. Even now, travelling down this line, you see the occasional large boat lying among the tropical vegetation well inland – obviously pushed there by the wave 13 years before.

The man I met in Galle had lost his daughter in the tragedy. He was full of praise for 'the British' who, he said, had donated more to rebuild the local economy than anybody else. He was also a Muslim, from the picturesque walled centre – and there was, he claimed, not a hint of tension between the communities in his town. The tragedy served to bring them together, he said; everybody had pitched in to help during and after the disaster, Muslims and Sinhalese alike. 'We rose above our differences,' he said. 'Food, water, we all helped each other bring the things we needed then, at that terrible time, to stay alive.' Since 2004, there have been occasional allegations that Muslims and Tamils were discriminated against in the rebuilding process, but here in Galle there are few signs of this (although the anti-Muslim violence fanned by right-wing Buddhist groups in Kandy did briefly spread to some outlying areas of Galle in 2018).

Galle's Muslims are particularly visible in the southern part of the old town, where crumbling mansions fringe the old sea walls and men pick coconuts fresh from the tree. The midday call to prayer rang out as I enjoyed perhaps the finest 'curry and rice' of all on the rooftop of the famed 'Mammas' restaurant, looking out over the colonial rooftops to white mosques and the Indian Ocean beyond.

POSTSCRIPT: This chapter revolves around my visit to Sri Lanka in September 2017. Whilst writing it, in 2018, riots in Kandy and other areas of the country erupted, which I cover in the passages above after correspondence with one of the people I had stayed with in Sri Lanka. Then, on Easter Sunday 2019, a devastating series of bombings perpetrated by Islamic extremists struck targets across the country – but particularly Colombo, and Negombo, with its large Christian minority and mixed population. Over 100 people were killed in St Sebastian's Church in the town, and many Muslims (a large proportion of whom were themselves refugees and asylum-seekers) fled their accommodation as a result of the subsequent tension and persecution.[68] Farah Mihlar, writing in *The Guardian* shortly after the attacks, argued that all the cycles of violence experienced in Sri Lanka's recent history – although distinct – are connected by a thread of state failures and disregard for human rights. She concluded: 'Ten years after the war ended it is clear that Sri Lanka remains in a state of conflict. This is the time for national reckoning. We need to rise above the narrow nationalistic and extremist positions held by all ethnic and religious groups, and build a peace premised on justice and equality for all.'[69]

CHAPTER 6
'XHOSA NOSTRA':
THE INTERSECTION OF LANGUAGE
AND POLITICS IN POST-APARTHEID
SOUTH AFRICA

The townships of Bushbuckridge are the perfect distillation of the past 50 years of South African history. Stretched out along a low line of hills for mile upon mile, the place exemplifies the popular image of the legacy of apartheid, with its rows of shacks, some 'improved', some still in their original favela decrepitude. Its lush Lowveld surroundings lend it a *rus in urbe* feel, as smoke plumes rise into the still air from charcoal fires, acacia and jacaranda trees break up the sometimes squalid urbanism of township ribbon development.

Its hopelessly impractical sprawl and inconvenient topography – all valleys and ridges – is redolent of the most depressed corners of the South Wales valleys, marooned miles from anything vaguely prosperous, and mitigates against the development of any kind of central business district. Instead, little micro-centres of vibrancy and entrepreneurialism dot the landscape: here, a shack selling cheap beer, there a hole in the side of a house dispensing dust-covered vegetables. These are still called 'spaza' shops, derived from the Zulu word for 'hindrance', a derivation that, despite its linguistic origin, smacks of the iniquities of apartheid (no doubt they were seen as 'hindrances' by those from more privileged areas).

So far, so typical. But, unlike many townships in South Africa, which lurk unseen, miles away from typical tourist itineraries, Bushbuckridge is superficially familiar to many foreign visitors because its outer fringes span the edge of the vast Kruger National Park (which is, inevitably, 'the size of Wales'). This means that its outer edges are often traversed by luxury four-wheel-drives whisking groups of tourists along the bumpy roads as fast as possible to their dream safaris; the big cats and the air-conditioned tents, the township passing in a brief blur of poverty voyeurism, if it is noticed at all.

Very few stop to get out. Unlike the handful of famous townships which adjoin the major urban centres of South Africa, like the globally renowned Soweto (the 'South Western Townships' of Johannesburg), Bushbuckridge has the unique misfortune of being right next to a world-famous tourist attraction but never, realistically, able to profit from that proximity. Whereas visitors to Johannesburg will often append a carefully managed Soweto trip to their itineraries, the long drive out to Kruger means almost all foreigners maximise their time in the park (that is, if they drive there at all – the park also has its own internal airstrip for the seriously well-heeled).

All of which made the fact that I was driving through the middle of it, hopelessly lost, in a small but very conspicuous hire car (a fetching shade of lilac) somewhat unusual. I was on the way to meet a man called Thomas Shivambu, a Tsonga-speaking resident of the township and something of a local historian with a distinctive activist's take on the history of South African bantustans.

***

Under apartheid, 10 'bantustans' were established in South Africa. They formed the urban centres that now still tend to be known as 'townships' (although this is not a strictly accurate conflation). They were a controlling attempt to concentrate ethnic minority communities into distinctive, sequestered enclaves in the guise of providing them with a version of political autonomy. The result, which was presumably intentional and is hardly surprising, was that the black population was almost entirely deprived of any role in South African political life, and was kept distant from the urban centres. The fact that Bushbuckridge feels so atomised and sprawling, and in a sense so 'rural', is a function of this: it was intended to be marginal to the mainstream of white South

African society, stuck on this twisting ridge high up in the furthest reaches of Mpumulanga province (formerly Transvaal), at the exact point where it meets the managed wilderness of the Kruger and the northern, poverty-stricken province of Limpopo.

A certain amount of forced 'clearance' was associated with the formation of the different bantustans, which in some ways echoed the experience of Scottish Highlanders in the late eighteenth century, but in other ways was closer to that of the former Yugoslavia in the 1990s. This is because the clearances were partly designed to render the bantustans more ethnically and linguistically 'homogenous', and partly for equally sinister 'administrative' reasons: almost always, the measures were driven by the white population's controlling instincts and the fundamental iniquities of apartheid. For example, virtually all native tribes were removed from the Kruger, now one of the biggest game reserves in Africa, in the early years of the twentieth century (although some remained in remote corners until the 1960s). The experience of the Makuleke over the course of the twentieth century is a case in point. They are a Tsonga-speaking tribe who were forcibly removed and pushed against their will into the newly established bantustans fringing the edge of the new national park. Post-apartheid, they had some of their lands restored and they can sometimes now be seen around the edge of Kruger engaging in educational tours, part of a fairly ambitious eco-tourism project which acknowledges the crimes of the past.

The geographical and cultural diversity of the tribal groups in this corner of South Africa was extraordinarily complex even before the old regimes – both colonial and apartheid – began carving up the land and population to suit their wider political and economic goals. Groups of Tsonga speakers merge with Siswati, Sotho, Sepedi and Tshivenda speakers at various points in the far north-eastern corner of modern South Africa.

Look at a linguistic map of the country – it will immediately strike you as colourful and unusually diverse when taken as a whole – but note how that diversity gradually increases away from the relative monoculture of the Afrikaans-speaking Cape in the south-western (opposite) corner and grows in complexity until the borders of Mozambique, Swaziland and Zimbabwe are reached in the north-east. There, a patchwork quilt of colours illustrates the fragmented reality on the ground.

The bantustans were the apartheid regime's attempt partly to manage, but primarily to exploit, this diversity: to use the diversity within South Africa as a kind of 'divide and rule' tool, although – again – this characterisation is a slightly reductive explanation of a very complex reality. Each bantustan was supposed to be designated to each ethnic group, so Zulus were supposed to gravitate towards KwaZulu, for example. The Swazi equivalent was KaNgwane, hard up against the border with Swaziland itself, with a complex apartheid history which saw serious attempts to formally transfer it to Swaziland in 1982.

Bushbuckridge – the area I was now driving through – formed part of Gazankulu bantustan, an even more complex geographical unit with – like KaNgwane – numerous exclaves geographically separated from the main heartland. In this case, the exclaves and the predominant make-up of the unit as a whole, were XiTsonga (or just 'Tsonga') speakers: Gazankulu was supposed to be the Tsonga 'homeland', in other words.[70] Even at the time, this was pushing it a bit: there were indeed a lot of Tsonga speakers in the region, but there were also thousands of speakers of other indigenous languages, and, of course, there were also hundreds of thousands of Tsonga living in other parts of South Africa far removed from their newly designated 'homeland'. As in the Balkans, the picture of ethnic and linguistic 'homelands' is never as simple as it first appears. And, as in the Balkans, people with different linguistic and cultural identities to the majority group inevitably feel threatened when that group is suddenly placed in a position of dominance. As with the Serbs in Croatia (two-thirds of whom left during the 1990s conflict), minority groups tend to move to areas in which they themselves form the majority, even if it is not where they come from, not their original home.

Language, as a marker of ethnic identity, came in for special attention and some have suggested it was mobilised by the apartheid regime to create compliance among the black population: a classic case of deliberately encouraging disunity, preventing black South Africans from formulating a united anti-apartheid position, or that was at least the intention. In reality, the concept of unity was never successfully extinguished, and the struggle against apartheid had the fairly obvious effect of strengthening it.

The globally celebrated post-apartheid national anthem, 'nkosi sikeleli'iafrika', although written in Xhosa, is effectively a paean for African unity – the perfect rallying point for anti-apartheid campaigners. Its composer, Enoch Sontonga, was inspired by the Welsh hymn 'Aberystwyth', composed by the Merthyr-born Joseph Parry in the late nineteenth century. Sontonga took the beautiful tune, possibly because he had a Welsh teacher at his missionary school in Johannesburg, adapted it, and added the Xhosa lyrics ('Lord bless Africa') pleading for unity. It was most famously sung at Nelson Mandela's inauguration in 1994, where it encapsulated the desire to transcend ethnic conflict of all kinds – not just that between white minority and black majority.[71]

Now, everybody in the world feels they know something about the recent history of this country and, in that respect, visitors arrive with a powerful set of preconceptions based on a blend of popular culture and fragments of twentieth-century memories. This, again, is another explanation for why my lilac hire car was driving over sandy potholes in the middle of a remote township in direct contradiction of every piece of advice ever given to foreigners in South Africa. I was conscious of not wanting to fall into that trap. Instead, I wheeled out the old travellers' cliché: I wanted to see things for myself.

***

A lot has been written about South African crime, some of it exaggerated, some of it accurate, some of it with more than a hint of bravado, some of it politically motivated. One thing is verifiably true: it is not a good idea to take a wrong turn in a township. This is precisely what I had done. I was on the wrong side of the tracks in what I think might have been the Hoxane district: a Tsonga-speaking area.

I had been warned not to take the standard, blindingly obvious, route through Bushbuckridge towards Kruger (I had arranged to meet my contact Thomas Shivambu at a community centre on the road out towards the national park). Instead, my German hosts told me in my White River hotel, you should 'go straight down the main road to Hazyview and make your way up towards Kruger from there – that's the way everybody goes these days'. When I asked why, they said that the direct route was almost impossible to follow because of over-running roadworks and lack of signs, before finishing with what, in South Africa, becomes a familiar warning about 'bad people' living nearby.

Just before I arrived in the area, there had been an incident on the road towards Kruger supposedly involving an attack on a tourist's car. But the balance between hyperbole and reality is arguably harder to achieve in South Africa than anywhere else and, by association, calibrating your own behaviour to take account of this is perhaps harder than anywhere else. It is a very fine line to tread as a visitor, the personal negotiation between caution and curiosity that characterises most travel is acute and hard to calculate. On the one hand, it would be foolishly naïve to suggest that the reports of crime are always exaggerated by a media and public who may have a vested interest in doing so (as with almost everything else in this country, crime is an overtly

127

political issue). On the other, the reality is that most of the victims of crime here already live in desperate circumstances, usually in the townships. Indeed, this latter reality is so well rehearsed that it has itself almost become a cliché. So, it is a tricky balancing act.

In terms of my own approach to navigating a route through the complex geography of South Africa, I ignored the advice and travelled direct, not so much because of a natural insouciance, but more because my onward route led far more directly through Bushbuckridge and Mr Shivambu, my Tsonga contact, lived on the Limpopo side at the furthest end of the township. Within minutes I was encountering a series of dusty tracks where the road should have been. A mound of earth had once been a roundabout but the road was in an advanced stage of redevelopment. Nobody was working on it, midweek at around 10am; indeed it looked as if the work had been abandoned in a hurry with tools lying around and piles of sand representing additional hazards to the motorist.

When I finally met Thomas, I felt as though I had been driving round the township all day. My car was covered in dense red dust, to the point that it was hard to see out of the windows. My stress levels were high, the road markings and signage either non-existent or hopelessly confusing to an outsider like myself. My mobile phone worked, but was cripplingly expensive as I had not bought a local SIM card. I knew that the community centre was some way removed from the township on its northern edge, as it spills over from Mpumulanga into Limpopo province, and the sprawling nature of Bushbuckridge then became more of a help than a hindrance, as I continued heading in that vague direction. At a busy crossroads that seemed to have open bush to one side, ignoring all the advice given to tourists, I stopped the car and got out, asking for directions at a shack selling the local version of fried chicken. My hunch, that the open countryside indicated that I was near, was correct – and a very precise set of directions was provided by the middle-aged woman who was only just setting up to start lunchtime preparations. The community centre turned out to be very close; it was indeed almost at the exact point that the edge of the township became the open bush, and there was Thomas, sitting on a red bench outside the newly built centre.

Over a cup of tea, he began to talk about the history of the bantustans, but not quite in the way I had expected. It quickly became apparent that here was a fully-fledged Tsonga patriot: for Thomas, his identity as a Tsonga speaker was crucial to his sense of belonging to this region. 'Look, there are around 300,000 Tsonga speakers here, in the township and around it, but what people fail to realise is that there are also many, many in other parts of South Africa and in our neighbouring countries. There are nearly 300,000 Tsonga people in Johannesburg, which is not what people think of when they think of a Tsonga heartland.' The Tsonga, who marginally dominate this part of South Africa, present a less unified face to the world than, for example, the Zulu. This is partly because of the historic fragmentation of the community, of which this journey was the perfect example.

Thomas agreed with what I feared might be my rather one-dimensional impression of Bushbuckridge as a 'complicated' place. 'Yes, and what you see here, what you see with the politics, is what is causing the problems.' He did not elaborate, I suspect for diplomatic reasons (and because we were not alone, and I later discovered that another 'activist' did not share his pro-Tsonga sentiments). But I understood these 'problems' to mean the inter-ethnic tensions that often characterise modern South African politics. Perhaps the best example of this, at present, centres around this north-eastern region. The EFF ('Economic Freedom Fighters') is a radical and frequently divisive Marxist–Leninist group led by Julius Malema, and dominated by the Sotho with its powerbase in Limpopo and this border region with Mpumulanga. This is Malema's homeland, and he is the archetype of the controversial African politician, convicted for anti-white hate speech among various other misdemeanours (to name some: singing 'shoot the Boer' in public, and repeatedly blurring the line between 'metaphor' and incitement to violence against the white population).[72]

Malema himself is a Northern Sotho, or Pedi. This 'ethnicity' seemed to me to encompass an incredibly diverse and complex group of linguistic communities. Thomas, although himself a Tsonga, agreed: 'What you see here and further north, what they are, are the Sotho of the Lowveld. It's hard to generalise, but most of the Sotho – from tribes like the Pulana and Kutswe – have been here for a long time. I mean, their families came here a long time ago.' Later, in the Kruger itself, I read about the Portuguese pioneer Joao Albasini, who purchased land from a Kutswe leader, Chief Magashula, in the 1840s.[73] That land is now familiar to thousands of safari-goers around the Phabeni gate.

By contrast, the Northern Sotho of the Highveld (the inland plateau around Gauteng) are, according to Thomas, immigrants from the west. I do not think he intended this to be a slight, more a factual comment, although it may have related to his perception that it was his group, the Tsonga, that were rightful custodians of this corner of the country. The reality, as so often, is that this part of Africa has seen waves of migrations for centuries. We are conditioned to think of population migrations as a Western phenomenon: in reality they occur globally, and have always occurred globally.

Thomas had two colleagues with him, who – apart from a gracious welcome – had not said much. While we spoke, I could see that one of them, a middle-aged woman called Colen, was getting agitated, clearly wanting to interrupt but unwilling to break Thomas's flow. It turned out that she was a member of EFF, Malemba's controversial party, but that she disagreed with Thomas's occasional attempts to marginalise other black South Africans, even other Tsonga speakers. I later contacted her via Facebook, where she was willing to elaborate: 'We speak of taking over the economy yet we are not united. We attack each other based on ethnicity each chance we get. One of my forever mistakes is thinking we are capable of forming a united front.' She claimed that, from her perspective, the EFF was all about 'sharing the struggle' and that attempts to divide, or even to discuss the 'ethnic' or linguistic make-up of South African communities was not only counterproductive, but continued to damage the country, and indeed an entire continent. 'This kind of thing sure brings out the hatred within us as black people, African people.'

Colen herself had immense faith, not just in her party and its leader, but in the concept of African unity encapsulated in Sontonga's anthem with its Welsh tune. She also, as I quickly discovered during our subsequent social media chats, put great faith in what Manuel Castells dubbed the 'network society' back in the 1990s.[74] Her relationship with media technology, made clear in our interactions on Facebook, defined the simultaneously global and local nature of movements like the EFF, or at least the way in which such movements mobilise their network via social media. She retained an optimism about the platforms that has faded in the post-Trump, post-Brexit Anglosphere. My take on it, after numerous interactions, was perhaps inevitably mixed. On the one hand, networked communication lent these activists real power to take on elite structures and attract wider attention; on the other hand, it frequently gave rise to 'group think' and, quite often, overt racism (some have accused the EFF of black supremacist tendencies and policies). Even a relatively superficial engagement with this kind of online debate reveals that any public sphere ideal, that of a neutral space for debate, often (but not always) degenerates into ad hominem abuse.

Any discussion about ethnicity in South Africa quickly reveals that Colen's idealism is not shared by all, but neither is it the case that linguistic and ethnic divisions are always perceived negatively or exclusively. Thomas, for example, answered my question about spoken language by saying that '100% indeed I speak Tsonga. I'm a very proud Tsonga or changani or whatever word people wish to use to describe us.' Did he think the Tsonga were properly represented in modern South Africa? 'No, but I do my best to change that, personally, me. I am multilingual, I fit where ever I go in South Africa and I represent my people and my language. I'm not, never, ashamed of myself.' It is also true that, despite Colen's protestations to the contrary, the reality is that the EFF is not only occasionally overtly racist, but also has its powerbase very firmly located in Limpopo, despite its theoretically all-encompassing Marxist–Leninist philosophy.

Thomas continued the theme, perhaps conscious that he had portrayed himself initially as a Tsongan patriot – he suddenly seemed keen to emphasise his South African pride and idealism: 'Why do you think there are 11 official languages in South Africa? Can any other country, anywhere in the world, say such a thing?' But he also took issue with criticism of Malema, linking it (as many do) to Jacob Zuma, often disliked in this north-eastern region because of his Zulu powerbase. As Thomas put it: 'Before we talk about Malema, what about Zuma, the ultimate Zulu nationalist? Or Mbeki?' Thabo Mbeki, one of the most high-profile and globally renowned post-apartheid figures, was frequently critical of what he sometimes saw as Zuma's Zulu imperialism. But Mbeki himself, according to Thomas, also surrounded himself with fellow Xhosa speakers from his eastern Cape homelands. This particular clique was sometimes dubbed, rather brilliantly, the 'Xhosa Nostra'. One clue to the regional success of the EFF might be contained within the reality that every post-apartheid president of South Africa has been either a Zulu or a Xhosa; it is easy to exploit the resentment that naturally results.

It was hard to know precisely where Thomas Shivambu stood on these issues, as he frequently backtracked from some of his more outré statements, clearly conscious of their implications and potency. In essence, his pro-Tsonga position was a reasonable one, which revolved around the fact that the Tsonga present a less unified face than the Zulu or Xhosa, and are less well known beyond the boundaries of South Africa. This clearly rankled, and he defined the issue in local terms, observing that 'we don't have a homeland to call their own', meaning that the bantustans of modern Limpopo and Mpumulanga, and subsequently this particular township of Bushbuckridge, never had a majority Tsonga population. Indeed, such is the sprawling nature of Bushbuckridge that it encompassed three different bantustans during the apartheid era and, even today, it is a truly dizzying amalgam of different tribes and linguistic groups, tiny exclaves and a complex and fascinating demography. In the 37 wards within it, no one language dominates: numerous wards speak the northern variety of the Sotho language, numerous wards speak Tsonga, one or two speak Swazi, Sotho and Zulu.[75] Even by South African standards, the diversity of this part of Mpumulanga is truly startling. Instead, from Shivambu's perspective, and as he was at pains to point out, the Tsonga are distributed 'everywhere', meaning that exclusivity is likely to be even more disastrous in South Africa than it is elsewhere.

For an example of a unified group, he suggested I try visiting the Swazi (often called SiSwati), which – after a three-night sojourn in the vastly contrasting Kruger, shorn of all ethnic tension, indeed shorn of its human population – is where I travelled next.

***

The spiritual home of the Swazi encompasses more than just the landlocked state of Swaziland itself: the three million or so SiSwati-speaking peoples span both sides of the border. I had arranged some meetings with journalists in the border town of Barberton, and had booked into what looked like a fascinating guesthouse on the edge of the town, where its outer suburbs run out of flat building plots before the land rises steeply to the

133

Makhonjwa mountains, which continue all the way to the Swazi border.

But before heading to Barberton, I wanted to visit Swaziland itself, so I took the long road to the Josefsdal border crossing, which lies on a broad mountain pass. This had been resurfaced: until recently, it was a rutted track suitable only for four-wheel drives; now it is immensely civilised. It feels like driving in Switzerland, and the wonderful mountain scenery does little to quell that illusion. But, just minutes after leaving Barberton it gradually dawned on me that there was something very strange about the route. The border post is clearly indicated on all signs, but the road is so extraordinarily quiet that it feels like a 40-kilometre private drive on the smoothest tarmac imaginable. South African roads are rarely very busy, and usually in good condition (indeed, motoring is one of the unheralded joys of the country), but this was downright weird.

Not only weird, but a combination of factors meant that it suddenly became unexpectedly worrying. I had left Graskop that morning, and stopped in a petrol station for provisions: the classic South African snack of beef biltong, as well as a dozen apples, and a Mozambican/Portuguese hybrid sandwich known as a 'prego'. I am usually in the habit of filling a three-litre bottle of water before I begin any long drive, particularly when it is 40°C degrees in the shade. But, as I stopped to enjoy my lunch at a viewpoint overlooking the De Kaap valley, I realised I had left the bottle in Graskop. Suddenly, the prospect of a drive through uninhabited semi-desert mountains, at midday in a ferocious summer drought, along a completely empty road, did not seem quite so attractive. I told myself that I would have to hope something was open on the Swazi side, although this was more for psychological reasons than any realistic conviction.

Above, a jackal buzzard wheeled, black and white tail feathers etched on the deep blue of the sky. No clouds. The heat of this unusually extreme start to the Transvaal season had begun to dissipate while I was in Limpopo, but was now starting to build again, as if steeling itself for a final blast before the summer rains arrived. It was now early afternoon and about as hot as it gets in this region as I began to climb into the Makhonjwa mountains: a dry and dusty 40°C with the road visibly starting to buckle as the tarmac melted; suggesting it might not remain in its current state of Swiss smoothness for long.

The drought had already lasted months, the radio news bulletins were full of it. Water shortages throughout Mpumulanga, hosepipe bans in Gauteng, restrictions on daily intake, spokesmen urging restraint: it was getting desperate across the country. As was I. Luckily, I had a survival strategy; that bag full of leftover apples bought from the petrol station from which I began to suck the moisture.

The journey back to Barberton was one possibility. But I was committed to crossing the Swazi border at Josefsdal: it seemed such an unusual and appealingly remote way of reaching it. And finally, after 40 kilometres without passing a single car, person or house, and with no mobile signal throughout, a collection of two or three buildings marked the border at the top of the pass. These were the first signs of life that I had seen in over an hour, but I still couldn't see a human being; it was extraordinarily quiet as I turned the engine off and looked around for somebody to let me out of South Africa.

I wrote at the time: 'This must be the quietest border crossing on earth, so quiet that it allows for the unprecedented phenomenon of "Border guard banter".' I checked the ledger on the South African side: two cars had passed through the border before me that day; or was it the day before? I had never seen anything like it: both sides of the border were absurdly tranquil, yet fully staffed (although none of the staff were foolish enough to be outside in the midday sun, which was one reason for the silence).

Nothing came, nothing went. A female border guard approached me after I had received my South African exit stamp, languid and immaculately dressed in blue shirt with ponytail and cap, obviously amused by the single unkempt man in a hired Hyundai, and asked me to open the boot. 'Is that fruit?' she enquired, a hint of a smile on her face, indicating the bag full of apples I was using to hydrate myself. She asked for one, ate it, then waved me through after asking me why I was going to Swaziland (the subtext: why now, at this precise moment, in the heat of the midday sun during a damaging country-wide heatwave? You are ruining my siesta). A short section of gated no-man's land separates the South African side from the Swazi border, flanked by enormous fences topped with rotating spikes. But this is high in the Mkhonjwa mountains, with steep-sided peaks rising all around and very little water: not an obvious place for desperate economic migrants to pass through.

After a few minutes of driving down this eerie deserted road, surprisingly lengthy for a section of no-man's land, with those high fences and deliberately planted pine trees blocking the views on all sides, the entrance to the home of the Swazi people is marked by a truly dilapidated manned border post. The man tasked with raising the single barrier into the country (no automation here) was dressed in an open-topped white shirt and fast asleep under a metal awning. He was literally asleep, not resting or escaping the midday sun with a half-hearted siesta; I had to rev the engine to wake him up. To his left, a cow wandered past the Swazi 'traffic information' sign (pictured on p. 173). You know the sort of thing: when you pass into Germany from France, say, a series of symbols outlines the subtly altered set of traffic laws, speed limits and the like, by way of universally understood semantic conventions. Here in Swaziland, the sign was comically battered and indistinct, just a faded notice not to exceed 70kph, a hilarious – possibly deliberately ironic – injunction given the state of the roads in Hhohho province. The grass below it was literally being grazed by farm animals, the text almost entirely illegible.

The border post itself was as delightfully civilised as the South African side, not unrelated to the fact that, again, it was staffed almost entirely by women. Inside, a huge picture of the Swazi king in ceremonial dress, a box of free condoms, and a handy pictorial guide to the nation and its customs. Swaziland itself is, famously, an absolute monarchy: one of just a handful in the modern world (Brunei, Oman and Saudi Arabia are really the only other examples, although by different measures the UAE, Qatar and the Vatican City qualify for this extremely dubious accolade). I had always equipped myself with ammunition for pub quizzes by adding Bhutan and Tonga to that list, but they have both apparently reformed in recent years. King (more properly Ngwenyama, which means 'lion' in Swazi) Mswati III, he of the posed photograph at the border post, has been 'in post' since 1986, and comes from the Dlamini clan, as must all Swazi monarchs, which immediately renders the country less than transparent in terms of its leadership recruitment process (although our own Saxe-Coburg-Gothas are recruited in precisely the same way). The affection for him seems genuine, although the reality is that the rulers are privileged people in what remains a desperately poor country, even by African standards, with the lowest life expectancy in the world (just under 50). Mswati is worth an estimated $200 million and drives a fleet of DaimlerChrysler Maybach 62 cars, each worth at least half a million dollars. The monarchs have become marginally more liberal in recent years, but this is, of course, relative: that said, Mswati has a mere 13 wives, far more modest than his predecessor's 125.[76]

Regardless of the system of government, my problems were more immediate and connected to the road surface which, in a hired Korean saloon car (not a DaimlerChrysler Maybach 62) posed serious problems. The road degenerates instantly, straight after the border post, and is little more than a potholed trench and alarmingly steep as it descends towards Bulembu. My Hyundai, which I had already tested to destruction on the gravel and dirt tracks of the Kruger national park, began to struggle – weaving round the deep potholes became impossible as I approached the village and the implications of a puncture (or worse) in this remote spot, far from call-out garages or the scope of insurance claims, did not bear thinking about.

Bulembu is, however, a surprise: at least at first glance. A planned community and an experiment in low carbon, environmentally sustainable living – which is why I had wanted to cross the border at this point in the first place. It struck me as a kind of idealised African future, albeit perhaps seeing it from a hopelessly Eurocentric perspective. But it certainly seemed to be a model that works: neat houses, extraordinary tranquillity, an intrinsic appeal to a manageably small number of tourists.

The downhill drive from the border post, just a few miles, had taken at least 20 minutes, considerably slower than my usual walking place. The potholes were cavernous, sometimes merging to form one giant road-width pothole, the surface virtually non-existent. But my car had made it, and I pulled over outside what looked like a conference centre, incongruous and perched below Emlembe, Swaziland's highest peak, which bestrides the border with South Africa.

I was hungry, and wandered round the entirely deserted building. Later, I found the colonial hotel (called, with some inevitability by its British originators, the 'Country Lodge'). I sat in manicured gardens after ordering 'French toast' in the restaurant, which – along with all the buildings, apparently converted managers' houses from the old mining days – was completely deserted. Two charming assistants served me as I relaxed in front of a wonderful view of jacarandas and, beyond, Emlembe.

The local Swazi are a little reticent about discussing the history of the town, I discovered. My eye had been drawn by the rows of neat terraced bungalows spread over the hillside across the valley on the drive from the border. After lunch, I walked through the village, which sprawls across a steep valley, and headed up to those terraces. Most of the bungalows were completely abandoned, and the reasons for this, as well as the unusual feel of the place more generally, gradually became apparent as I pieced together fragments of evidence during my stay.

The town was built around a chrysotile mine, founded in the late 1930s and still extant until going bankrupt in 2001. After this catastrophic economic meltdown, combined with additional factors (not least, AIDS), Bulembu (once a thriving 10,000 strong) was decimated, with just a handful of people remaining (and this in a country with one of the highest HIV infection rates on earth at this time). I had never heard the word 'chrysotile' before, and it was only back in South Africa that I discovered it is essentially the most commonly occurring form of asbestos. At once, the reluctance of locals to discuss the town's recent history became clear.[77]

I walked back to the lodge to find the same ultra-helpful waiter, George. When I asked him about Bulembu, he did not say much beyond 'nice place, boss', and pointed me to a brochure which outlined the vision behind the new, revived community. As I had suspected, it was essentially an idealistic (and admirable) experiment which acknowledges the economic and environmental devastation wrought by the mine and instead tries to find sustainable solutions to Swaziland's problems. Bulembu seemed to be a kind of model that could be rolled out in the rest of the country – although that was not directly articulated, it did seem to be the subtext behind the brochure, which had a tendency to universalise the town, as if it formed that potential gilded future for the rest of Swaziland. Next day, as I sat on the lawn outside the lodge, drinking tea below the purple flowers of a jacaranda tree, its idyllic isolation, high up in these border mountains of Hhohho above the beautiful Komati valley, seemed perfect for such an 'experiment'.

You would never suspect, wandering round the town, that, not only were you in one of the poorest countries on earth, but that the AIDS crisis in Swaziland was so bad in the 1990s and well beyond, that over 40% of the population is now infected with HIV and a nationwide orphan crisis continues to devastate communities across the country.[78] You would also never suspect that Bulembu was once the site of an asbestos mine which had a predictably devastating effect on the health of those unfortunate enough to have worked in it, as well as the community as a whole: indeed, I had no idea myself until I was safely removed from it. Neither the brochure, nor George, made any reference to it. And despite the frequency of references to 'sustainability', it was never linked to the mine, although it made perfect sense when I was finally able to join the dots back in South Africa.

***

The Swazi people themselves transcend the border. My initial plan had been to drive further into Swaziland from Bulembu, but I was forced to give up this idea just a few miles down the road to the less than alluringly named village Pigg's Peak, the next community on from Bulembu, as the road was literally impassable, it had been damaged by flooding almost half a year before. So after a couple of days enjoying the extraordinary tranquillity of Bulembu I crossed back into South Africa.

Although descended from a range of different Nguni clan backgrounds, the contemporary Swazi are united by language. All speak SiSwati, regardless of whether they come from Swaziland itself, or the neighbouring part of Mpumulanga where I now based myself. All seem loyal to the concept of the monarchs Ingwenyama (the 'lion', or the king) and Indlovukati (the rather wonderfully named 'she elephant', or Queen Mother).

'Xhosa Nostra'

Their language, SiSwati, is divided into numerous dialects, hardly surprising given the region's complex topography, as well as the fact that the three million strong community is divided in two by the political boundary separating Swaziland from South Africa. The centrality of the language to Swazi identity is obvious to anybody spending time in Swazi lands on either side of the border, and was emphasised in 2018, when the Swazi monarch changed the name of his country to eSwatini – finally removing the colonial overtones to the Swaziland moniker (eSwatini means the same thing, land of the Swazis, but in the native tongue rather than English).[79] The name change echoes other post-colonial changes but took people by surprise as it came so 'late', long after throwing off the imperial yoke. Botswana, by way of comparison, changed its name from the colonial Bechuanaland as soon as it gained its independence. It seems possible that the delay might have had something to do with those varied dialects, as well as the fact that the Swazi people themselves transcend the border, so 'home of the Swazis' will always be a somewhat contentious way of referring to the country. There is, apparently, a 'pure' form of the language spoken in the north; or at least that is what people in Bulembu said. This seemed to me to echo 'High' and 'Low' German – the prestigious standard form and the bastardised form.

In Barberton, where I ended up, the local Swazi people spoke a fairly standard version of the language but with (I was told) a distinctive intonation and rhythm; a distinction that reflected their origins, separated from the 'home' of their people.

I had arranged to stay outside the town in what was essentially an annexe to a private home. Directions were obscure, and involved a long drive up a single track lane towards a dirt track. This punished my car almost as much as the roads in Swaziland had, and led to the annexe, which was completely isolated with its own land and a private verandah: I had the place to myself.

Barberton itself was a surprise: I had been expecting a sleepy colonial town, bungalows and manicured lawns. But in fact the local Swazi lend a vibrant edge to the place, which I discovered on inadvertently walking into a shebeen[xii] on a quest to get a bottle of wine with which to relax on my verandah that evening. Inside, riotous scenes, with dozens of men in an advanced state of inebriation despite the hour (mid-afternoon, with the sun high in the sky). I later found out that many of these men were Mozambican migrants illegally working on the edge of the town, and the full story behind this became apparent later that first evening.

After being unceremoniously ejected from the shebeen (they are not generally places for white tourists, no matter how adventurous or open to new experiences you might be) I finally procured a bottle of red at a nearby off-licence, which I had missed on my first walk round town. As I sat on the verandah with a glass of Pinotage, shirt off as the weather became intensely humid, even though dusk was falling over the De Kaap valley, I became aware of a persistent banging sound, fairly distant but rhythmic. It was unexpected, jarring in this tranquil spot, even slightly disturbing. Then, another, closer this time – almost in parallel to the first. The banging, not quite rhythmic enough to be from a machine, but almost too regular to be human, then continued for hours. I knew that Barberton was a gold-mining town but it was not until the next morning, when I went for a walk into the hills above my 'house' that I discovered the link.

---

xii South African shebeens were originally a response to apartheid-era restrictions which prevented black Africans from entering bars. Typically, they sold home-brewed alcohol and were often run by women. They are now legal, although they continue to play an important cultural and social role in the community. Interestingly, given the subject of this book, the word 'shebeen' derives from Irish Gaelic, meaning illicit whiskey.

Rounding a corner in what I presumed to be virtual wilderness, high above the edge of the town, I saw a man with deep bloodshot eyes carrying a pickaxe over his shoulder. He had an orange bucket strapped to his waist and his blue overalls were covered in a reddish dust. Gold miners! The sounds suddenly made sense.

Later, the owner of the property came up to the annexe to introduce himself. Tim had British ancestry but was, entirely informal, deeply committed to his community (and, as I would go on to discover, the entire continent). There is, unavoidably, an echo sometimes a faint whiff of colonialism to this outlook, the idea of 'putting something back' seems linked at some level to a kind of patrician superiority. But perhaps it is better to suspend the cynicism and see it as an unambiguously positive progression from concentrating on exploiting mineral resources.

The heat was building yet again and the next evening was just as stifling, close and humid. From the verandah, I watched the sun set over the mountains and the broad valley beyond. But, as it got dark, the beauty and tranquillity of the scene was marred – not by the tap-tap-tap of pickaxes this time – but by a vivid glow of white light directly below, on the edge of Barberton. It looked like floodlights over a football or cricket pitch: indeed, that is what I initially took it to be. But after a while I realised that it was far too extensive for that; a glow was cast over a large section of the entire town.

'Oh, that's just the township,' said Tim, as we shared a glass of Pinotage. 'The lights are an anti-crime measure, they stay on all night. You get used to it.'

Earlier in the evening, I felt a pang of envy for Tim's family as I watched the three young children playing in the garden with the children of an Afrikaaner single father who arrived later to stay the night in the other rooms of the annexe, giving me some lively company for a change. 'Blind snake!' the youngest boy cried excitedly at one point. Their relationship with the natural world was genuine and completely unforced. True, their father was a wildlife guide specialising in small-group tours to the Kruger (renting this bungalow was just a sideline for him and his British wife, Emma). But these children clearly derived pleasure from monitoring the species around their home; Tim had set up a camera trap at a distant point in the garden and had recorded all manner of species over the past few years. The snake was small, I would never have noticed it, but we all went over to take a look and Tim proudly confirmed that his young son's identification skills were developing nicely – it was indeed a blind snake. So, I began to idealise this lifestyle: for a carefree, nature-centric child's life entirely removed from Xboxes and iPhones, my own children's indoor diversions of choice. Instead, these kids were plugged in to the natural world in an admirable way.

But now, looking out over the 'township', imagining life there, whilst listening to the insistent tapping of the pickaxes (it had started again, around 8pm this time) wielded by desperate Mozambican migrants on the hillside directly above, pools of light suggesting they worked through the night, I had second thoughts. My offspring may be urbanised and divorced from nature, but I do not have barbed wire round my house, or grilles on the windows, and I am not kept awake by security lights or the sound of illegal mine workings.

***

Again, though, there are plenty of traps for the unwary observer of South African life and culture; it pays not to make too many assumptions. 'The last thing the Mozambican migrants want is to draw attention to themselves,' said Tim. The sounds were annoying, and the presence of desperate men unnerving, he admitted, but 'they've never given us the slightest bit of trouble'. I believed him, although the issue clearly played on his mind, as it frequently cropped up in conversation during my stay.

Indeed, the next morning he told me, sotto voce, that he had helped bring an injured miner down from the hillside the week before. They had been sitting around their 'braai' in the evening when they heard a commotion from the hillside. An argument among the miners. Tim had walked up the hillside, unnerved again given its proximity. He had lived in Angola as a teen so spoke a bit of Portuguese:[xiii] one of the miners had fallen in what are hideously dangerous shafts, re-opened illegally and jerry-built. He was being carried down the hillside on a makeshift stretcher, it seemed possible that he had broken his back.

Tim's anecdotal account of this accident, and the lives of the Mozambicans more generally, seemed to say something profound about the nature of migration and the movement of labour. It is frequently framed as a local problem, in the sense that people are concerned about its impact on their respective countries: listening to the media in Britain, one could be forgiven for thinking that every migrant on Earth has but one desired destination. It is actually, of course, inescapably global – alongside climate change, perhaps the biggest global political issue of the twenty-first century.

I later found that many of Barberton's residents had a real issue with the Mozambicans in the mines – one of the reasons why Tim was probably right, they kept a deliberately low profile and kept themselves apart from some of the shebeens

xiii As a former colony, Portuguese remains a lingua franca in Mozambique – although as in most of sub-Saharan Africa, the majority of people speak indigenous languages through choice. In Mozambique, Portuguese is more common in urban areas, as in the other Lusophone African countries of Angola and Guinea-Bissau. In fact, most of the Mozambicans in Barberton are Tsonga from the south of the country, and spoke XiTsonga, in common with the Bushbuckridge residents mentioned earlier in this chapter, another indication of the way in which linguistic and cultural realities transcend colonial boundaries in Africa.

in town, let alone the few wealthy white residents living higher up with their far-reaching views over the De Kaap valley. As is usually the case with desperate migrants, the Mozambicans made a convenient scapegoat for impoverished locals. The Swazi had little natural affinity with them and regarded them as an unwelcome, alien and potentially criminal element – rather like the Roma are viewed in Western Europe.

Indeed, migration into South Africa provides a form of unity for its less tolerant politicians. We may be linguistically diverse, runs this version of populism, but at least we are unified by our common supranational identity as South Africans. The subtext (sometimes covert, sometimes overt) is that migrants from Mozambique, Zimbabwe and beyond are merely exploiting our tolerance and (relatively) high standards of living. It is an obvious truism to observe that such sentiments are globally all-too-common in the contemporary world with its internal fractures and massive movements of population. The pre-eminent European point of comparison may well be Italy: famously regional, famously divided by internal variations in dialect and cultural practice, but 'unified' by unscrupulous populist politicians attempting to exploit a latent distrust of the huge recent wave of migration to the country from Africa and the Middle East. Fortunately, in Italy as elsewhere, tolerance tends to prevail for the majority.

CHAPTER 7
MOLDOVAN FRONTLINE:
TRACING THE MARGINS OF THE
USSR'S LATIN OUTPOST

Handing over one's passport to a border guard who is not really a border guard, at a border post that is not really a border post, to enter a country that is not really a country, gives one pause for thought.

I will be more specific: it is deeply disconcerting, troubling, borderline scary. But the process of gaining entry into the phantom country of Transdniestria is never likely to be a reassuring experience. Control freaks would be well advised to give it a wide berth: your documents will be removed for some time, and you are in effect deliberately placing yourself beyond the normal channels of diplomacy when you cross that chimerical border.

As the only foreigner on a shared minibus, I had been marched outside and taken to a small white building, somewhere between bungalow and builders' shed in architectural style, when we reached the border. I noticed the Russian flag on the guard's sleeve as he took the passport out of sight into a back room. Time passed slowly: it is a dreadful cliché, but it always does in such circumstances, and it really is true that you develop a kind of hyper-awareness of your surroundings, noticing the spider climbing the wall of the office, the dried-up potted plant, the tobacco smoke rising in curls from the bored young man doing some filing at the back.

The diesel engine of my 'marshrutka' (Russian for shared minibus, a form of transport still common across the former Soviet Union) continued to splutter over, belching noxious fumes. That was good. I had been assured that marshrutkas normally wait for any foreigners foolish enough to cross the border independently, although my source (who was the receptionist at my Chisinau hotel) had estimated numbers of those independent foreigners at 'several' a week, which was hardly reassuring. For a few moments I was helpless, away from my only means of transport, and outside the reach of embassies without a passport, until – at last – the guard slid it back towards me with the tiniest of grunts, along with a digitised strip of paper outlining my name, nationality, and the precise time of entry – as well as the exact second that I had to leave by.

Foreigners do not get much time in Transdniestria, which would almost certainly win any notional pub debate about the most obscure and unexplored corners of Europe. Its continuing obscurity is a little puzzling these days, however, as its very existence speaks to a much broader truth about contemporary geopolitics. It is, in short, significant.

It is not an exaggeration to say that the border that I was passing through is the frontline between what we still refer to as 'the West', the European world represented on its outer fringes here by the sovereign state of Moldova, and the sphere of Putin's Russia. Not quite a new 'Iron Curtain', but instead a cultural fault-line rather like the one running through eastern Ukraine, stirred up and exploited by Putin's regime, with a blend of official Russian troops on the ground, and shadowy versions of the same thing (flags on sleeves have a tendency to give the game away, as do giant flags painted on border bridges). It is also a cultural fault-line that is widening, not narrowing, and as a result my visit seemed unusually well timed coming, as it did, not long after two epoch-defining events driven by identity politics: the UK's vote for Brexit and the Russian annexation of Crimea, not far away across the plains of Bessarabia.

Some context is probably necessary at this stage: Transdniestria is, formally and legally speaking, part of Moldova. Moldova itself was once one of the stranger corners of the former Soviet Union and remains one of the least known and least visited countries in Europe even before its two most notable geopolitical quirks, Transdniestria in the east and Gagauzia to the south, are added to the mix. Its people are, essentially, Romanians, with all that implies: they are Latin, not Slavic, with a taste for the finer things in life and a Romance language that finds echoes in Italian and French. Transdniestria (the country on 'the other side' of the Dniester river – there are several alternative ways of spelling its name in the Roman alphabet) always had a majority Russian population, however. While that population was happy enough in the old Soviet Union, even if it was as part of its strangest Latin outpost, the break-up of that Union changed their outlook. They had been comfortable as a minority within the Soviet Moldovan SSR but wanted no part of an independent Moldova, seeing it as a direct threat to their linguistic and cultural identity, and also seeing a risk – as they perceived it – of Moldovan 'reunification' with Romania. Language was absolutely central to this, with the Roman alphabet swiftly introduced by the Moldovans, and the prospect of Russian losing its status as an official language of the country. Following a brief conflict in 1994, which went almost unnoticed in the wider world, distracted as it was at the time by more noticeable upheavals following the collapse of Communism, Transdniestria declared unilateral independence from Moldova and became, de facto, a separate state.

That state remains phantom, however, unrecognised by almost every nation on earth (there are some exceptions, although those exceptions tend themselves to be in the same geopolitical trap – Abkhazia and South Ossetia, for example). Like those entities, and the better known Eastern Ukraine, an uneasy Transdniestrian peace is kept by a trilateral force, including Russian and Russian-backed forces who blur the boundaries between formal and phantom, lending the border area a surreal feel, with its hidden tanks and ominous warning signs. And, like Eastern Ukraine, Transdniestria represents that fundamental ideological frontline between Putin's sphere of Russian influence, and the European, Western-facing world. As outliers of a much larger community, their marginal status is fused to a sense of bombastic Russian pride, rather like that of some Sri Lankan Tamils – minorities where they live, but always conscious of their status as fringe members of a much larger whole. Often, this tends to make the brand of patriotism simultaneously defensive and aggressive; a potentially dangerous combination when threatened.

I left the white bungalow masquerading as a border post and rejoined my marshrutka, which now drove off into the buffer zone which remains on the 'Moldovan' side of the Dniester. This was established in 1992: the only part of Transdniestria on the right bank of the river. Almost immediately, the outer suburbs of Bender are reached: its unusual name deriving from its earlier occupation by the Ottoman Turks.

Bender's ambience is distinctive, and particularly noticeable as it is encountered immediately after crossing the border. The Moldovan side has that characteristic feel of a down-at-heel Eastern European country, potholed roads, litter, peasant farms and rural shacks. But Bender is very different. *The Truman Show* movie kept coming to mind as I wandered round its manicured streets, disconcerted at the eerie cleanliness, lack of traffic, and seemingly coordinated silence. Slightly dazed by it all, I wandered into a large branch of the 'Sheriff' supermarket on the edge of the city centre: the shop was entirely devoid of people, but stocked with shelves of exceptional, high quality produce from across the former Soviet Union. Expensive brandies (row after row of Klimt, the locally produced brand, which is excellent and justifiably famous across the region), smoked salmon, caviar: all immaculately presented above polished floors. Nobody wandered the aisles, which were unbelievably clean, with marble tiles that gleamed.

My thoughts kept wandering back to the film: the supermarket looked staged, completely false, as if nobody ever bought any of these products, that they were all just for show. As if one person – an unwitting part of a wider drama – would be led into the shop at any moment, smiling inanely at the goods on offer, like a Slavic Jim Carrey.

A little booth offered me the chance to swap my Moldovan Leu for some rubles. Inevitably, Transdniestria has its own phantom currency, and a potted history of this currency provides a convenient micro-guide to the oddness of the place itself. When the 'republic' was first established in 1994, it began to use old Soviet notes – which had flooded the place after newly independent ex-Soviet countries like the Baltic States and the Central Asian 'stans' cemented their independence by issuing their own banknotes. In an effort to maintain 'Russian-ness', it seemed an obvious decision to keep using the Soviet rubles – so the Transdniestrians fixed an adhesive sticker of Suvorov (the founder of Tiraspol) to the back, and hey presto, a new currency was created from old banknotes. What could be simpler?

Sadly, this did not go entirely to plan: inflation quickly sky-rocketed as a partial result of the enclave's isolation, and a 500,000 ruble note became necessary. New rubles were introduced at the turn of the millennium, but there was a problem: Transdniestria did not have its own Mint. And, as an unrecognised country, it could not ask neighbouring countries for help as to do so would imply 'recognition' of this formally unrecognised state. Eventually, and somewhat surprisingly given the political climate at that time, the Polish Mint in Warsaw stepped in: coins were struck in Warsaw and transported through Ukraine to Transdniestria. The Moldovan government, enraged at this tacit acceptance of the breakaway republic's status, complained – to which the Poles responded that they were merely producing 'tokens', not coins, because Transdniestria was not an independent state.

This must have been a rather weak excuse, because Ukrainian customs – keen to support fellow ex-Soviet allies against this rebel Russian, Soviet-tinged outlier – seized thousands of Transdniestrian coins as they passed through the country, handing them over to the Moldovans. It threatened to turn into an international incident, with the reputation of Poland as a fully-fledged independent European state at stake. The contract was duly cancelled, and a Mint was later opened in Tiraspol itself.[80] The machinations, twists and turns inherent within this little tale encapsulate the difficulties of maintaining 'independent' status while remaining unrecognised by all your neighbours: it is not easy.

As a result, it is impossible not to have some grudging admiration for this weird little place, even if you are made slightly queasy by the twenty-first century version of Russian populist patriotism that it seems to embody at times (although – in yet another bizarre twist – the creator, lodestone and personification of that unpleasant brand, Putin himself, does not 'officially' recognise it either).

Apart from the currency, Transdniestria's flag is an even more overt hymn to Soviet nostalgia. If the hammer and sickle was not enough, a red star graces the top left hand corner, and the green and red bands directly mimic the original flag of the Moldovan Socialist Republic – of which, you'll remember, Transdniestria was very comfortable being a part. It is the independent Moldova which is not quite so much to its taste, and the Moldovan state whose flag it refuses to fly (you will not find its characteristic yellow, blue and red anywhere once you cross the border).

In a place like Transdniestria, symbolism becomes crucially important. Flags are the most obvious manifestation of this and, in an act that was both telling and amusing, the government passed a motion in 2017 to make the Russian tricolour (with an undetectably minute adjustment to the colour ratio) its 'second flag'. This followed an earlier referendum in which 97% of the population voted in favour of closer ties with Moscow as a means of guaranteeing its independence from Moldova and, by extension, the Western world and the European Union.

As ever with results of this kind in authoritarian countries, it is fascinating to speculate on the identities of the 3% voting against: might they be closet Romanian–Moldovan unionists? Undercover Europeans? Agents provocateurs?[81]

***

Given its proclivities, and its general ambience and appearance, it is easy to assume that Transdniestria must be some kind of Soviet throwback – a planned economy with strict controls over private enterprise. This, however, would be a mistake. Instead, it is a peculiar and possibly unique hybrid in which the Sheriff corporation acts as a kind of private-enterprise extension of the state, establishing a monopoly that has only very recently been challenged. Instead of state-run shops, Sheriff run the supermarkets. Instead of a state-built sports stadium, the huge complex I later passed in a second bus journey was built and is maintained by Sheriff (Moldova's best football team, FC Sheriff Tiraspol, play here and will be familiar to students of the outer fringes of European competition). The mobile phone network? That is controlled by Sheriff too.

There are very few advertisements visible, making the streets redolent of modern Cuba (the only contemporary comparison that my personal experience could come up with, although in all other respects the two are temperamental opposites, there is little live music in Tiraspol's bars, and exuberant hip gyration will not get you very far with the locals). Sheriff's virtual monopoly presumably renders advertising redundant – not so much a one-party state as a one-company state, and yet another reason *The Truman Show* kept coming to mind as I wandered the streets. Those who have seen the film will recall the Omnicam company as the ever-present corporate hand behind the wilder fringes of reality TV that the movie explores. The sci-fi writer Philip K. Dick covered similar terrain a lot earlier, in 1969, with *Ubik*. I was a big fan in my teenage years: Ubik (the 'ubiquitous company' of the title), begins each chapter advertising a different product, until the final chapter claims that it created the universe itself, and directs all events within it. It has been years since I gave the book much thought, but if there is one place guaranteed to bring it flooding back, it is Sheriff-dominated Transdniestria.

Across the road from Bender's Sheriff hypermarket is a huge war cemetery which serves two related functions: it is partly a commemoration of former Soviet glories, partly a commemoration of the short-lived violence ('the war of Transdniestria') which gave rise to the curious phenomenon of this country in 1992. The two fuse together in a celebration of Russian nationalism then-and-now: indeed, that chronological framework is crucial to the Transdniestrian's sense of themselves as an embattled minority sealed into their strip of land by forces beyond their control. The link with the Soviet past is best interpreted in that way – it is not necessarily nostalgia for the certainties of the Communist system (although there is an element of that, as there is elsewhere in the former USSR). But there definitely is a nostalgia for the Russian-dominated reality that the era represented, or, being more charitable, a nostalgia for the notion that a single powerful ideology could hold different peoples together. Concepts like this are always more appealing if you find yourself in the majority, of course, not always quite so appealing if you see it as a threat to your identity and language.

Transdniestria as a whole is a treat for those nostalgic for the symbolism and urban ambience of the former Soviet Union. The Soviet nostalgia (paralleled in what the Germans call 'Ostalgie') goes way beyond the usual wistfulness here, and the architecture of Transdniestria remains frozen in aspic as a result: it is all wide boulevards, brutalist buildings and Communist statues perfectly maintained by enthusiastic civic workers. One of the most notable of these statues is round the corner from the Soviet railway station in Bender (itself a perfect example of its kind, completely unchanged and advertisement-free – I was warned not to take pictures within, as shadowy guards with huge brimmed hats patrolled the empty platform). A bright green Lenin stands in a park opposite the Soviet cinema, his hand raised in characteristic pose. I've seen similar examples everywhere from Bishkek to Kharkov, but there is one startling difference here: Lenin is green, a vivid shade of emerald green. On seeing the picture, a friend of mine commented that 'it looks like he's been carved from a gigantic bar of carbolic soap', which perfectly describes his verdant smoothness.

I continued to walk around the immaculate streets, and after leaving the railway station (the ambition inherent in the Soviet rail network is still discernible across the former USSR, from the most obscure outpost, like Bender, to the grandeur of Kharkov, Kiev and Moscow) I entered a street pockmarked with bullets, with one long building in a state of near-collapse, vegetation devouring the internal walls. This was jarring and puzzling amidst the generally immaculate streets, and it reminded me of provincial Bosnian towns like Jablanica, where civic restoration has not yet got round to filling in the shell damage and bullet holes. Violence in Bender, and the rest of the entity was short-lived and not remotely comparable to the Balkans, but I was later told that this street was deliberately left in this condition, like the General Post Office in Dublin, its bullet holes sacred and untouchable reminders of the Easter Rising.

***

After leaving the town of Bender, I got a second marshrutka for the short journey to Tiraspol, the entity's capital and by far its biggest city. The bus crossed the militarised zone, an everyday occurrence for the other passengers but an unusual one for me, with camouflaged 'Russian' troops wielding guns and more than one armoured car. Barricades were present on the 'Moldovan' side of the river, along with abundant graphic instructions clarifying that photography was banned. I was not tempted, even when I spied a Russian tank hidden below camouflaged netting: the price of an interesting Instagram post seemed likely to be a night (or several) in the cells. Once on the bridge itself, over the Dniester, I immediately saw what must have been a precursor to the 'flag decision', the ultimate in pro-Russian sentiment: the large arched iron bridge is painted red and green on one side, and red, white and blue on the other: the flags of independent Transdniestria and the 'mother country' side by side in everlasting unity.

On the 'left bank' was that huge sports stadium, the home of Sheriff Tiraspol and perhaps the best example of the bizarre influence this company has in the republic. For obvious reasons, the Moldovan national team cannot play there – and are forced instead to play at Zimbru's ground, a dilapidated and small venue on the outskirts of Chisinau. In fact, Wales played there in a World Cup qualifier shortly after my visit.

***

'Would you like some Moldovan olives?' asked a man in the immaculate central market in Tiraspol. He spoke in perfect English, one eyebrow raised and a hint of a smile on his lips. The 'Moldovan olives' were actually walnuts, giant ones, so unfeasibly big that I would never have identified them as such. 'These are the best nuts in the world,' he added with, I felt, a hint of double entendre. The market seemed to encapsulate the paradox of Transdniestria: on the one hand, it was piled high with opulent and superb produce, boasting spanking new green stalls, a computerised system of bookings, and produce charts far more sophisticated – and much more appealing – than my local market at home. Indeed, in some corners of the market, specialists gathered: honey stalls here, walnut stores there, all peddling slight variants on a theme, and in that sense it reminded me of a high-end farmers' market in the UK or New England.

On the other hand, however, it was simultaneously redolent of old Russia, the former Soviet Union, with babushkas selling mushrooms they had clearly gathered themselves, dressed in big hats and old coats, despite the warm September sunshine.

Those who enjoy a dash of quirky geopolitics when they travel will be enchanted by Tiraspol. Not for them the boulevards of Paris or the majesty of Venice: instead, the Transdniestrian tourist finds pleasure in the faded Soviet mural, or the giant billboard portrait of the latest pro-Russian populist to seek election. Indeed, it has become something of a pilgrimage for the very small number of adventurous travellers who are likely to be lured by the magnetic charge of visiting a phantom country which is filed alongside the likes of Northern Cyprus as an unrecognised state (although it is much harder to visit). Assuming the visitor enjoys this sort of thing, the attractions are endless: the Soviet memorabilia is ubiquitous, but my personal favourite 'sight' in Tiraspol is the double embassy of South Ossetia and Abkhazia. The two stand shoulder to shoulder in the centre of Tiraspol: the embassies of two unrecognised countries in the capital of an unrecognised country, their flags fluttering proudly, the yellow, red and white of South Ossetia, and the more striking Abkhazian flag made up of green and white stripes with a red inset and raised 'Ulster-style' hand, supposed to mean 'hello to friends!'

Keen observers of contemporary geopolitics will spot the link between all three entities. All of them are de facto independent, but not recognised by the rest of the world. All were once part of the Soviet Union, with the movement of population and legacy of diversity (linguistic, religious, cultural) that implies. All are propped up by Russia, and entirely dependent on it for their continued existence. And all lie formally on the territory of a pro-Western, Europe-leaning nation. Moldova in the case of Transdniestria, Georgia in the case of South Ossetia and Abkhazia.[82] I noticed that the embassies had bilingual signs – but that the Russian and Moldovan were both rendered in

Cyrillic, a telling detail because Moldovan is generally written in the Roman alphabet nowadays.

Unpicking the complexities of all these frozen conflicts would take some time; suffice to say that all three boil down to the same contemporary reality; a way in which the Putin regime can flex its muscles, subtly (or not so subtly) extend its influence whilst also reflecting a very real cultural distinctiveness that really does feel threatened by the Western direction of the state in which it finds itself. In other words, it is too trite to dismiss them entirely as figments of Putin's mischief making and manipulation, and also inaccurate to say that is not itself a significant factor.

Language is, again, the key. The Transdniestrians speak Russian, with a smaller minority of Moldovans. The Ossetians – who are essentially Orthodox Christian Iranians – speak Ossetian, not remotely related to Georgian, or indeed any living language, although it does have Eastern Iranian roots. As previously explored in this book's Caucasus chapter, the Abkhazians (of whom there are only around 200,000) speak Abkhaz, an Abazgi tongue characteristic of the ultra-linguistically diverse north-west Caucasus. There is even an Abkhaz diaspora across the Middle East and, as if that were not enough, three very distinct dialects of the language rejoicing in the names Bzyb, Sadz and Abzhywan.[83]

***

As opening conversational gambits go, 'my grandmother dated Yuri Gagarin' is pretty good. Svetia, who was responsible for it, was one of those quintessential products of the old Soviet Union. Chisinau born-and-bred; her first language was Russian, but she also spoke fluent Moldovan (which, as we've already established, is really Romanian). She was around a decade younger than me, in her late thirties. I had been put in touch with her by a mutual media contact – she combined PR work with Russian-language journalism in Moldova and beyond, and her mixed heritage gave her a wry and detached view on contemporary Moldovan politics.

The line about granny and Gagarin, which I suspected she had used numerous times before, arose because we had arranged to meet in a Ukrainian restaurant across the road from a famous statue of the ultimate Soviet space hero in Tiraspol. Apart from being amusing, and a great story, it was actually rather instructive – could there be a more effective way of semaphoring influence in the former USSR? It simultaneously implied a nostalgia for those days whilst also sending up the hypocrisy of a theoretically classless society that was as obsessed with networking and influence as anywhere else. Her family were archetypal products of the old Soviet Union; comfortable with their Russian identity, and yet still comfortable in the Moldovan SSR where they were surrounded by Romanians – moving seamlessly between the two languages.

Independence changed all that. While they had never been threatened by the new-found nationalism of the independent Moldovans, the old influence borne of those carefully cultivated contacts and the inbuilt advantages of being part of the Russian intelligentsia was gone. In its place came the need to scratch a living on the edge of the new Europe, and that meant that some awkward decisions had to be made by ethnic Russians in Chisinau.

'All of us pretend to be Romanians now anyway,' said Svetia. 'It doesn't matter whether we're Russian speaking or Moldovans going back generations, we all pretend to be Romanians.' I did not even need to ask the reason. We were in a taxi, and she knew the driver: a working-class Chisinau lad of Russian heritage. She turned to him to illustrate her point, and after a brief conversation in Russian she translated for me: it was clearly her way of explaining how universal the process was, not just a middle-class ploy by those who had the cultural capital to draw on. The driver was indeed changing his citizenship to Romanian, despite his Russian heritage and the fact that Moldovan/Romanian was not, and would never be, his language of choice. The process of gaining Romanian citizenship for people like him was, he explained through Svetia, rather tedious and complex although entirely feasible and therefore very common among his peers. Gaining that passport is an obvious and achievable 'holy grail' for young Moldovans of all linguistic backgrounds. As counterfeit 'Romanians' they become EU citizens, with all the rights of free movement that entails. Indeed, my Wizz Air flight from Luton to Chisinau had been packed with Moldovan migrant workers, almost all of whom seemed to be travelling under Romanian passports (I could not help noticing as I nosily looked around at the passport covers as we queued to get on the plane).

***

Moldova's geopolitical situation could hardly be more sensitive. First, there is the obvious geographical problem of isolation, tucked away, landlocked, in the most marginal corner of south-eastern Europe. Second, there are the minorities within it. This diversity is not unusual in itself – but what is unusual is the fact that both 'minorities' within Moldova look to, and are actively backed by, Putin's Russia to bolster their respective cases for self-determination, whether that be devolution, autonomy or effective independence. It is a classic example of Putin's tactics, to destabilise Europe, to encourage those opposed to west-facing EU-aspirant states. It is also a classic legacy of the Soviet state, which encouraged internal migration and the deliberate mixing of linguistic and ethnic groups. Idealistic and noble, in many ways, but never likely to pass smoothly through the revival of identity politics without destabilising newly independent states like Moldova, Georgia and Armenia.

If Transdniestria is the archetypal example, next on my Moldovan travel agenda came Gagauzia. If Transdniestria is an obscure corner of Europe, Gagauzia takes the pub quiz element up several notches. The Gagauz are the second group of separatists in Moldova, although there are few similarities between them and the Transdniestrians either in language and ethnicity, or the political reality of their 'autonomous' status. Unlike Transdniestria, the Gagauzian border is merely marked by a series of signs. These sit oddly in the flat, agricultural landscape of endless ploughed fields, but are hardly a barrier to entry, and are far removed from the tension and hostility of the Russian-patrolled border further east.

I had taken a morning marshrutka from Chisinau. These shared minibuses are now generally known as 'rutierele' in Moldova, an indication of the politics of language if ever there was one, as many people still describe them by their old Soviet (in other words, Russian) title. As with several of these Soviet-era terms across the region, the desire to assert independence extends to the translation of what were once multinational and universally understood descriptors, even if they were in a 'colonial' tongue (indeed, there have even been attempts by some on the Moldovan nationalist fringe to take this to the next level by claiming their language is entirely separate to Romanian, attempts dismissed as 'politically-motivated absurdity' by linguists[84]). Whatever the rutierele are called, they still serve as the main means of transport in most former Soviet countries: they are crowded and sometimes uncomfortable but they are also convenient and fast, assuming you can penetrate the complex inner workings of the systems.

The journey from Chisinau passes through typical pastoral Moldovan scenery, largely flat with low linear hills crossing the landscape at intervals, and interspersed with a few dried vineyards and wooden shacks. It is not the most exciting corner of Europe, physically, and in some ways it is strange that such a flat landscape should mask such an intriguing level of cultural diversity. But even if the landscape had been more exciting, I would have struggled on this journey – because travelling by marshrutka tends to induce a kind of narcoleptic nausea in me: it is a hideous combination, sweaty claustrophobia in the tiny buses (tip: do whatever you can to avoid sitting above the wheel arch), an urge to vomit occurring simultaneously with a crushing eyelid-weighting tiredness with no relief in sight. If you are foolish enough to combine this with a weak bladder, or the self-inflicted pain of a litre or two of beer in advance of the journey, torture will ensue. The soporific nature of the landscape in this part of central Moldova certainly did not help.

The Gagauz border is marked by a twin concrete pole, 40 feet high – which represents significant altitude in these parts – with the Gagauzian sky blue crest at the top. Below, large red letters leave you in doubt that you are entering a different region; GAGAUZIA, it announces in capitals, with 'Komrat Dolayi' pinpointing the district of Comrat, to which the bus was heading (Comrat being the region's only real town). The radio station switched to echoing and atmospheric Gagauz music.

There are dozens of competing theories about the Gagauz, their ethnicity, their origins, their ancient movements: some suggest they are essentially Turkicised Bulgarians who retained their orthodox Christian religion. Under this interpretation of their origins, which is probably the most widely accepted, they are descended from Oghuz Turks in present-day Kazakhstan. Tribal warfare caused them to migrate westwards, ending up in the obscure Bessarabian margins of Europe – under the control, in that medieval era, of Bulgaria. Later, under Russian rule, the Gagauz were moved to their present homeland as part of the kind of geopolitical ethnic population 'swap' common at the time (in this case, a population of Sunni Muslim Nogai people were removed from this flat corner of southern Moldova and transplanted elsewhere). Later still, in 1906, Gagauzia anticipated the 1917 Russian Revolution by staging a mini-revolution of its own: declaring independence as the 'Republic of Comrat', an entity that lasted for five days, and one which must qualify as one of the least known but most interesting entities in the history of European politics.[85]

Like Transdniestria, the central issue for the Gagauz revolves around language and identity, with the key concern being the possibility of Moldova uniting with Romania – and what their status might be under such a putative state, which would essentially be a kind of 'greater Romania'.

The region declared independence again on the day of the Moscow coup in 1991. This was never likely to be accepted by the Moldovan government, although it did eventually concede a degree of autonomy to the region. Its size and dimensions were apparently determined by referendum, although the resultant 'map' is so absurdly complex that it is very hard to imagine precisely how this process worked. It is currently split into four separate enclaves, the largest of which was the one I had now passed into (although even this is tiny, just a few kilometres across).[86]

It is almost as if the residents were intent on rendering the country as unwieldy and eccentric-looking as possible. There are echoes of Terry Pratchett's *Discworld* about a territory that rejoices in two exclaves no larger than two miles across in the middle of 'standard' Moldovan territory (check out Samurza on Google maps if you feel the need for proof of life imitating [comedic] art). Tiny exclaves separated from the 'mother country' are common in linguistically diverse corners of the world: indeed, my travels in the Ngabe-Bugle comarca in Panama saw me reflecting on the contemporary implications, with social media having the potential to connect them. And while the Gagauz versions are absurdly microscopic, they are at least occupied by some people – albeit not very many. By contrast, when travelling in the Caucasus in 2012 I passed through two former Azerbaijani exclaves in present-day Armenia that have long since been denuded of their former Azeri Muslim residents (after the Azeri–

Armenian conflict of 1994, a vast and largely unreported exodus of both peoples saw a tragic population transfer which continues to have implications, and cause tensions).[87] Indeed, if this all seems impossibly 'exotic', perhaps it should not. Further west, dozens of European enclaves still exist, general peacefully and uncontroversially (although there are always exceptions). Land exchanges and other deals have, over the years, ironed out some of the eccentricities, but many remain.

There are tiny German enclaves within Switzerland, for example, and the little Spanish community of Llivia is located on the French side of the Pyrenees. I visited Llivia with my family in 2016, and was struck by the presence of the place, proud of its Catalan heritage, surrounded by a sea of Frenchness.

Within Wales, too, Flintshire was once noted for its peculiar enclaves, particularly up in the Anglicised north-eastern corner of the county bordering Chester. The English Maelor, which occupies the 'Welsh panhandle', and is marooned several miles away from what we might call 'rump Flintshire', has an identity that still resonates today – but there were also other, smaller enclaves further north and west in the Dee valley near Gresford, which muddled the cultural and physical geography of the country still further. The introduction of Clwyd in 1974 ironed out some of the quirks, but echoes remain.

The Flintshire enclaves date back to Edward I's formation of the county in 1284, although the English Maelor was only fully absorbed within the parent county in 1536 (having earlier been part of the Principality of Chester). Three separate pieces of land that were not particularly closely associated were brought together under the Flintshire umbrella. Some authorities say that another, Englefield, was Edward's attempt to obliterate the ancient Welsh cantref[xiv] of Tegeingl (not so very different from

---

xiv The cantrefi were medieval land divisions in Wales. The literal meaning is a hundred towns (cant=100, tref=town, although this would have denoted a settlement of any kind at the time). They varied

the motivations of nationalists in the Balkans and the Caucasus in the 1990s). Hopedale was the third portion, a tiny enclave south of Chester, and it was separated from the much larger exclave of the English Maelor by the Maelor Gymraeg, which remained part of Denbighshire.[88]

As their names suggest, the two Maelors were (and are) culturally distinct and, although the old enclaves relate mainly to patterns of land ownership, an obvious linguistic division was (and is) also present – echoing the absurdly tiny Gagauz enclaves through which I was now travelling, which can be identified by their tri-lingual signage (Russian, Moldovan/Romanian, and Gagauz). In the English Maelor, there are few occurrences of the Welsh suffix 'Llan', for example. Indeed, there are few Welsh place names of any kind in the area – in contrast to intensely Welsh villages like Rhostyllen and Rhosllanerchrugog just a few miles away in the Maelor Gymraeg. In fact, when it was commonly known as 'Flintshire detached', English Maelor residents supposedly told a boundary commission in the 1880s that they wished to merge with Shropshire.[89] This never happened, and that curious wedge of land poking into England remains a familiar and distinctive feature of Welsh maps.

In Gagauzia, a referendum in 2014 threw up the startling result that 99% of its tiny population supported independence if ('if' being an important qualifier here) Moldova joins Romania, or the wider EU. Gagauzia is ruled by the Communist party, which favours close ties with Russia along Transdniestrian lines – including joining Putin's customs union – and the vote should be viewed in that context.[90] Whatever the reality of the situation, however, a strongly independent streak cuts through these bizarrely atomised little communities.

---

considerably in size, leading some to suggest that the boundaries were primarily linguistic, tracing the borders of different Welsh dialects, as well as (in the Flintshire cases cited here) the frontiers between Welsh-speaking areas and more Anglicised districts.

Wandering round the streets of Comrat in crystal-clear September sunshine, I was struck by the trilingualism, the old ladies selling Kvass in national dress, and the general difference in tone from Chisinau. Lenin again graces the streets, this time in proletarian garb of overcoat and cloth cap outside the Gagauz 'parliament' building. Rusty red stars still adorn the lamp posts, and there are Afghan war memorials and other carefully maintained symbols of the Soviet era all over Comrat and even some of the smaller villages. But there are also numerous Turkish crescents, complete with references to the Turkish government. It is very clear that Turkey sees Gagauzia as part of its natural sphere, much as the Russians do, although in this case that is for cultural links and the extension of 'soft power' rather than political reasons. It is immediately obvious that Gagauzia relies on foreign aid, and it does not take much effort to work out where that aid comes from.

A side street reveals a nursing home, immaculate, entirely refurbished and rejoicing in its new – albeit unwieldy – moniker: the Reccep Tayip Erdogan home, named after the arch-populist leader of Turkey. Gagauz Foreign Minister Vitali Vah has been quoted as saying that 'we have two strategic partners. Turkey is good for business, Russia for access to the market.'[91] There's a small, but brand new, Turkish embassy and indications of its soft power everywhere. Indeed, it is somewhat surprising that the phenomenon of contemporary pan-Turkism, that extension of the Turkish worldview, is not more widely known. After the collapse of the Soviet Union, Turkey somewhat opportunistically set up 'TIKA' (its international cooperation and coordination agency) in 1991.[92] Offices were set up in all those corners of the former Soviet Union that Turkey saw as its natural sphere of influence: essentially, all the countries dominated by a Turkic-speaking majority along with some, like Gagauzia, that weren't but were clearly Turkish in origin or linked in some way to Turkish culture. I remember, for example, visiting the Lithuanian town of Trakai in the late 1990s and being intrigued (in those pre-Google days) by the community of Crimean Karaites associated with the town. Not only did they have their own ultra-obscure Kypchak Turkic language (now critically endangered) but they were Jews with a coherent food culture and specific set of cultural traditions, and they were distributed in tiny numbers across any number of unlikely locations on the fringes of Eastern Europe, from Lithuania to the Crimea.

Less obscurely, Central Asia and the Caucasus see the most obvious expressions of the more recent pan-Turkic movement: Azerbaijan, Kyrgyzstan, Kazakhstan, Uzbekistan, Tajikistan and Turkmenistan are all encompassed within this pan-Turkic worldview. When travelling in Kyrgyzstan in 2012, its capital Bishkek struck me as a simultaneous expression of the ambition inherent in the Soviet empire-building in Central Asia, alongside a resurgent 'Turkishness', which often revolve around cultural links and flights to Istanbul.

The Gagauz language is called Gok Oguz, and again the obvious linguistic links are exploited by Turkish nationalists in some online propaganda, although the unfortunate fact (for pan-Turkic nationalists) is that not many people speak it. It sounds like 'Turkish backwards' according to some linguists, as they struggle to describe its unique characteristics. But despite the reality that more people in Gagauzia speak Russian than Gok Oguz, the militant Gagauz leader Stepan Topal – a former road worker who was elected president during Gagauzia's brief period of independence in 1994 – has no doubts about where the nation's loyalties lie. 'The Turkic brotherhood is an ancient race, like the Jews. In the future, Turkic people and nations are going to rise up and become more important.'[93]

Sounding more like Erdogan or Putin than a defender of a tiny minority people, Topal is also quoted as saying that 'what the Europeans call democracy isn't real democracy', encapsulating the 'war of ideas' that characterises contemporary politics in this corner of Europe, notions exploited by the current leaders of both Turkey and Russia.[94] Gagauzia looks set to continue its tightrope walk between those two giants, while ignoring (or at least marginalising) the EU and the Moldovan state in which it finds itself. It continues to play Turkey off against Russia, all too aware of its strategic and symbolic importance, like Transdniestria, a tiny barrier of anti-European sentiment ripe for exploitation by the populists of both countries.

For the Moldovans, the negotiation of this internal diversity – in such a tiny and fragile state – is problematic. For Veaceslav Craciun, it is a question of compromise: 'it's evident that given the multinational character of southern Moldova, a flexible linguistic policy is essential if we're to build stable and sustainable social relations'.[95] But despite this (itself an obvious indication of Moldova's desire to join the EU by 'proving' its tolerance of diversity) there have been more mischievous moves to give official status to all the minority languages in the region, often advanced by separatists who perhaps see it as a route to destabilise the state. For example, in 2013 a proposal to make Bulgarian an official language of Gagauzia was put forward (which would have made the signs in Comrat quadrilingual), despite the fact that Bulgarian is the mother tongue of just 5% of the Gagauz population, all concentrated in a few tiny villages.[96] The origins of the proposal are murky and disputed, but it illustrates a wider point: the accommodation of minority languages can be exploited by those with ulterior motives. 'Sustainable social relations' is a laudable aim and one that tends to be reached at a certain point in that trajectory from conflict to compromise; but liberal policies such as these require buy-in from the entire community if they are to prove sustainable.

Colour illustrations

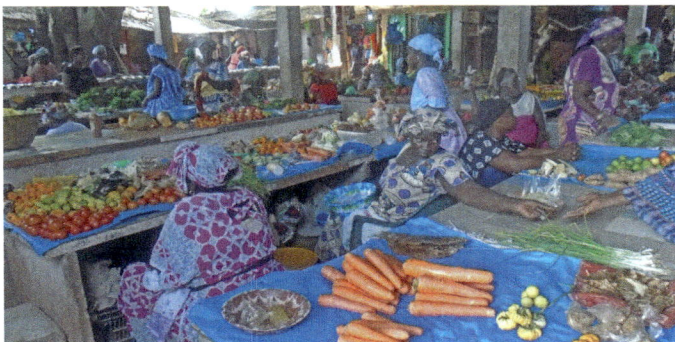

Chapter 1: Kafountine Market, Casamance, Senegal

Chapter 1: The author at The Gambia–Senegal border

Chapter 1: Mobile technology in Senegal

Chapter 2: Chazhashi, Svaneti, Georgia

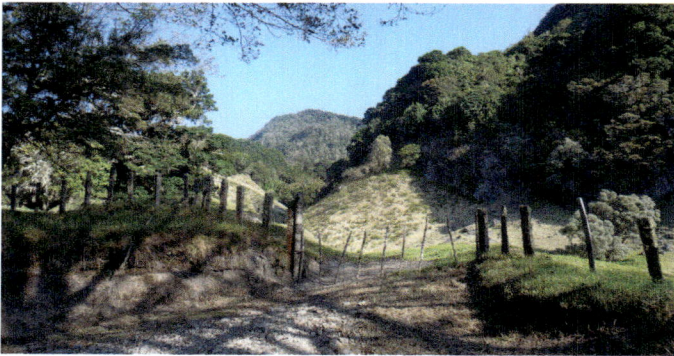

Chapter 3: Above Boquete, Panama

Chapter 4: Albanian iconography in Pogradec

Colour illustrations

Chapter 4: Pestani, North Macedonia

Chapter 4: Statue from the Albanian isolationist period

Chapter 5: Near Haputale, Sri Lanka

Chapter 5: Tea plantation, Sri Lanka

Chapter 5: Trilingual shopfronts, Haputale, Sri Lanka

Chapter 6: Bulembu, Swaziland

172

Colour illustrations

Chapter 6: Swaziland border with driving instructions

Chapter 7: Lenin statue in Comrat with Gagauz
and Moldova flags, and trilingual signage

Chapter 7: Catalan independence flag and the entrance to Llivia

Chapter 7: Tiraspol, Transdniestria

Chapter 7: The embassies of two unrecognised countries, Abkhazia and South Ossetia, in the capital of an unrecognised country, Transdniestria

Chapter 7: Transdniestria and Tiraspol flags on the Transdniestrian Parliament Buildings in Tiraspol

Colour illustrations

Chapter 8: Monument celebrating the centenary of the Welsh colony in Trelew, Patagonia

Chapter 8: Patagonian coast near Puerto Madryn

Chapter 8: Ysgol yr Hendre, Trelew, Patagonia

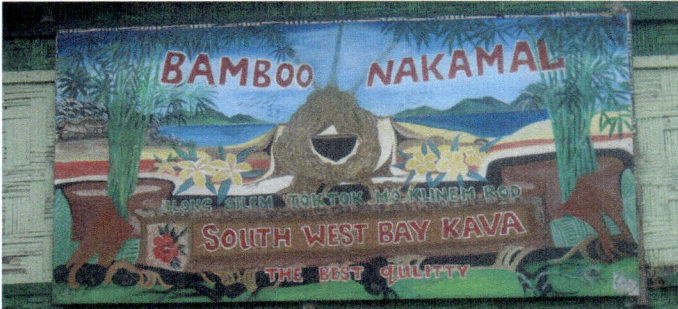

Chapter 9: Nakamal, Vanuatu

Chapter 9: Totems in Vanuatu

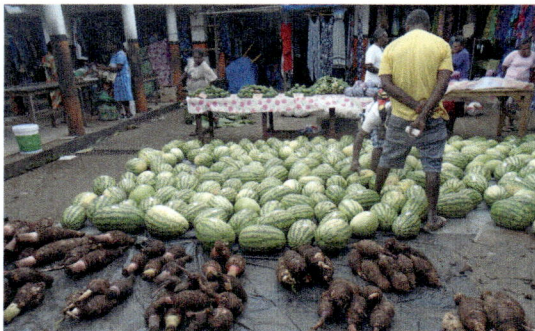

Chapter 9: Port Vila Market, Vanuatu

CHAPTER 8
Y WLADFA: THE INEVITABLE
PATAGONIAN INTERLUDE

Has there ever been a group of people more intensively studied than the Patagonian Welsh? Every member of that community must, at some point, have felt the intrusion of a TV camera, an annoying academic, a persistent journalist. Those that have not met a Welsh-speaking celebrity making a documentary for the mother country must be vanishingly few.

Scrutinised for years, its past trawled over and micro-analysed, its mythologies continually rehashed, it is hard to have an original thought about the place if you have any kind of grounding in Welsh culture. Outsiders sometimes try – Bruce Chatwin famously brought his distinctive (partially invented, some say) gaze to bear on the place in his classic 1980s travelogue, for example. And the enormity of Patagonia as a whole, its alluring sense of remote weirdness, has always guaranteed it attention from all manner of foreign adventurers from hardcore mountaineers to wannabe gauchos.

But for the Welsh, Patagonia has always been about something more fundamental: the only meaningful outlier of Welsh-speaking culture, a tiny sliver of what might have been, an inspirational reminder of the resilience of 'yr hen iaith', the old tongue. So it was inevitable that the 150th anniversary of the colony in 2015 saw another raking over the bones of the South American Welsh experience, another flurry of visits from news readers, actors and sporting icons. Another attempt to burnish the living myth.

And while it might be hard to make observations about this community that sidestep the usual tired clichés, a visit to Y Wladfa ('the colony') has the destabilising effect of simultaneously confirming one's preconceptions whilst also demolishing them. By that I mean that the essential poignancy of chapels in the desert, bara brith, and tea shops framed against the alien azure skies of the deep south is all there. But so is the contemporary Argentinian reality. Trelew is a big, rather bog-standard Latin American city: 200,000 people from a diverse range of backgrounds. It is a perfect illustration of the obvious reality that the south of Argentina echoes the American West. This is frontier-land, with the same pioneer spirit and the same sense that nobody really belongs here (the native Tehuelche were largely exterminated by the Europeans on their drive south, in another uncomfortable parallel with the US).

And preconceptions are demolished in other ways too. Some crucial things have changed in recent years, and they are perhaps not the things that most immediately come to mind. Large-scale immigration, for example, has been happening in Patagonia for multiple decades: the Welsh have long since been absorbed into a vastly larger melting pot, their identity engulfed, numerically at least. But while many predicted the obliteration of the linguistic community following those waves of migration (such fears were commonly voiced at the time of the colony's centenary in 1965), it has not happened. Instead, the community exploited unexpected external developments to survive and evolve. And in recent years it has even begun to modestly expand, to the point where it might accurately be described as 'thriving'.

The factors behind this are many and varied: the most obvious being the slow liberalisation of Argentinian public life and an associated acceptance of identity politics – seeing the essential melting-pot diversity of the country as something to be celebrated rather than suppressed. But, a little less predictably, the advent of social media has also played a crucially important role.

It is something of a truism to observe that, since the launch of platforms like Facebook and Twitter, social media's direction of travel has been wild and unpredictable. Its political and cultural impact has varied dramatically depending on global context – from the optimism of the Arab world in 2011, when those platforms were seen as tools by which committed, tech-savvy networks of activists and students could reverse ancient power structures to take on authoritarian elites in developing countries, through to the unexpected adoption of the same technologies by the white male majority in the developed, Western world (the most unscrupulous and persuasive of whom somehow managed to frame themselves as representing the 'network' of ordinary people, in opposition to a notional 'elite').

It has certainly been a bumpy ride. In 2011, few predicted the role of social media in the populist revolts later encapsulated by the election of Trump and the vote for Brexit; or the associated mobilisation of identity politics by the white majority, framing *themselves* as threatened, and using social media to challenge the primacy of the 'mainstream media'. But in the context of fragmented minority language groups, of which the Welsh in Patagonia are the archetypal example, two tiny communities separated by 1,000 kilometres of desert, it all looks a little different.

Far from threatening Welsh in Patagonia by the dominance of the global linguistic juggernauts of Spanish and English, Facebook has offered it a crucial lifeline. On my third day in Chubut, I met community leader and activist Anna Rees in the infamous Touring Club bar in Trelew. Rees is closely involved with the community as a whole, and more specifically with the Welsh-medium primary school in Trelew, which is now oversubscribed, despite the fact that a majority of the students have no Welsh heritage at all. She told me that while much of the communication is done initially in Spanish, there is always an attempt to communicate with parents in Welsh, whether they speak it or not. Not only this, but Facebook acts as a mildly politicised focal point for the community as a whole. We spoke in broken Welsh, our mutual lingua franca (very broken in my case), surrounded by faded pictures of old Chubut, mugshots of long-forgotten outlaws, and row upon row of obscure spirits, from gaucho favourite Fernet Branca to an old bottle of Lagavulin from distant Islay.

The trappings of Welshness are far more visible further up the Chubut valley, in touristy towns like Gaiman. But before my final pilgrimage to those tea shops up the valley, I found myself hopelessly attached to the Touring Club. A more evocative setting would be hard to imagine. It is one of those places that myths and half-truths inevitably attach themselves to. Any bar with a lot of history, globally, tends to have this kind of alluring baggage, emphasised and perhaps exaggerated to appeal to tourists. Think of the Lamb and Flag in London, where the poet Dryden was supposedly attacked in the seventeenth century. Or the Bodeguita del Medio in Havana, haunt of Neruda, Marquez and other Latin-American literary greats (and, less appealingly, the site of an anti-tourist bombing in 1997).

Trelew does not get many tourists, so the Touring Club does not need to give too much prominence to its most high-profile anecdote, which revolves around the visit of Butch Cassidy and the Sundance Kid in the early twentieth century (although the bar was rebuilt in the 1920s by Agustin Puyol and his wife Anita Jones, the daughter of Welsh colonists). Inside, its walls are lined with memorabilia, Welsh rugby posters among them, and the ambience is redolent with the pioneer spirit of the Argentinian south (which – it seemed to me, sitting there with a whisky – mirrors the American West in more ways than I had initially imagined, not least the romanticisation of the cowboy/gaucho and the obvious tension between that romanticisation and the knowledge that native people were virtually exterminated by that process).

'Most of the parents in the school don't speak Welsh', Anna conceded in Patagonia's distinctive Spanish-accented, non-colloquial Welsh, after I asked her about the celebrated Ysgol yr Hendre, located not far away from the Touring Club in the backstreets. 'But we want them to see that we operate in Welsh. It's good for people to understand that, and Facebook is a good way for that to happen, for them to see that Welsh is a modern and vibrant language that can give something to them.' There may be a degree of tokenism in this, in the sense that most of those accessing the school's pages will initially read the Spanish version, but Anna offered a clear rationale: 'I do everything I can bilingually through Facebook', adding that it transcends age in Chubut: 'Some old people also use Facebook to find out what's going on – it's very interesting, very useful, very quick and they understand that.'

A long-established web-based newspaper called *Clecs Camwy*, which now acts 'as a kind of online archive for the community' according to Anna, is now defunct, superseded by the convenience and ubiquity of Facebook.[97] But its rationale, to bring geographically atomised groups together, remains. In the context of a diasporic group, the idea of preserving a society through time becomes a feasible and fundamental role for the media. The Welsh language media in Patagonia have always conceived of their role in that way, it is a distinctive feature of the cultural landscape. Indeed, preserving the community via an articulation of a form of identity politics was a fundamental underpinning principle behind the nineteenth-century establishment of Welsh newspapers, dozens of which were established across Y Wladfa. This long established tradition of community newspapers is as old as the colony itself, and goes some way to explaining the contemporary impact and function of social media.

It is not counter-intuitive to suggest that social media provides a survival strategy for minority languages, although this is far from universally true, and plays out very differently in different geopolitical environments. In Iceland, for example, the indigenous tongue, famously unadulterated, ancient, and resistant to imports even when new terms for technological advances are required (coining words like 'hladvarp' for 'podcast', for example [a combination of the Icelandic words for 'charge' and 'throw']) does seem threatened by social media. *The Guardian*'s Jon Henley suggested in early 2018 that Icelandic was facing 'digital extinction', drowning in an online ocean of English.[98] Like Welsh, Icelandic faces an obvious problem: all its speakers share another common language – and that other language is global, not local. The concern is that the native tongue therefore becomes obsolete in certain aspects of people's lives, particularly those of the young, the so-called digital natives. In Iceland, the prognosis according to some pessimists is grim.

But in Patagonia the opposite seems to be the case. All Welsh speakers in Patagonia share another language – and, like English, Spanish is global and hugely influential online. But social media transcends the barriers of physical geography that have always separated the Welsh speaking communities in Patagonia, the hundreds of kilometres of desert between the Gaiman and Esquel was an insurmountable barrier for the development of a unified political voice for much of Y Wladfa's history. Now, they can be drawn together – just as other fragmented linguistic communities I have visited on my travels, the Gagauz of Moldova, the Ngabe of Panama, the Swazi of Southern Africa and the Tamils of Sri Lanka have been, if only in a modest way – by social media.

A META-NET study of 2017 conceded that in the digital era, Europe's rich linguistic heritage, its mosaic of minority tongues, 'faced challenges' but went on to suggest that the new communicative world offered 'many possibilities and opportunities'. It found that language technology support varied dramatically from 'weak or non-existent' for some small languages (including Icelandic) to 'fragmentary' for languages like Basque, where a clear political dimension adds an extra facet to the notion of preservation.[99]

For George Rehm, 'there are dramatic differences in language technology ... the gap between 'big' and 'small' languages still keeps widening. We have to make sure that we equip all smaller and under-resourced languages with the needed base technologies, otherwise these languages are doomed to digital extinction.'[100] The mass of data required to introduce voice recognition technology like Siri is harder to acquire for minority tongues with fewer speakers. But language technology of this kind is only part of the full story, and a rather technocratic and structural one at that. The man in Struga whom we met in Chapter 4, deliberately using his local dialect when tweeting, was just a small example of a much larger phenomenon. While minority languages might be starved of the investment required to invest in big-scale language technology, at grassroots level people do understand the role and importance of social media in maintaining and diversifying the use of minority languages. As META-NET itself conceded: 'linguistic borders often do not coincide with political borders'.[101] Herein lies the true value of social media, as the recent experience of Y Wladfa proves. The pre-web reality saw fragmented communities struggling to articulate a coherent political position as a result of geographical separation. Social media has supplanted the local newspaper reading tradition of Welsh Patagonia and now forms a meaningful public sphere, which transcends geography and looks set to maintain and perhaps develop Welsh speakers' sense of community and political representation.

***

I had reached Patagonia by bus from Buenos Aires: a 20-hour journey. In Argentina, however, a journey of this magnitude is not the traumatic prospect it would be elsewhere: the better class of 'ejecutivo' coaches make horizontal travel a possibility, seats turn into beds, and complimentary wine and snacks ease the pain still further. Most of the journey passed in a Malbec and Fernet Branca-fuelled haze, the rather monotonous scenery sliding past hypnotically as the 'wet pampa' gradually gives way to the aridity of the 'dry': it was all rather pleasant. That said, I still decided to fly back. But before returning to the capital, I visited the uninhabited coastal wilderness of Peninsula Valdez, fetching up at its stunning north-easterly tip – known as Punta Norte – where I was greeted by the exhilarating sight of a giant petrel, flying just a few feet above my head as I watched sea lions and elephant seals haul themselves away from the immense crashing surf. It seemed to me at the time to be the ultimate expression of the wild South Atlantic.

There is a small museum in nearby Puerto (or Porth, as it originally was) Madryn which encapsulates the reality of that wildness for the first Welsh settlers on the *Mimosa*, the clipper which sailed from Liverpool in 1865. It is absorbing throughout, perched on cliffs with the limitless Atlantic visible through every window. The poignancy of that view brings a lump to the throat – it takes no particular leap of the imagination to consider the realities of the *Mimosa*'s landing which my experiences at Punta Norte magnified. The museum's old-fashioned explanatory panels do not need to lay it on thick; the view is adequate, it is explanation enough. The utter lifelessness of the shore in these parts – bleached desert rocks, the absence of greenery, indeed the absence of any kind of vegetation – must have been bewilderingly alien. The only feasible escape route was the vast ocean that had just been crossed: a two-month voyage from Liverpool. But what really set me off, apart from the male voice choir piped through every room, was the painfully familiar laid out tea service on vintage nineteenth-century furniture: a scene I remembered from childhood. Even though Puerto Madryn is now a large town, its remoteness and the hostility of the coast is never far away. And the vulnerability of the tiny dark oakwood table next to the Atlantic breakers, with its brown tea pot and red tea cosy, neatly arranged on a tablecloth, was one of the most powerful things I had seen – more so than the more famous, but more touristy, tea shops of Gaiman. My thoughts went back to Punta Norte and its windswept shore as I examined the modest collection of artefacts preserved from the first settlers – bibles, oak chairs, old photographs of Bala, Llanrwst, Nefyn. It is hard to imagine a bigger contrast; the hilly greenery of the North Wales valleys to the endless bleached steppe of the Patagonian coast.

In Puerto Madryn itself, Welshness lends the visitor a mild celebrity status, and this despite (or perhaps because) the town is now a standard Patagonian coastal community, which receives cruise ships en route to Antarctica, eco-tourists en route to Peninsula Valdes, as well as the usual sun seekers (although I visited in February, high summer, and did not see too many of the latter, although perhaps I am comparing it to the Costa Blanca or Côte d'Azur. There is an awful lot more space in Patagonia – a great deal of coastline for a small number of tourists to inflate their airbeds in). There is also the experience of entirely unexpected but entirely genuine links that sometimes happen in the unlikeliest of surroundings. 'My great grandparents were on the *Mimosa*,' said the receptionist in the hostel I was staying in (hip, with exposed brickwork and craft beer behind the bar). The casual mobilisation of Welsh heritage, which occurs fairly frequently even in these modern Argentinian melting-pot cities, takes some getting used to. As we have established, the majority of pupils at the celebrated Trelew Welsh medium primary school have no Welsh heritage at all; but those that can cite some distant link with the earlier settlers are generally very keen to do so. Depending on who you believe, there are at least 50,000 Patagonians that claim some kind of Welsh heritage – around 10% of whom have some level of ability in the Welsh language.[102]

***

The Welsh experience in Patagonia has been romanticised, almost fetishised, by the Welsh in Wales for several decades. The notion of a still-extant group of politicised migrants, intent on preserving the language and culture in an alien environment has obvious traction, which was particularly relevant in the post-1960s context of resurgent Welsh political and cultural identity. Since Welsh devolution in 1997, and the 150th anniversary of the colony in 2015, the totemic significance of the Patagonian Welsh has further increased. This trend has not always been interpreted positively, with Mici Plwm describing Chubut as a kind of 'Disneyland for the Welsh middle classes' in the early 1990s.[103] Others have observed the lazy reliance on language, ancestry and nonconformity as lenses through which to interpret Y Wladfa, which ignores the complexities of Welsh identity in Patagonia and beyond.

Social media potentially acts as a corrective to such reductive tendencies. The focus on Patagonia from within Wales has also coincided with a genuine, organic growth in the confidence and assertiveness of the Welsh community in Chubut. This is currently – at least in part – facilitated by online media, which is intrinsically suited to the demands of numerically small linguistic communities as it provides an obvious communicative hub, a vital public sphere.

The importance of newspapers among the Patagonian Welsh, since the earliest days of the colony, is also crucial to understanding the renewed impetus that social media platforms have lent to the cultural and political coherence of the community. The foundation of the colony in the 1860s coincided with a growing awareness of the potential role of the news media in providing a sense of political and social coherence to small migrant communities, and the establishment of dozens of small-scale newspapers must be viewed in the context of an instinctive understanding of their role in community building.[104] These traditions neatly fused with the advent of social media, which has altered the balance between personal space and community space across Chubut, and provided users with new means of expression and connection.

CHAPTER 9
'UNITY THROUGH DIVERSITY':
HOMAGE TO VANUATU

Flying to the South Pacific from Wales is like being fired to the ends of the Universe by a cosmic catapult, the closest thing to interplanetary travel without the pressure of signing up for NASA. It is painfully distant: there is something that borders on the unsettling about first enduring the rigours of the 22-hour double flight to Brisbane, then heading an extra three hours across the limitless expanse of the Pacific, punctuated – very rarely – by collections of tiny islands, microdots of terra firma, like constellations of stars in an infinite blue galaxy.

I had come all this way on something of a pilgrimage to the ne plus ultra of linguistic diversity: Vanuatu. Its remote collection of islands marooned in the middle of the world's biggest ocean harbour an astounding range of languages – 138 at the last count, most of which are microscopic in scale, spoken by tiny numbers of people.[105] Some of them are threatened, but many – perhaps counter-intuitively – either actively thrive or at least continue as the everyday languages of choice for a high proportion of the population. I wanted to find out why. And I also wondered whether it would be naïve or accurate to view Vanuatu as a yardstick, a model of uncontested linguistic diversity.

Certainly, Vanuatu typifies the kind of superabundance that arises when geography dictates the sequestered evolution of peoples and languages. Its entire population is less than that of Swansea – 270,000 people – but that population is spread across a vast swathe of the Melanesian Pacific, occupying dozens of islands, each of which is a world unto itself, largely cut off from its distant neighbours – even if they are fellow Vanuatuans. And, of course, the entire archipelago, and indeed Melanesia itself, is just a small part of the unfathomably huge oceanic whole (it is, for example, 1,200 kilometres away from Fiji, its closest

Melanesian neighbour to the east, and at least twice that to the closest Polynesian island of Samoa).

Unesco's linguistic diversity index – which suggests that Vanuatu has the most languages for its size on the planet – uses a complex series of metrics to come up with its results. These kind of indices are endlessly debatable, of course, but are essentially based on the number of speakers of each language as a proportion of the overall population. Or, to put it another (probably more meaningful) way, the probability that two people selected at random from the country's population will have different native languages.[106]

On scales like this (Unesco's is not the only one – there are other methods of measuring the same thing), Vanuatu's status at the top of the linguistic diversity tree is only threatened by other similar South Pacific countries, most obviously Papua New Guinea, which has a similar mixture of infrastructural, cultural, historical and topographical factors promoting superabundance – but is, crucially, far bigger both in area and population.

The negotiation of that abundance, the sensitivity of the tightrope walk between preserving cultures as living museums, sealing them off from the modern world, and providing those on remote islands or hidden valleys with some of the benefits of twenty first-century life, is arguably more acute in the South Pacific than anywhere else in the world.

***

Port Vila, Vanuatu's rather ramshackle but charming capital, has a kind of frontier-town feel, despite its idyllic tropical location facing the sunset on the western shores of the island of Efate. It reminded me of other places where a remote settlement is the biggest thing for thousands of miles – Murmansk, perhaps, or Darwin, Puntas Arenas, Manaus. There is the same sense of constant flux, the same sense of being on the edge of something big: somewhere empty and yet significant that lies just beyond the urban fringe. That something or somewhere may be the Amazonian jungle, or the edge of Antarctica or, here, the Pacific Ocean. Walking around the streets, there is also the distinct feeling that for many of those visiting from elsewhere in the region this is the biggest place they will ever see; the most cosmopolitan, loudest, busiest, exciting town they will ever visit. There are no more than 40,000 inhabitants in Port Vila; there are no chain stores, no McDonalds, no universities, and no traffic lights. But migrants from across the Vanuatuan archipelago have flocked there in recent years, attracted by the relative boom in tourists (there still are not many, and they are almost exclusively Antipodean) and the relative sophistication of the place.

As a result, you could easily make an argument that Port Vila is one of the most diverse and multi-cultural towns on the planet. Casual visitors might not immediately realise it: almost all of the inhabitants share the dark skin and distinctive features that make this archetypal Melanesia (Melanesia literally refers to 'islands of black people', to distinguish the region from other parts of the South Pacific). But, get talking to the taxi drivers, or the waiters, or the shop assistants, and it quickly becomes apparent that they are all immigrants from every corner of Vanuatu, united only by a love of the psychoactive drink called 'kava' and a wonderful lingua franca – which takes the form of a charismatic pidgin known as Bislama (arguably a multiethnolect in an unusual context). Within Port Vila itself are scores, perhaps even hundreds, of different linguistic and cultural communities. The best place to hear the reality of this is at the market near the waterfront in town. There, the people gather to sell vegetables, fruit and flowers, all with their own product specialities and all speaking at least three languages, moving seamlessly and constantly between them. English for the Australian tourists, Bislama for the Vanuatuans beyond your own kin, with your own mother tongue reserved exclusively for your own community.

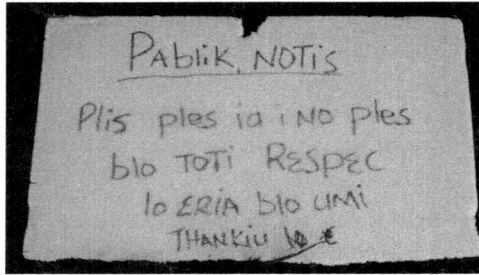

Figure 3: An example of Bislama pidgin

The market is the obvious first point of arrival for any visitor, a short hop from the tiny Bauerfield airport through recent developments spread in linear fashion along the few roads that radiate out from the busy but tiny city centre. There is only one real road on Efate, the main island and the focus of the country, but haphazard development around Port Vila – with all those internal migrants from elsewhere in the country keen for a slice of urban action – has led to the rapid development of dirt tracks and inadequately surfaced roads criss-crossing the hills above the town. The migratory nature of the place is apparent immediately, even before you begin to speak to the people who live there, in the sense that many of the ramshackle houses are obviously new, and Port Vila as a whole is clearly rapidly expanding.

As ever, the moment you do start to converse with the locals, eyes begin to open and insights are gained. One of the first people I met, as I sat with a cold drink on a patch of fishy-smelling waste ground on the sea front opposite the market, called himself John – a shambolic, elderly figure carrying a huge shopping bag, with matted hair and long leather shorts, which struck me as an unlikely South Pacific take on Bavarian lederhosen. In a very mild South Pacific sort of way he was a hustler for the small number of day tour packages sold to visitors on Efate, which is why he approached me. Mild to the point of inertia, mind, as John was more interested in mythologising his own past than selling tours

(I would guess he was around 70, not an obvious candidate for such a job). 'Ah, the mother country,' he said when he found out where I was from, with a smile and – I felt – a distinctly satirical tone. 'I shook the Queen's hand in 1974,' he added by way of a well-polished mini-anecdote, 'when she came to our special island.' It is true that Queen Elizabeth did indeed visit the New Hebrides (as Vanuatu was known before its independence) in 1974, but it became clear that John was referring to Pentecost, his home island, of which he was very proud, and not Vanuatu as a whole, or Efate (which is where we actually were). I have no idea what the Queen's itinerary was, but it seemed unlikely to me that she would have had the time, or her entourage the inclination, to visit the outlying islands of this remote Pacific outpost. John disagreed, and was adamant that he had met her as a young(ish) man: 'Everybody in the world knows my island,' he then claimed. A slight exaggeration, perhaps, but as Pentecost is the home of land diving, the precursor of bungee, his statement had a vestige of truth. Land diving is a horrendously risky test of manhood for the teenage boys of Pentecost, and islanders have suggested that the familiar modern form of globalised health-and-safety-approved bungee in which young people throw themselves off bridges for the benefit of social media posts is a classic case of cultural appropriation. It is certainly true that the Pentecost original version, in which tree vines are tied to the ankles and the jumps made to ensure a good yam harvest, has featured on a fair few TV documentaries over the years. For John, it was commercially-inspired appropriation, pure and simple: 'It is our tradition, New Zealand tourist saw it, he took it, we get nothing.'

Although I was unable to visit Pentecost (it is a 90-minute flight from Port Vila, or a couple of days by the 'Big Sista' boat that links the islands), I met four different Pentecost-born Vanuatans during my stay, all of whom were intensely proud of their homeland, and all four of whom had different native tongues (the island has five main languages – Raga, Apma, Sawa, Ske,

191

Sa – but a total population of less than 18,000).[107] Pentecost serves as a useful exemplar, both of the reality of linguistic diversity in Vanuatu, and the reality of the multicultural nature of Efate, as it increasingly lures intra-island migrants.

Edgar Hinge, who I was able to interview at the Vanuatu Cultural Centre, was a Pentecost islander and a native speaker of Raga – the dominant tongue in the north of the island. Why do you refer to it by its colonial name, Pentecost, I asked? 'We don't. We call it Raga,' he said, pointing to a giant map of the islands with their (supposedly) indigenous names on it. But, I was later told, even this is contested and illustrative of the island's linguistic diversity. Raga actually refers to the north of the island, to the people that live there, their language and their culture, not Pentecost as a whole. 'In history, we did not have much contact with each other,' Edgar later admitted, referring to the other groups on Pentecost. 'Sometimes, the differences in our languages was deliberate, we were kept apart to keep our special identities.' The implication being that there was a concerted effort on the part of tribal elders to preserve language and culture through isolation, long before such diversity was celebrated and protected by government. He also said something that I had read before: 'The difference between our languages is the same as there is between your languages – between English, French, Spanish. We do have some words the same as Apma and Sawa but we cannot understand each other.'

As a speaker of Raga, the numerically dominant tongue, it is perhaps not surprising that Edgar took an optimistic view, as surveys suggest it is buoyant, indeed actively growing on the island. Perhaps the most astonishing fact about Pentecost's languages is that each of these tiny languages splinters off into multiple dialects, some of which are almost incomprehensible to other speakers. So the ultra-obscure language of Sa, for example, spoken in the south of the island by around 2,000 people, has four distinct dialects and that, according to Edgar Hinge, 'is probably an underestimate, it is a very complicated place'. The linguistic difference is paralleled, as is often the case in Vanuatu, by significant cultural differences. Language is, as ever, the 'badge of nationhood', but that is complemented by what Edgar referred to 'as different clothes – grass skirts, (penis) sheaths' worn by the speakers of Sa.

***

Despite, or perhaps because of, this extraordinary diversity, the ni-Vanuatu[xv] are these days fairly unified in the political sense. This notion is pushed quite strongly by most politicians, unsurprisingly given the country's mixture of language and culture. I saw several government-issued green T-shirts bearing the slogan 'unity through diversity' being worn by various ethnic groups across the islands, including the man operating the little boat across to Lelepa island (I noted that T-shirt with interest, because it was so unseasonably cold at that point, with the wind whipping off the open Pacific, that I had cause to wear a coat, not something I was expecting to be hauling out of my rucksack on this trip). The boatman's shirt seemed doubly appropriate, as it was the islanders' skills as canoe makers and sailors that helped cement this unity in the first place, or at least the government claims that it did. In the National Museum in Port Vila, a display of traditional canoe designs concludes with the somewhat idealistic claim that 'through trade and other voyages, inter-island canoes allowed for the renewal of kinship affiliations and the dynamic exchange and diffusion of languages, ideas, knowledge and culture that has led to the great cultural diversity seen in Vanuatu today'.

---

xv Literally meaning 'of Vanuatu', this is now the accepted term to describe residents of the islands, because it is intended to capture the fact that the multiple linguistic groups on the islands (mostly) share the same Melanesian origins despite the subsequent development of separate languages. That said, the term is only used in English and French, not in the indigenous languages of the islands.

The contradiction inherent in such a claim seems obvious, and has occasionally boiled to the surface in recent times. Indeed, even the otherwise celebratory occasion of Vanuatu's independence in 1980 was marked by a bizarre secessionist rebellion on one of the bigger islands, Espiritu Santo, led by a charismatic rebel leader called Jimmy Stevens. Government vehicles were commandeered, bridges blown up, and radio stations set up to broadcast Stevens' thoughts – which ran the gamut from a belief in older customs and a desire to preserve them, through to plans to turn his home island of Santo into a tax haven.

Jimmy had 27 wives, dozens of children and hundreds of devoted followers (most of whom were apparently his own progeny). He was said to be a mixture of Melanesian, Polynesian and European heritage and, at the time, said that his movement wanted to see 'island for island independence'. Questioned by journalists, he said 'we don't want to mix up'. His plan for dozens of tiny statelets, run in the old way, by hereditary chiefs, was rumoured to have received financial backing from the Phoenix Foundation, a ferociously anti-Communist organisation based in Nevada that had a vested interest in the promotion of tax havens dominated by the gold standard. Others suggest he exploited tension between the French and British sides of Vanuatu's island life.

His Polynesian heritage was said to have given him an oratorical edge, a kind of sharpness that his Melanesian followers were swayed by. He was, in essence, a populist – but one with a highly specific cause. His cult movement, Na Griamel, eventually blossomed into the full secessionist drive, a sort of fusion of ancient beliefs and modern politics (he was also something of a proto-environmentalist, opposed to agribusiness and land clearance). He was eventually arrested and sentenced to 12 years in prison, just as the modern state of Vanuatu was born.[108] Lini, the new Prime Minister who had seen off Stevens, perhaps conscious of his influence and the nature of the state he was founding, then tried to steer a pragmatic course between tradition and modernism as he laid out something of a manifesto for the new state in 1980: 'We shall need guidance not only from God but our own custom and traditional values. We are moving into a period of rapid change like a canoe entering a patch of rough water; God and custom must be the sail and steering paddle of our canoe.'[109] And it is that emphasis on custom, more commonly rendered 'kastom' in the pidgin, that remains heavily promoted by the government and must go some way towards explaining the sustainability and vibrancy of the multiple linguistic and ethnic groups on the island. Their 'kastom' is celebrated, and is never seen as a threat to the centre. Perhaps Jimmy Stevens' rebellion had a legacy after all.

The most basic and universal result of this is Vanuatu's celebration of its kava culture. Kava is a drink with immense cultural traction and an entire mythology connected to its origins, as well as the daily ritual of drinking it. This was outlined to me by Sam Eman, who I met in the nakamal (kava bar) near my lodging just after I had penetrated the complex rituals involved in its consumption and sampled my first shell. For Sam, kava was part of his everyday routine – although 'never before 5pm and never too much'. He claimed (correctly, it transpires) that Vanuatu is the home of kava, the place where it was first consumed. From here, it travelled the South Pacific as far as Hawaii. But Vanuatu remains the lodestone of kava culture, and its kava is still renowned as the strongest and purest. The effects of the drink are rather hard to articulate, but suffice to say that it promotes a kind of gentle conversation, which was how I met Sam, also alone and sitting opposite me in the nakamal. As the drink took effect, Sam (who spoke good English, like most men in Port Vila) patiently outlined the 'kastom' myth still told about kava on the islands: 'A jealous man killed his wife and buried her in the garden. An unknown plant grew from her loins [I think he said 'loins', although on reflection it seems an unusual choice of words]. A rat ate the plant every evening, and every evening that rat would stagger away and go to sleep peacefully – so we say that because kava had risen from the body of a woman, it must be tabu for women to drink it.' Not entirely understanding the logic of the story, I looked around. Women were clearly drinking it. Not many, but I saw two, and indeed I was served my shells of kava by two women hard at work, dredging the unappealing green liquid from the murky depths of a huge yellow bucket. For Sam, who had to agree, this was simply an indication of Port Vila's cosmopolitanism: 'Yes, here in Port Vila you see women drinking the kava, it's modern, we have tourists. But on my home island, on Tanna, this never happens. It is tabu.' In fact, I later discovered that it is taboo for women even to see kava being made on Tanna, or to see men drink it.

The word 'tabu' (generally rendered that way in Bislama, although usually spelt 'taboo' in English) was imported into English from Captain Cook's travels in the South Pacific, probably from Tonga. It is very useful, and has stuck for English speakers – although in Bislama it is a common word in everyday language and serves multiple functions, from the traditional – as in Sam's example above – to the modern, where it more broadly stands in for 'not allowed' or even simply 'no' (no smoking signs, for example, are rendered 'TABU blong SMOK long ples ia': an exact transcription of a sticker I saw above the urinal in the Vanuatuan cultural centre).

Whether taboo for women or not, I had seen the roots of the kava plant, *piper methysticum* ('intoxicating pepper', literally) across the island of Efate and watched its preparation, a fairly arduous process which reminded me of tea making – albeit in giant buckets, and demanding unusually rigorous stimulation of the leaves (or roots in this case) whilst steeping it in water. It has sedative and anaesthetic qualities, although its most notable immediate effect is the numbing of the mouth and its appallingly bitter taste. According to Sam, 'there are more and more kava bars across Port Vila, and now we don't drink beer at all'. This was not strictly accurate, but it is certainly true that – as migration from the outlying islands increases – kava consumption does too, almost as if it acts as an anchor, a reminder of island culture and a badge of identity for all Vanuatuans. It is also an obvious unifier; something that all linguistic groups can share.

My own consumption of kava took off exponentially. Two half shells on the first night, two full shells on the second, and three full shells on the third night. Happily, that was as far as I got, because one of kava's many unusual properties is reverse tolerance, the exact opposite to alcohol, so no increase in dosage was necessary. The culture and practice of kava drinking is highly specific, and takes some learning. I observed proceedings before diving in; sticking out like the proverbial sore thumb but completely accepted by all the locals. The British pub equivalent is well known to all of us, and was most famously fictionalised by the Slaughtered Lamb scene in the film *An American Werewolf in London*. We are all familiar with the concept of the stranger entering a local pub to hostile glances and muttered imprecations. Here was its South Pacific equivalent: to be precise, the Bamboo nakamal in the Nambatu (number two) district, a collection of ramshackle huts serving the kava (and snacks to take the foul taste away) and a kind of courtyard where you sit, post-kava, relaxing.

But, either because the locals are accepting and nice, or because kava has that kind of effect and they are all under its influence, or a combination of the two, I was left to my own devices – which was just as well because, in the words of the wonderfully-named nineteenth-century British-born mariner and cartographer William Twizell Wawn, who wrote about the effects of the drink in 1870, 'a pint of strong kava will make a man desirous of being left alone and allowed to sit quietly'.[110] It did indeed, and it also makes the imbiber sensitive to loud noises and bright lights – hence the low murmurs of conversation and the muted blue light which indicates that kava is available within. Rarely have I drunk in a more atmospheric place. At a little booth (which never opens until the kava is prepared from the plant roots and the sun begins to set, around 4.30pm) money is handed to a man who gives you a token depending on the size of shell desired. At a second booth, two women dredge the bucket and pour the green fluid in. Then, crucially, you take the shell to a kind of trough, turn your back to the rest of the customers, and drain the shell in one whilst standing up – spitting copiously into the trench in a vain effort to mitigate the revoltingly bitter taste and the numbing effect on the mouth. Then, you retire to the courtyard to think about life, or perhaps engage in gentle conversation, until ready for another shell.

You are told, by everybody, never to drink kava on a full stomach: it leads to nausea and lessens the effect. But on that third night, I had wandered into town after two shells, pleasantly relaxed, ate a delightful meal cooked by local women in the seafront market – boiled poulet fish, coconut milk, manioc (cassava), rice – and then, unwisely, stopped off for a third full shell as I returned to my lodgings. Once back there (I had a kind of studio flat overlooking the lagoon east of Port Vila) I began tussling with the baffling front door lock, as I had done all week. This time, I really could not open it – it was not the kava, which tends to focus the mind, it really was not opening. Desperate for bed, I kept turning and turning, forcing the key further and further until I finally contrived to snap it, embedding its useless remnants in the lock. Outside, the tropical night swarmed with insects. I was tired (kava has a sedative effect) and at a loss as to what to do. There were no other guests, and the owner – a rather taciturn Australian called Ian – was not there, evidently away on a night out (it was Friday).

By sheer good fortune, he returned after an hour of me being devoured by insects. He was less than thrilled to be torn away from his weekly night in town (he had only come back for some extra cash, and was dressed in a very loud Polynesian-style shirt), and even less thrilled when he realised the full magnitude of what had happened. Was there a side entrance? Yes, but it's locked from the inside. Could the remnants of the key be removed by pliers? We tried hard, but the answer was no. Could I have a different room? Possibly, but all your belongings including your passport are inside this one.

So we found ourselves, in the small hours of the morning, dismantling one of the windows with a small screwdriver and the light of Ian's mobile phone. With three decades of rock climbing experience, and at a rough guess half of Ian's weight, I was the obvious candidate to climb through the tiny gap which now appeared, quite high in the side wall of the flat. But, still somewhat becalmed by the kava, this was easier said than done. Here's the 1870 observations of W. T. Wawn again: 'When his knees give way, a man discovers that kava acts in a contrary way to alcohol. The latter effects the head, kava goes straight to the legs. Alcohol excites, kava sooths, and then stupefies.'[111] Not ideal for novice cat burglars, then, as I quickly discovered, legs dangling over the gap, the narrow window frame cutting agonisingly into my abdomen. You don't get this in a Premier Inn, I reflected as I squirmed and twisted through the gap like a spawning salmon.

***

Kava notwithstanding, it would be naïve to conclude that the linguistic and cultural diversity within the migrant, melting-pot town of Port Vila is always entirely harmonious – the spirit of Jimmy Stevens has not entirely disappeared. Quite quickly in Vanuatu I stumbled across a rather amazing little 'proxy war' based – of all things – on the World Cup, which seemed a perfect illustration of the ways in which the locals, drawn from tribal origins across the archipelago, negotiate and express their differences. The fact that this proxy war was based on the Football

World Cup also seemed to represent something fundamental about the impact of globalisation on people's lives, even in the remotest corners of the globe, surely the least likely hotbed of football allegiance and passion.

On my first short trip out of Port Vila, to Mele Bay in the north-west, I had noticed a huge Argentinian flag towering above a characteristic straw hut, typical of the ramshackle village houses in the interior. Then, another one, slightly tattered but flying proudly to its left. Further on, two German flags. Then, a cross of St George next to a small Brazilian flag. As I continued my journeys around the island, seeing Belgian flags, Spanish flags and even a lone Uruguayan flag, the relationship between these nations, all of which seemed unlikely in the context of the South Pacific, gradually began to dawn on me. My trip was in September 2018, two months after the World Cup Final: the flags were the flags of all the favourites.

I was travelling by minibus, the only realistic way for an independent traveller to get around the islands. There are hundreds of these narrow old Japanese buses, marked with a red 'B' in case you're unsure. There are no set routes – they all ply the single rough island ring road in both directions so it is just a case of waving one down and negotiating a fee, which you may or may not deem acceptable: it is hard to get lost or disorientated in a country with one road.

Every time I got in a Vanuatuan minibus, I was taken aback by the humour and intelligence of the drivers. Rarely have I encountered such pleasant people. I started off by asking where they were from, always finding the answers intriguing (it was never Efate, even if they had lived there since they were toddlers). But I soon realised that their origins were absolutely core to their sense of identity, their sense of self. In fact, there was no need to ask – they volunteered the information, everybody on Efate does, whether you ask them or not. Minority languages are central to identity and everyday life in a way that reminded me of parts of Gwynedd or the Basque interior; although in the case of Vanuatu, we are talking hundreds of separate identities forged through language, not one.

My initial journey to Mele was a standard trip and Keith Ganae, my driver, immediately noticed me looking at the flags. Even by the standards of Vanuatuan bus drivers, Keith was excellent company and I asked him whether the flags were connected to the World Cup. He nodded: 'My team was Brazil,' he turned to me with a mock pouty face for comic effect. 'I didn't go out for a week after they lost. I stayed inside my house. I even turned my phone off.' Things had got heated in the villages and in parts of Port Vila, he added. 'Look at the people that picked France – have you seen what they did?' I had certainly noticed the number of Tricolours since arriving, emblazoned on cars, huge stickers on the side of minibuses, flags flying from shacks. But I had assumed that was because of Vanuatu's colonial ties. It was only later, seeing those Argentinian and Brazilian flags, and a few rather forlorn, almost apologetic German flags, that I started to put the pieces together: the French flags were symbols of victory for those Vanuatuans who had backed them. Almost everybody across the island had picked a side, and then – very firmly and quite literally – pinned their colours to the mast. Two months on, they were an inescapable feature of the landscape, still flying on many of the houses, whether winners or losers, Germany or France, so I could only imagine how many flew during the tournament itself. I assumed there must have been some financial, gambling element to this but Keith was evasive on the subject, conceding only that something 'serious' had been going on.

I am familiar with Malaysians, Thais and Indonesians getting very exercised about the English Premier League: it's a classic symptom of globalisation and the capitalist sporting juggernaut exemplified by the EPL and Sky. But this, on the remotest of islands, just seemed deluded, borderline insane in terms of the level of commitment to a cause that was not your own: unless there was another explanation. I pressed Keith on the topic. Initially, he just repeated that it was 'serious' and that the French followers were, by this token, displaying their victory over their rivals. I was never quite able to ascertain whether there was a linguistic element to the proxy 'conflict' revolving around island origins among the migrants of Efate, although Keith certainly hinted that there was, as he pointed to the French sticker in his car, which I had not initially noticed. 'Do you know why that's there?' he said. I shook my head. 'Because this is my boss's minibus, not mine. I usually work in the airport, but they don't need me at the moment. I am driving while I have this holiday, I am driving this bus for my new boss – he's from Santo so he supports France. I'm from Ambae so I support Brazil.' Assuming that Keith's assertion that things got 'serious' was a tad exaggerated, or lost in translation, it all seemed a rather interesting way of maintaining friendly rivalries and negotiating the tensions inevitable when groups of people with different tribal and linguistic origins converge in one place.

When I finally reached the tiny settlement of Mele, there was another surprise, and one that seemed to typify Vanuatu: the people here are isolated Polynesians, and speak an outlying branch of the Polynesian language family called Mele-Fila, unrelated to the Melanesian tongues that surround it (Mele and Fila are, you guessed it, two separate languages although just about mutually intelligible). The reasons for this are complex and disputed, but after speaking to numerous people I gathered that it might relate to the (relatively) famous Lapita culture – a series of ancient migrations in the Neolithic era, undertaken by a remarkable people who are thought to have originated in Taiwan and, through ingenuity and a command of oceanic navigation, spread across the South Pacific ultimately to settle Polynesia further east. Indeed, even among the Melanesian languages in Vanuatu, certain life 'themes' contain numerous Polynesian borrowings that suggest earlier contact – tellingly, the two most obvious themes are words connected to the preparation and consumption of kava, and words connected to seafaring. The village was also the only place I saw the cross of St George, emblazoned on the side of shacks, flying from rooftops: backing England in the World Cup must have been, I assumed, another way of demonstrating this Polynesian distinctiveness.

I arranged to meet Keith later that day for the return trip. As we passed a brand-new building, much bigger than anything else around it, windows still covered with plastic sheeting, he began to get agitated. 'Look at this, look at it. What do you think it is?' A hotel? I ventured. It was near the sea, and although a bit gaudy and dated it seemed the most likely option. We were some miles north of Port Vila in open countryside, although the 'beach' nearby was black volcanic sand, not particularly appealing – and the entire location had a rather windswept and bleak feel. 'We think it's a Chinese hotel, but we don't really know,' Keith said. There were hard-hatted Chinese staff present, making last minute adjustments by the look of it. I had seen other Chinese men in suits at other sites, and investment was clearly increasing. For Keith, it was sinister: 'Our government takes their money but they don't tell us what they do with it,' he said, before drawing what initially seemed a rather misplaced comparison with colonial-era Australia, suggesting the Chinese were gradually colonising Vanuatu with hard cash. 'I've been to Australia. Brisbane, twice. You know what happened to the 'blackfellas' there. This could happen to us.' The idea that the diversity of Vanuatuan indigenous life might be wiped out by the Chinese, in the same way the indigenous languages of Australia were (largely) destroyed by the experience of colonialism, not surviving contact with Europeans, seemed far-fetched, although Keith's comparison was not quite as wild as it first appeared. In April 2018, the *Sydney Morning Herald* ran a story entitled 'On the ground in Vanuatu, monuments to China's growing influence are everywhere', outlining the 'sheer ubiquity' of China's presence on the islands.[112] The debt to Beijing is already very big, the opportunities for local people not particularly obvious. So Keith's concerns were real. The worry is that China might seek to increase the pressure on an indebted Vanuatuan government, and that its real motive is some kind of military presence, given the strategic and sensitive nature of Pacific geopolitics. Whatever the reality, and it's very hard to come to informed conclusions, the Chinese embassy on the opposite, southern side of Port Vila is astounding in its scale.

I came across it by accident, on a run one morning, down to Erakor beach from my accommodation near the lagoon. A huge white building, brand new, intensely secured with high walls and barbed wire – looking as if it should be in Kabul rather than the South Pacific. Bearing in mind that the UK, along with many other European countries, does not even have a consulate on Vanuatu, it seems grotesquely out of proportion, an inflated monument to an ambition that is not entirely clear.

***

If this is the new postcolonial realpolitik for Vanuatu, it is not surprising that the locals are worried. Partly, this is because of the country's history, which saw it treated as a kind of exotic titbit by European powers keen to export their own version of civilisation, and increase their own influence on the other side of the world (in this sense, at least China's designs on the country have a little more geographical integrity – although this is highly relative).

The evidence for this comes in the still extant colonial names for the islands. Espiritu Santo ('Holy Spirit' in Portuguese), for example, was named by the first European to land on Vanuatu, Pedro Fernando de Queiros who – in one of those spectacular misunderstandings common in this period of global exploration – thought he had landed in Australia. This was 1606 – and a long gap then ensued before Captain Cook came up with the rather bizarre 'New Hebrides' moniker in 1774.[113] As a descriptor, it is not that great, although as an enthusiast of the original Hebrides and north-west Scotland (I spend a week there every May) I can perhaps discern a certain similarity in terms of the pristine beaches, clannish people and clear aquamarine water. Vanuatu does get a lot of rain too. But the hibiscus flowers, palm trees, kava and tropical fish are a little harder with which to draw parallels. Despite the inherent arrogance of naming places after the imperial power, it became widely accepted, rather like 'Wales' and 'Welsh' became accepted despite the derogatory and colonial overtones (Welsh being the term Germanic peoples apply to 'foreigners'). Indeed, the New Hebrides name was only dropped on independence in 1980.

Vanuatu's colonial history is just as quirky as its indigenous cultural mix. It was essentially shared between France and Britain – who jointly declared it neutral territory in the late nineteenth century. But this declaration, nice in principle, led to problems in practice largely because of its extremely remote location. Because there was no real government, marriages (for example) could not be recognised, unless the couple travelled to New Caledonia (if they were French – 400 miles away across the Pacific), or Fiji (if they were British – 750 miles away in the opposite direction). Eventually, this unsatisfactory, pseudo-anarchic position led to the residents taking matters into their own hands and, eventually, the creation of a rather remarkable construct – the independent 'country' of Franceville. This was, essentially, modern day Port Vila, with its own flag and its own president. But most notably, it was also the first self-governing nation to grant universal suffrage to all men and women, and all races. Perhaps unsurprisingly, not much information on this entity exists, even in the national museum of Vanuatu – but apparently a red, white and blue flag with five revolutionary stars was raised, and the idealistic nature of the construct was made clear from the outset. Both the French and the British disapproved of it, as tended to happen with distant upstart colonies, and it lasted less than a year.

After this came another awkward entity, once described as 'a country where crime cannot be punished, or payments of debts enforced [which] could hardly hope to attract a good type of settler'. This was the view of Margaret Rodman, who wrote a book about the chaotic nature of governance in the New Hebrides during the nineteenth and early twentieth centuries.[114] The Anglo-French 'condominium' was more commonly called the 'pandemonium' by residents, who had to contend with what was described at the time as a 'Tower of Babel tribunal'. Other contemporary writers described the New Hebrides as 'high musical comedy ... one of the strangest political situations in the modern world' as French, English and indigenous languages and legal systems battled for supremacy. The hybrid legal system just added to the absurd complexity of the place – and religious, political and colonial divisions were simply laid on top of the existing linguistic and ethnic diversity of the islands.

Port Vila itself was always something of an anomaly in a country without any kind of urban culture. As a result, those attracted to 'settle' the island, many of whom were former prisoners as Rodman implies, used the chaotic mixed legal system to their advantage, turning Port Vila into a lawless new town. Indigenous people were traded, or even used as gambling chips (indeed, entire plantations were lost in games of poker). While in the Secret Garden (a strange open-air museum in the middle of nowhere) I came across a potted history of Port Vila at this time written by R. J. Fletcher, a British visitor in the 1920s. His account reveals much about the overt racism and disregard for the Melanesian population as a whole, let alone any sensitivity to cultural differences within that community. Given that this was the 1920s, not the 1820s, the account reveals much about the aftermath of the chaotic political situation on the islands. Fletcher mentions the notorious 'Bloodhouse Bar' in 1920s

Port Vila, observing slave labour recruiters playing poker and drinking champagne after a successful season: 'The regulation method is to shout a case, kick the lid off and open the box with an 18-inch knife. The stakes are merely the recruited niggers who are ranged solemnly around the walls and change hands many times during the night. Guns were fired at targets set up on the other side of the road.'[115]

***

Christianity infiltrated the islands in an intriguing way, embedding itself into the culture despite unpromising beginnings when more than one missionary ended up in the pot – indeed a group of Erromango islanders officially apologised in 2009 for the awkward fact that their ancestors clubbed to death, and then ate, English missionary John Williams in 1839.[116] Remarkably, Williams' descendants recently travelled to the island for what must have been a somewhat strained 'ceremony of reconciliation', which presumably began with something along the lines of 'sorry for eating your great, great, great grandfather'. A vivid painting of the killing, or artist George Baxter's feverishly imagined version of it, is held in the National Library of New Zealand.

Edgar Hinge, at the Vanuatu Cultural Centre, had this take on it as we chatted about belief systems and cultural practice: 'When Christianity arrived there was conflict between missionaries and the local people. My ancestors thought they would spoil us, that we'd lose our language and our culture. But after some time we realised that what they said was the same as what we said. Our kastom was about peace, unity, respect, same as Christians.'

Maybe, maybe. In the centre of the centre, as it were, a large traditional canoe bears the slogan 'God and Kastom, Working Together' which sums up the official tendency to somehow fuse the two together as if they have always been natural bedfellows. The official position describes it thus: 'The foundations of the Ten Commandments are in synergy with our foundational cultural system. There were some things that our ancestors practised that they were happy to abandon and the missionaries also believed that they were no good.' Although not mentioned on the canoe, these included: infanticide, black magic, internecine warfare and ancestor veneration in the form of life-sized mannekins called Rambaramps.

The epicentre of this, home of the strangest cultural practices of all, remains the island of Malekula – and not all those practices have gone away, despite the presence of Christianity. I did not know this until I met a man from the island, yet another taxi driver, called Henry, as I tried to get back to Vila from a trip to the eastern edge of Efate. 'No tourists go to Makekula,' he said, with a frown and a hint that I should have known the reason why. 'Even I don't go back there much, the people there don't like it when we leave and they don't like people from other islands.' Or tourists, I assumed.

I was curious, and looked into the possibility of getting there, but it was tortuous and sadly impossible given my schedule. According to a plaque in the Secret Garden (which is consistently less airbrushed than the national museum, an uncensored take on local life) the island 'has a dark and forbidding demeanour and its history encompasses cannibalism and continuous tribal warfare'. Its people have a reputation as 'stubborn, conservative and strongly resistant to European influence over their lives and trespass on their lands'. This made it irresistible to missionaries, who made it their business to convert the coastal villages, at least. Inland, old traces remain – tribal people speaking multiple languages, known as the 'Big Nambas' and 'Small Nambas' (a reference, I'm afraid I have to tell you, to the size of their penis sheaths). These coverings are not to be taken lightly, as 'to tear away a man's penis sheath is an insult only requited by death'. The penis is considered particularly susceptible to magic, meaning that when the sheath is removed, in private, the eye of the penis is covered with a finger. As a result, the sheaths have a complicated and foolproof fastening system, since slippage would be disastrous. This is fine, but makes urination tricky – although apparently 'it gets easier with practice'.

In remote corners of their mountainous domain, still holding out against external influences, ancestor veneration through Rambaramp effigies continues. These are commemorative effigies of important chiefs, some of which I was able to see: life-sized and fashioned from tree fern, wood and bamboo, overlaid with finely ground vegetative compost and capped with the decapitated skull of the deceased, tampered with and modelled to make it look as if the individual is still alive (as you might imagine, this 'tampering' only has the effect of making it more grotesque and terrifying).

Bodies of those to be honoured are placed on a platform in the jungle and allowed to 'drain', then placed in the rafters of the family home until dried and smoked. The body is moved several times back to the jungle, every time marked by the carving of figures in black palm, and then it is handed over to the Rambaramp maker, who works silently on the effigy for several weeks, eventually placing the cleaned and stylised original skull on top of the figure. A large feast is then held, the figure placed in the Kastom house, after which the spirit supposedly returns to the skull. Whilst not entirely unique, the fact that something akin to it is said to continue among the Small Nambas on Malekula certainly is – one of the most bizarre and grotesque (to some outside eyes) of South Pacific cultural practices. The impenetrable nature of these customs is linked to the astonishing range of languages – there are 12 'interior' languages on Malekula, all unique, at least four of which are reserved for the Small Nambas, with still more spoken around the coastal regions. In this case, as always in Vanuatu, the preservation of language is inseparable from the preservation of unique cultural practices.[117]

***

The strange and the grotesque is never far away in Vanuatu. Towards the end of my stay, I was able to visit the remarkable island of Lelepa, which, along with its neighbouring island of Eretoka is a world heritage site, the domain of Roi Mata, an influential thirteenth-century Melanesian chief who united Efate and surrounding islands. It became famous for the gruesome nature of his burial site after French archaeologist José Garanger excavated it in the late 1960s, finding 50 skeletons including Roi Mata himself, his numerous wives, and his chiefly entourage. Garanger based his excavation on centuries of oral evidence, which spoke of a large kava drinking ceremony and hinted at the huge scale of the event. The evidence suggested the oral testimony was right, and more than one of those buried had been trying to raise their hands based on the position of the skeleton, 'struggling to raise herself out of the grave': buried alive, that most primal of human fears.[118]

Of all the languages examined in this book, Lelepa is the tiniest. It is healthy, and in everyday use – I heard it spoken by every person I met on the island – but as there are less than 400 residents, it is very small indeed.

The islanders are not the easiest people to talk to, perhaps for obvious reasons, but while there I met a man called David, who outlined the island's distinctive political system. 'On the island, we have five tribes – octopus, taro, coconut [sadly, I did not catch the names of the other two]. I am a coconut. All the chiefs come from the taro tribe. In the past, the chief looked out for the community and presided over important sacrifices and ceremonies, but now that we are Christians the Pastor looks after religious activities and the Chief looks after the community.' It is a kind of parliament with the chief in control. The 'Royal' line runs through the taro clan and its integrity is assured by matrilineal inheritance, rather like Jewish identity. However, Royals can be married into by other tribes via rather complex arrangements, which struck me as a model of democratic fairness, with all five clans having some kind of stake in leadership.

David told me that the island children learn in their native Lelepa tongue 'until year two' (it was not entirely clear when that was, but it seemed to be aged 10 or 11) before switching to English. For Andrew Grey, who worked as a schoolteacher on Pentecost, the problem then becomes that the system leads to 'a generation of young people who are not fluent in the language that they are literate in, and not literate in the language they are fluent in' and that this means that exam results are inevitably poor. From the little I saw on Lelepa, this did not seem to be the case, although the tension between oral and written languages is a real one for speakers of tiny languages like Lelepa, languages that will never have a literature.

The alternative view is that placing an emphasis on vernacular languages – as they seemed to do on Lelepa – is hugely beneficial for the students and, of course, simultaneously helps preserve fragile and irreplaceable languages, fundamental elements of the cultural ecosystem, what it means to be human. Wales, again, is an obvious model for this. Learning through Welsh as a child does not pose a threat to that child's subsequent, or parallel, development as an English speaker. In other words, picking up the globally dominant mega-tongue is not a problem, either for Welsh children or those on Lelepa: it will happen anyway.

That is also the case with Bislama, Vanuatu's national pidgin, closely related to English, which poses a risk to Lelepa and the other vernacular tongues. I was told that local youngsters use words borrowed from Bislama without realising those words are 'borrowed', in much the same way speakers of British English pepper their speech with Americanisms without realising. Or, in a closer parallel, the way in which colloquial Welsh uses English borrowings. In places like Pentecost, intermarriage – a mother that speaks Ske and a father that speaks Raga, say – leads inevitably to Bislama replacing the indigenous tongues as a convenient lingua franca. But on Lelepa, according to David, that is much less of a threat – its tiny scale means that one language continues to dominate.

Lelepa struck me as a kind of model. Of course, brief visits only allow for an airbrushed and idealistic snapshot, but that aside, it proves that there really are ways of negotiating the tensions inherent in twenty-first century life, that the export of global English can be accommodated. In that sense, although the scale and setting are different, the Welsh model remains a point of comparison: English (or perhaps the pidgin English of Bislama) provides the means of communication with the outside world, but the indigenous tongue remains sustainable.

The vibrancy of Lelepa and its language seemed to illustrate a way of preserving a unique and irreplaceable culture whilst embracing limited and sustainable levels of contact and modernity. The islanders themselves organised small group tours of the island: very small scale, fewer than 10 people, with a small boat to transport them across, once or twice a week. There are no other ways of getting to the island. The modest stream of income from that contact was enough to render the village comfortable, meaning that the push factors which often see agrarian communities of this kind lose their young people were not present, or were not sufficiently attractive to lure them away from the island. Dozens of children of all ages – even some in their mid-teens – played with analogue toys, small cars, bicycles and the like. The contemporary cliché, 'low impact', seemed genuinely applicable and as I returned to the mainland on that small boat I could not help indulging in a spot of idealism. This was low impact, this was sustainable; this was – just possibly – the way to maintain a language without destructive compromise.

CONCLUSION:
AN ANTIDOTE TO EXCEPTIONALISM?

In her celebrated book about Italy and its citrus fruit, *The Land Where Lemons Grow,* Helena Attlee references, en passant, Grecanico, an archaic language derived from medieval Greek which is still spoken by 5,000 people in Reggio Calabria at the southern extremity of peninsular Italy. Attlee was told that the little village of Galliciano, high above the Ionian Sea, is inhabited almost entirely by Grecanico speakers, and that the 'ndrangheta, the Calabrian mafia, take their name from a Grecanico word for 'manliness'.[119]

This book provided my reading material on a trip to the Italian Alps in the summer of 2019. As a lifelong mountaineer, I have been visiting obscure corners of the Alps since the late 1980s and this time plumped for the Orobie range north of Bergamo, rarely visited by British climbers. After returning from a three-day traverse of the dominant peaks, Pizzo di Coca and Pizzo Recastello, my friend Steve and I were relaxing with a cappuccino in the large village of Valbondione when we heard the driver of a bin lorry shout to some pedestrians in a language that definitely was not Italian. After this, I heard its distinctive intonation everywhere in the village, and in some of the larger towns further down the valley. It was Bergamasque – one of dozens of Catalan-style languages widely spoken in the mountainous regions of the north. This is incomprehensible to a speaker of standard Italian, yet would not be considered (by most) to be anything more than a dialect – which is also the word Attlee uses to describe Grecanico.

These micro-anecdotes are merely to prove an obvious, but important, point about the scope of this book: debates about the scale and status of minority languages can never have an end point, as linguistic diversity spirals off in infinite variety across the globe. True, some regions are more diverse than others – just as some regions are more biodiverse than others – but linguistic diversity remains a defining feature of the geopolitical make-up of many contemporary countries.[xvi]

As a result, the book aimed merely to 'take the temperature' of a globally scattered range of linguistically diverse environments in a post-web world. But, as the Italian examples prove, even defining what is meant by a 'language' is fraught with difficulty. It is a fruitless task to attempt to separate language from dialect, or to formulate some kind of methodology of definition. The old cliché is that 'a language is a dialect with an army'.[120] When considered in the context of this book, that aphorism is not particularly helpful – but the point that it tries to make is. Consider the core Scandinavian languages, for example: there is a high degree of mutual comprehension between the three and yet Danish, Swedish and Norwegian are always considered to be separate languages. Some Slavic languages are very close to each other, and there are frequent claims that the status of 'language' is conferred by the existence of a written literature, although this too is a highly problematic definition in many parts of the world. Often, differences between languages are more political than real (what used to be called Serbo-Croat, and is now 'Serbian', 'Croatian', 'Bosnian' and 'Montenegrin' is an obvious example[121]).

At the other end of the spectrum are many languages that outsiders might wrongly think to be mere dialects – and these are typically small, minority languages. In short, there are no universally accepted criteria for the definition of language – dialect and language exist on a continuum, with status more often than

---

xvi Large-scale migration and multiculturalism are also, of course, defining features of most developed – and many developing – countries. The extraordinary linguistic mixture thus created (over 250 languages are currently spoken in London) is fascinating and immensely significant both culturally and politically, but beyond the scope of this book, which has instead attempted to explore 'indigenous' minority languages (whilst acknowledging that this concept is itself slippery, and fraught with definitional difficulty).

not a political question. Scots (the Germanic tongue spoken in the Lowlands, as opposed to the Gaelic of the Highlands) is a classic example of a tongue that exists somewhere on the boundaries of language and dialect, subject to furious debates for decades.

Italy, of course, has hundreds of languages spanning a broad spectrum from dialect to language. Anybody familiar with the country, which was unified over the course of the nineteenth century, knows that it is almost the definition of *regionalism*, which now comfortably co-exists alongside an umbrella national identity. Italians are happy to celebrate as Italians when they win the World Cup, but simultaneously ferocious in their defence of region and internal diversity. This ranges from mild affirmation via language, cuisine and culture, through to driving a tank into the Piazzo San Marco in a dramatic appeal for the re-assertion of Venetian independence (an armoured vehicle constructed by Venetian separatists was seized by police in 2014, echoing a celebrated incident in 1997 when the world-famous bell tower was occupied for eight hours by another generation of radical Venetians).[122] Multiply Italian regionalism ad infinitum across numerous global contexts and you have something approaching the spirit of this book; a snapshot of that diversity in the contemporary wired world.

***

It is a common observation that globalisation and nationalism are two opposing poles in the contemporary world; and that the tension between those poles increasingly defines politics in many countries. Conflicting ideologies about language and integration are at the heart of debate; and what we mean by 'belonging' varies accordingly. But this book tries to make a case for the kind of open-minded regionalism that often characterises the outlook of minority language speakers – cherishing their uniqueness whilst remaining open to the rest of the world, an openness that simultaneously emphasises the importance of preservation.

George Steiner, writing many years ago in the context of the collapse of the Soviet Union, identified an emergent 'self-authenticating autochthony'[xvii] between neighbouring tongues'.[123] Certainly, in the context of Eastern Europe, the Caucasus, and Central Asia, this proved prescient. The instinct to preserve is intense, in the face of a world language, English, whose reach far exceeds any earlier equivalent (Latin, Greek, French). This instinct appears to be strengthening not weakening, despite (or because of) the effect of globalised social media.

In a celebrated academic argument, way back in 1973, radical geographer William Bunge predicted the 'soundtrack' of a notional future globalised society: 'Clearly a world culture of international youth is arising … it appears that from the younger generation everyone will speak English … the world culture probably will be technologically Western European, heavily electronic with free electricity. It is less clear but likely that African music and dance forms will be the dominant world-wide forms … people the world around are voting with their feet, so to speak, for this dance and music.'[124] Prescient in all ways except one: Bunge did not anticipate bilingualism; that English would become merely the media-driven global lingua franca, not a replacement for linguistic diversity.

Central to this is the question: how should the speakers of minority languages negotiate the relationship with global English? If that form of simplified lingua franca, often dubbed

---

xvii As a near-synonym for 'indigenous', the mobilisation of autochthony is highly problematic, and Steiner's use of the word here alongside 'self-authenticating' was presumably intended to convey the dangers of this in a different era. Notions of belonging will very often imply that some do not belong, that there are differing degrees of authenticity: not a sustainable basis for a tolerant society. In Ancient Greek, from which the word derives, 'autochthones' were the original inhabitants of a region.

Conclusion

Globish, is becoming universal, as it gradually but surely is,[xviii] accelerated by social media, we might look again to exemplars like Welsh to offer some kind of indication. The answer is that it is not a zero sum game: both can and will be accommodated. Consider the Dutch, or the Swedes – the way in which the vast majority in those countries can code-switch effortlessly between their mother tongue and English, and extend this to the speakers of minority languages. Wales is also a model for the way in which an overwhelmingly dominant culture can be accommodated whilst preserving and celebrating a fragile minority revolving around the centrality of language. And if, further to that, the experience of living with that dominant culture actually helps, because it reveals something about the value of diversity, the value of preserving that which is distinctive, then perhaps this is a model worth adopting universally. Looking outwards, if the speakers of *majority* languages might be persuaded to adopt a similar ideology, to accept that diversity, to accept their place in the global mosaic of language families, it would be a nice way of detoxifying 'big nationalism'. This idealistic worldview would mean English speakers looking across the North Sea to their Frisian-speaking cousins in the northern Netherlands (Frisian being the language that is closest to English) then accepting that, if Frisian is half way between Dutch and English, Dutch is half way between English and German,[125] and all are part of the modern family of Germanic languages, inescapably and intrinsically European.

---

xviii Not everywhere of course. In non-Russian parts of the former Soviet Union, Russian remains the lingua franca of choice – although even here that is changing, with those under 30 increasingly likely to speak English as an alternative. In other parts of the world, French, Spanish, Hindi and many other languages may occupy the same role, although in almost every instance the younger generation has an increasing tendency to speak English as the second language of choice.

A kind of global bilingualism, with English/Globish (or, in some places, a pidgin) occupying the role once envisaged for Esperanto, seems very likely. Globish becomes the lingua franca, with the rest of the world adopting the Welsh/Scandinavian bilingual model in which English co-exists comfortably with the mother tongue. Indeed, if anything, the ubiquity of English and its globalised form has a more debilitating effect on 'English proper', an observation first made by Steiner back in 1973.[126] This is particularly true in the UK – with Matthew Engel lamenting the disappearance of British English as its wit and distinctiveness sinks under a media-driven tide of Americanisms.[127]

***

As identity politics warps into Trumpian nationalistic self-interest, the basest form of political tribalism – we might usefully reconsider the place of minority languages, in the sense that they generally come from a defensive point of departure. This is not always pleasant or positive, but it does contrast with the strident nationalism (combined with laments for a lost period of former dominance) that characterises the version of identity politics we have recently seen emerge in the US, England, China, Turkey, India and Russia. If there is no former dominance to lament, the emotion is less toxic.

Minority languages tell us something crucial about the world – they remind us of an important reality, which is perhaps why they have so often been deemed a threat by the centre, who may be uncomfortable with the reality of an internal diversity that does not necessarily share their worldview. They offer a crucial riposte to the resurgent 'big nation' nationalism characterising contemporary politics: they are an antidote to exceptionalism, a reminder that the world is a complex place, and that simplistic solutions revolving around the assertion or reassertion of a dominant power is dangerously misplaced. If this book has any kind of message, it is that minority languages can act as a political corrective – a 'reality check' – to exclusive and bombastic nationalism when these forces are dangerously ascendant.

ENDNOTES

1   Irish Central (2019). How much Irish is spoken in Ireland? Retrieved from https://www.irishcentral.com/culture/education/how-much-irish-is-spoken-in-ireland

2   K. Katzner (1995). *The languages of the world*. London, UK: Routledge.

3   D. Crystal (2002). *Language death*. Cambridge, UK: Canto.

4   K. D. Harrison (2008). *When languages die: The extinction of the world's languages and the erosion of human knowledge*. Oxford, UK: Oxford University Press.

5   G. Tregidga (2019, Autumn). Levant and Kernow: 100 Years on. *Planet: The Welsh Internationalist*, p. 235.

6   L. Brooks (2019, 19 October). Gaelic close to "societal collapse" across Scotland despite an urban revival. *The Guardian*.

7   BBC News (2018, 22 September). "Encouraging" survey suggests rise in Welsh language speakers. Retrieved from https://www.bbc.co.uk/news/uk-wales-45611374

8   J. Meek (2019). *Dreams of leaving and remaining*. London, UK: Verso.

9   D. Goodhart (2017). *The road to somewhere: The populist revolt and the future of politics*. London, UK: C. Hurst.

10 A. Solomon (2019, 16 September). Against the wall: from Mexico to Calais, why the idea of division is taking hold. *The Guardian*. Retrieved from https://www.theguardian.com/books/2016/sep/16/against-the-wall-mexico-calais-division

11 R. Sutherland (2019, 7 January). Radio 4 *PM*.

12 J. Freedland (2019, 1 March). We now know the great prize of Brexit: Becoming Trump's prey. *The Guardian*. Retrieved from https://www.theguardian.com/commentisfree/2019/mar/01/brexit-trump-trade-hanoi

13 Meek (2019). *Dreams of leaving and remaining*.

14 See, for example, M. Castells, *Networks of outrage and hope: social movements in the internet age*. Cambridge, UK: Polity Press; P. Mason, *Why it's kicking off everywhere: The new global revolutions*. London, UK: Verso.

Endnotes

15   European Union (2019). META-NET White Paper Series. Retrieved from http://www.meta-net.eu/whitepapers/overview

16   J. Rifkin (2001). *The age of access: The new culture of hypercapitalism, where all of life is a paid-for experience.* New York, NY: Tarcher.

17   UNESCO (2019). Cultural and linguistic diversity. Retrieved from http://www.unesco.org/new/en/indigenous-peoples/cultural-and-linguistic-diversity/

18   BBC (2014). Senegal's Casamance MFDC rebels declare a ceasefire. Retrieved from https://www.bbc.co.uk/news/world-africa-27221999

19   Peace Direct (2017). Could zircon exploitation re-ignite the war in Casamance. Retrieved from https://www.peaceinsight.org/blog/2017/09/could-zircon-exploitation-re-ignite-the-war-in-casamance/

20   BBC (2018). Casamance: Thirteen dead in attack in restive Senegalese region. Retrieved from https://www.bbc.co.uk/news/world-africa-42592788

21   World Bank (2019). GDP per capita (current US$). Retrieved from https://data.worldbank.org/indicator/ny.gdp.pcap.cd

22   Global Security (2019) 1982–89 Senegambia Confederation. Retrieved from https://www.globalsecurity.org/military/world/africa/gm-history-09.htm

23   N. Ferguson (2003). *Empire – how Britain made the modern world.* London. UK: Allen Lane; E. Said (1978). *Orientalism.* New York, NY: Pantheon.

24   J. Aaron, & C. Williams (Eds.). (2005). *Postcolonial Wales.* Cardiff, UK: University of Wales Press.

25   A. Price (2009, 16 November). Wales, the first and final colony. Wales Online. Retrieved from https://www.walesonline.co.uk/news/wales-news/wales-first-final-colony---2070487

26   T. Anderson (2004). *Bread and ashes: A walk through the mountains of Georgia.* London, UK: Vintage, p. 55.

27   Soviet Red Book Summary (2019). *The red book of the peoples of the Russian Empire.* Retrieved from https://www.eki.ee/books/redbook/introduction.shtml

28   Ibid.

29 Human Rights Georgia (2008, 15 February). Nine years as "hostages" in Georgia's Pankisi Valley (Part I). Retrieved from http://www.humanrights.ge/index.php?a=main&pid=6999&lang=eng

30 T. De Waal (2010). *The Caucasus: An introduction*. New York, NY: Oxford University Press, p. 14.

31 Agenda.GE (2015, 14 April). Georgia celebrates Mother Language Day. Retrieved from: https://agenda.ge/en/news/2015/782

32 K. Pender (2017, 29 September). Abkhazia: Memory of war still looms large. Retrieved https://eurasianet.org/abkhazia-memory-of-war-still-looms-large

33 *National Geographic* (1990, March). Lenin quote cited on Map of Soviet Union.

34 Association Atinati. Retrieved from http://atinati.org/?lang=en

35 U. Ammon, N. Dittmar, & K. Mattheier (Eds). (2006). *Sociolinguistics: An international handbook of the science of language and society*. Berlin, Germany: Walter de Gruyter GmbH, p. 1899.

36 T. De Waal (2010). *The Caucasus*, p. 80.

37 J. Hall (2012, 8 October). Was she really 132? World's "oldest ever person" Antisa Khvichava dies in remote Georgian village. *The Independent*. Retrieved from https://www.independent.co.uk/news/world/europe/was-she-really-132-worlds-oldest-ever-person-antisa-khvichava-dies-in-remote-georgian-village-8202514.html

38 T. De Waal (2010). *The Caucasus*, p. 151.

39 S. Mateu (2016, September). Language policy in Abkhazia. *Nationalia*. Retrieved from https://www.nationalia.info/new/10844/language-policy-in-abkhazia-promoting-abkhazian-or-forgetting-georgian.

40 Ibid.

41 Anderson (2014). *Bread and ashes*, p. 81.

42 Few for Change (2019). Poverty statistics: Ngäbe-Buglé Region, Panama, and the world. Retrieved from https://www.fewforchange.org/blog/2015/10/poverty-statistics-ngbe-bugl-region-panama-and-the-world

Endnotes

43 La Estrella de Panama (2015, 23 August). La religión Mama-Tatda. Retrieved from http://laestrella.com.pa/estilo/cultura/ngabes-celebran-mama-tatda/23893352

44 One Planet Nations. Online map of Panamanian comarcas Retrieved from https://www.nationsonline.org/oneworld/map/panama-administrative-map.htm

45 L. Horton (2006). Contesting state multiculturalisms – indigenous land struggle in eastern Panama. *Journal of Latin American Studies*, *38*(4), pp. 829–858.

46 Ibid.

47 A. Cole, & C. Williams (2004). Institutions, identities and lesser used languages in Wales and Brittany. *Journal of Regional and Federal Studies*, *14*(4), pp. 554–579.

48 Crystal (2002). *Language Death*.

49 R. Macfarlane (2015). *Landmarks*. London, UK: Hamish Hamilton.

50 R. Elsie (2018). Albanian dialects. Retrieved from http://dialects.albanianlanguage.net/

51 Ibid.

52 M. Vickers (2014). *The Albanians – a modern history*. London, UK: I.B. Tauris.

53 R. Carver (2009). *The accursed mountains – journeys in Albania*. London, UK: Flamingo.

54 Ibid.

55 R. Denselow (2017, 12 October). Saz'iso: At Least Wave Your Handkerchief at Me review – virtuoso world music. Retrieved from https://www.theguardian.com/music/2017/oct/12/saziso-at-least-wave-your-handkerchief-at-me-review-virtuoso-world-music

56 R. Carver (2009). *The accursed mountains*.

57 K. Budina, & L. K. Hart (1995, June). "Northern Epiros": The Greek minority in Southern Albania. *Cultural Survival Quarterly Magazine*. Retrieved from https://www.culturalsurvival.org/publications/cultural-survival-quarterly/northern-epiros-greek-minority-southern-albania

58   BBC Scotland News (2017, 8 November). "Eh'll heh a peh" - Researchers have found that Scots dialects like Dundonian are "as good as a second language". Retrieved from https://twitter.com/bbcscotlandnews/status/928228128073203713?lang=en
59   Macedonian language. *Encyclopaedia Britannica*. Retrieved from https://www.britannica.com/topic/Macedonian-language
60   *Al Jazeera America* (2013, 28 November). Sri Lanka starts count of civil war dead. Retrieved from http://america.aljazeera.com/articles/2013/11/28/sri-lanka-startscountingthecivilwardead.html
61   BBC News (1998, 25 January). Eleven die in Sri Lankan temple suicide bomb. Retrieved from http://news.bbc.co.uk/1/hi/50366.stm.
62   IRIN (2012, 23 July). Bridging the language divide in Sri Lanka. Retrieved from https://www.refworld.org/docid/501005892.html
63   Euractiv (2009, 26 October). The Slovak-Hungarian dispute over Slovakia's language law. Retrieved from https://www.euractiv.com/section/languages-culture/opinion/the-slovak-hungarian-dispute-over-slovakia-s-language-law/
64   D. Shulman (2016). *Tamil – a biography*. Cambridge, MA: Harvard University Press.
65   Ibid.
66   Said (1978). *Orientalism*.
67   K. Sangakkara (2018, 6 March). Retrieved from https://twitter.com/kumarsanga2/status/971293153969000449?lang=en
68   M. Srinivasan (2019, 26 April). Scared refugees in Negombo flee their homes. *The Hindu*. Retrieved from https://www.thehindu.com/news/international/scared-muslim-refugees-in-negombo-flee-homes/article26950518.ece
69   F. Mihlar (2019, 23 April). There is a thread running through Sri Lanka's cycles of violence. *The Guardian*. Retrieved from https://www.theguardian.com/commentisfree/2019/apr/23/sri-lanka-violence-minorities-christians-muslims
70   South African History Online. The homelands. Retrieved from https://www.sahistory.org.za/article/homelands
71   Ibid.

72   BBC News (2019, 30 April). Julius Malema – South Africa's radical agenda setter. Retrieved from https://www.bbc.co.uk/news/world-asia-pacific-14718226

73   Kruger National Park Guide. Archaeology Kruger National Park – excavated ruins. Retrieved from https://kruger-national-park-guide.com/archaeology-kruger-national-park.html

74   Castells (2012). *Networks of outrage and hope.*

75   Bushbuckridge Local Municipality – final IDP 2015–16. Retrieved from https://bushbuckridge.gov.za/wp-content/uploads/2017/10/FINAL-IDP-BLM-2015-16-.pdf

76   T. Selander (2011, 7 August). I am a prisoner, says Swaziland's Queen No 12. *The Telegraph.* Retrieved from https://www.telegraph.co.uk/news/worldnews/africaandindianocean/swaziland/8686424/I-am-a-prisoner-says-Swazilands-Queen-No-12.html

77   Bulembu. Bulembu Choir USA Tour 2020. Retrieved from https://www.bulembu.org/

78   Unicef. Swaziland. HIV and AIDS. Retrieved from https://www.unicef.org/swaziland/hiv_aids.html

79   *Sky News.* (2018, 20 April). Retrieved from https://news.sky.com/story/king-of-swaziland-changes-his-countrys-name-to-eswatini-11338333

80   Pridnestrovian Republican Bank. Retrieved from https://www.cbpmr.net/content.php?id=1&lang=en

81   Michael Schwirtz (2006, 18 September). Transnistria votes on independence. *The New York Times.* Retrieved from https://www.nytimes.com/2006/09/18/world/europe/18RUSSIASUMM.html?mtrref=www.

82   Sergei Goryashko (2016, 8 August). South Ossetia: Russia pushes roots deeper into Georgian land, *BBC News.* Retrieved from https://www.bbc.co.uk/news/world-europe-45100160

83   Omniglot. Abkhaz. Retrieved from https://www.omniglot.com/writing/abkhaz.htm

84   M. H. Ciscel (2006). A separate Moldovan language? The sociolinguistics of Moldova's Limba de Stat. *Nationalities Papers*, *34*(5), pp. 575–597.

85 S. Benazzo, M. Napolitano, & M. Carlone (2018, 3 January). Gagauz resist Moldova's embrace of West. *Balkan Insight*. Retrieved from https://balkaninsight.com/2018/01/03/gagauz-resist-moldova-s-embrace-of-west-01-01-2018-1/
86 Ibid.
87 Minority Rights Group International. World Directory of Minorities and Indigenous peoples – Azerbaijan: Armenians. Retrieved from https://www.refworld.org/docid/49749d5b32.html
88 C. Williams (1961). *Flintshire: A hstory for schools*. Denbigh, UK: Gee.
89 Ibid.
90 Benazzo, Napolitano, & Corlone (2018, 3 January). Gagauz resist Moldova's embrace of West.
91 Vitali Vah quoted in E. Hardy (2016, 10 August). How Gagauzia, a tiny corner of Moldova, became the front line in Erdogan and Putin's war for influence. *International Business Times*. Retrieved from https://www.ibtimes.co.uk/how-gagauzia-tiny-corner-moldova-became-front-line-erdogan-putins-war-influence-1575063
92 TIKA. Retrieved from https://www.tika.gov.tr/en
93 E. Hardy (2016, 10 August). How Gagauzia, a tiny corner of Moldova, became the front line in Erdogan and Putin's war for influence.
94 Ibid.
95 IPN Press Agency (2018, 14 August). Europe, "anti-European" Gagauzia's main advocate, Op-Ed. Retrieved from https://www.ipn.md/en/integrare-europeana/92942
96 Minority Rights International. World Directory of Minorities and Indigenous Peoples. Retrieved from https://minorityrights.org/minorities/gagauz/
97 *Clecs Camwy*. Retrieved from https://clecscamwy.wordpress.com/
98 J. Henley (2018, 26 February). Icelandic battles the threat of digital extinction. *The Guardian*. Retrieved from https://www.theguardian.com/world/2018/feb/26/icelandic-language-battles-threat-of-digital-extinction

Endnotes

99   META-NET White Paper Series. Retrieved from http://www. meta-net.eu/whitepapers/overview

100 Ibid.

101 Ibid.

102 Welsh Language Commissioner. Retrieved from http://www. comisiynyddygymraeg.cymru

103 M. Plwm (1992, 23 April). Patagonia – Disney dosbarth canol Cymraeg, *Golwg* 4/32.

104 W. Brooks (2012). *Welsh print culture in Y Wladfa – the role of ethnic newspapers in Welsh Patagonia, 1868–1933.* Unpublished PhD thesis, University of Cardiff.

105 A. François, S. Lacrampe, M. Franjieh, & S. Schnell (Eds.). (2015). *The languages of Vanuatu: Unity and diversity* (Studies in the Languages of Island Melanesia 5). Canberra, Australia: National Library of Australia. The Languages of Vanuatu. Australia: National Library of Australia.

106 Ibid.

107 Ibid.

108 D. Reinhardt (1980, 21 November). Leader of New Hebrides rebellion sentenced. UPI Achives. Retrieved from https://www. upi.com/Archives/1980/11/21/Leader-of-New-Hebrides-rebellion-sentenced/8989343630800/

109 Walter Lini quotation on independence. L. Garae (2018, 24 July). Minister launches celebrations. Retrieved from https://dailypost. vu/news/minister-launches-celebrations/article_5ae8c8e4-cde0-5b34-92da-28c8855e6ea7.html

110 K. Kiple, & K. Orlenas (Eds.). (2000). *Cambridge world history of food.* Cambridge, UK: Cambridge University Press.

111 Ibid.

112 D. Wroe (2018, 9 April). China eyes Vanuatu military base in plan with global ramifications. *Sydney Morning Herald.* Retrieved from https://www.smh.com.au/politics/federal/china-eyes-vanuatu-military-base-in-plan-with-global-ramifications-20180409-p4z8j9.html

113 Palm Project. Background & history of Vanuatu. Retrieved from http://palmproject.org/about/background-history-of-vanuatu/

114 M. Rodman (2004). Traveling stories, colonial intimacies and women's histories in Vanuatu. *The Contemporary Pacific Journal*, *16*(2), DOI: 10.1353/cp.2004.0056

115 R. J. Fletcher quotation taken from The Secret Garden. Mele Cultural Centre and Nature Reserve, Mele, Efate, Vanuatu.

116 *The Telegraph* (2009, 8 December). Tribe apologises for eating British missionary. Retrieved from https://www. telegraph.co.uk/news/worldnews/australiaandthepacific/ vanuatu/6756656/Tribe-apologises-for-eating-British-missionary.html

117 Malekula languages (and note about material from museum) statistics taken from the National Museum of Vanuatu, Port Vila, Efate, Vanuatu.

118 Roi Mata Excavation, notes taken from The Secret Garden. Mele Cultural Centre and Nature Reserve, Mele, Efate, Vanuatu.

119 H. Attlee (2015). *The land where lemons grow*. London. UK: Penguin.

120 The quotation is generally attributed to Max Weinreich. Retrieved from http://www.olestig.dk/scotland/weinreich.html

121 *The Economist* (2017, 10 April). Is Serbo-Croat a language? Retrieved from https://www.economist.com/the-economist-explains/2017/04/10/is-serbo-croatian-a-language

122 *The Guardian* (2014, 2 April). Italian forces arrest Veneto separatists over alleged plot to attack Venice. Retrieved from https://www.theguardian.com/world/2014/apr/02/italy-arrest-veneto-separatists-plot-tank

123 G. Steiner (1992). *After Babel – aspects of language and translation* (2nd ed., p. 17). Oxford, UK: Oxford University Press.

124 W. Bunge (1973). The geography of human survival. *Annals of the Association of American Geographers*, *63*, p. 289.

125 R. Brooks (2017, 10 January). Which languages are closest to English? The Language Blog. Retrieved from https://k-international.com/blog/languages-closest-to-english/

126 Steiner (1992), *After Babel*, p. 495.

127 M. Engel (2017). *That's the way it crumbles – the American conquest of the English Language*. UK: Profile Books.